TACKLING TOUGH TEXTS

TACKLING TOUGH TEXTS

A Research-Based Guide
to Scaffolding Learning
in Grades 6–12

SARAH M. LUPO
DAN REYNOLDS
CHRISTINE HARDIGREE

THE GUILFORD PRESS
New York London

A Division of Guilford Publications, Inc.
www.guilford.com

Printed in the United States of America

This book is printed on acid-free paper.

For product and safety concerns within the EU, please contact *GPSR@taylorandfrancis.com*, Taylor & Francis Verlag GmbH, Kaufingerstraße 24, 80331 München, Germany.

Last digit is print number: 9 8 7 6 5 4 3

Library of Congress Cataloging-in-Publication Data

Names: Lupo, Sarah M., author. | Reynolds, Dan, author. | Hardigree, Christine, author.
Title: Tackling tough texts : a research-based guide to scaffolding learning in grades 6–12 / Sarah M. Lupo, Dan Reynolds, Christine Hardigree.
Description: New York : The Guilford Press, 2025. | Includes bibliographical references and index.
Identifiers: LCCN 2024025685 | ISBN 9781462555666 (paperback) | ISBN 9781462555673 (hardcover)
Subjects: LCSH: Reading (Secondary) | Reading comprehension. | Individualized reading instruction. | Language arts—Correlation with content subjects.
Classification: LCC LB1632 .L87 2025 | DDC 428/.40712—dc23/eng/20240718
LC record available at *https://lccn.loc.gov/2024025685*

To the teachers and students—too many to name—
whom we learned with and alongside
and who provided inspiration for this book.
We wrote this for you.

About the Authors

Sarah M. Lupo, PhD, is Associate Professor of Literacy Education in the College of Education at James Madison University. She has worked in education since the early 2000s, including as an ESL teacher, English teacher, reading specialist, and literacy coach in Washington, D.C., Arizona, Virginia, and even Istanbul, Turkey. Her research strives to position all learners as capable and as bringing cultural and linguistic assets to the reading experience, while putting theory into practice to find ways teachers can improve text learning in grades K–12.

Dan Reynolds, PhD, is currently a Senior Education Researcher at SRI International and former Associate Professor in the Department of Education at John Carroll University. Previously, he taught high school English and reading at public and Catholic high schools in Louisiana, Texas, Tennessee, and Ohio. His research has been published in leading journals of literacy education. Dr. Reynolds works in all areas of translational science in adolescent literacy—conducting primary empirical research studies, crafting policy recommendations, delivering professional development with districts and teachers, and teaching high school students. His particular research interests include scaffolding students' reading of complex texts and reading intervention for high school students.

Christine Hardigree, PhD, is Associate Professor in the Education Department at Iona University. She studies literacy education for linguistically diverse adolescents. Dr. Hardigree's work can be found in several peer-reviewed journals as well as practitioner-oriented texts.

Acknowledgments

We wish to acknowledge the following people without whom this book would not exist:

Our graduate assistants who tirelessly provided support, references, assistance, and feedback, especially Paige Knisely, Marissa Markham, Jules Perez, and all of the James Madison University Middle, Secondary, and Mathematics Education Graduate Assistants.

Our colleagues who lent their time and talent to review our work and refine our ideas, including Tricia Kievlan and Angela Webb.

Our families, for their patience and understanding of the sacrifices we made to bring this book to life, including Marshall, Annabelle, and Jacob Lupo; Laura, Mary, Bridget, Jack, Teresa, Joey, and Louis Reynolds; and Matt and Bette Hardigree.

Contents

Purchasers of this book can download and print the reproducible forms and handouts at *www.guilford.com/lupo-forms* for personal use and use with students (see copyright page for details).

CHAPTER 1

What Is Comprehension and What Should Teachers Know about It?

GUIDING QUESTIONS

1. What is comprehension?
2. What does the research say about how to teach adolescents to be better readers?
3. Does reading ability matter in disciplines other than English Language Arts?

"You know they're not going to read that, right?" Dr. Perch and his colleague are planning an upcoming unit in their biology class. Dr. Perch has selected a chapter from the textbook to cover the standards, but his colleague is dubious about their students' motivation to read. "Honestly, I don't even bother assigning the chapters anymore," she says. "I just link to some good videos and go over it in class. Kids today just don't read."

K*ids today just don't read.* How many times have we heard this from colleagues, news reports, and even students themselves? Is this true? Are students of today simply not reading? And what does that mean for teachers? The research indicates that this statement might be true. Students in grades 6–12 are spending an average of 10 minutes a *day* with their eyes on text—actually reading–across English language arts (ELA) *and* social studies classes (Swanson et al., 2016). That's total, not 10 minutes in each class. Students spend about 7.5 hours at school each day, and they are reading for 10 minutes. And, to make matters worse, approximately half of ELA and social studies teachers are spending *far less*, if any, time reading.

If you have picked up this book, you, like us, might be concerned about the lack of reading in middle and high school settings. Reading is part of the foundation of an education and one of the critical ways we learn. Reading is one of the ways that we become informed citizens, learn about great scientific contributions to society, and know and appreciate the craft of storytelling. How can our society continue to learn from our historical achievements and mistakes, invent new technology, appreciate good literature, learn about various aspects of the human experience, and stay apprised of national and international events without reading? The answer is that we can't. To provide a humanistic education that our children need and deserve, we must empower them with deeply meaningful knowledge of language and the printed word. We cannot allow only AI or video to convey knowledge and deprive our children of engaging with great voices from the past and present. Our students need the opportunity to learn—and think about what they are learning—directly from the sources that have shaped our society, rather than hearing someone else's interpretation of it. Written language *is* power, and our students need it.

You are likely wondering about how you can support your students in reading and learning from texts across content areas, particularly with challenging texts (looking at you, *Canterbury Tales*). We know how hard it can be to not only support students in understanding the complex and varied challenges of texts across ELA, science, and social studies, but also to recognize how difficult it can be to motivate students to *want* to read and learn from these texts.

How do we know? We've done it! Between the three of us, we (Sarah, Dan, and Christine) have 26 years of teaching experience with elementary, middle, and high school students all over the United States and even across the globe, including Arizona, Washington, D.C., Virginia, Louisiana, Ohio, Texas, Illinois, Pennsylvania, New York, Tennessee, and Istanbul, Turkey. Collectively, we have also worn many hats: We have taught ELA, Writing, Creative Writing, Journalism, English as a New Language, and ACT/SAT preparation, and we have served as reading specialists, literacy coaches, and administrators. Today, we continue to teach, but within our college classrooms as we prepare the next generation of teachers. Now, we're also researchers working to find solutions to the challenges teachers and students face with reading in everyday classrooms.

We came together to write this book based on a simple observation: Across our classrooms and our research studies throughout the years, we have observed some of our former students, although brilliant thinkers, struggle to make sense of written texts, not only in their ELA classes, but also in their other classes. We have taught adolescents (even in high school) who lacked complete knowledge of letters and sounds and struggled to sound out words. We have taught students who could read words beautifully, fluently, and quickly, but when we asked them about what they read, they couldn't tell us a thing. We've taught students who could understand literal ideas from a text, but when asked to think more deeply about what they read or to develop more complex interpretations, they froze. We've even taught students who were learning English *and* learning how to read for the first time. Some of those students were also taking chemistry, and U.S. History, *while* being asked to read Shakespeare in their ELA class. If you, like us, have had a difficult time supporting your readers in learning from texts in ELA, science, history, or another other subject, you are not alone (Biancarosa & Snow, 2006; Moje, 2008).

Thankfully, much research has been done to support teachers in helping their students successfully read and learn from texts across the disciplines. In fact, there is enough information from the research about supporting older readers in learning from texts to fill this entire book. The goal of this book is to share research-based practices to support readers of varying abilities to learn from—and even enjoy—texts across their school day. Our book is intended to serve as a guide to help 6–12 science, social studies, and ELA teachers ensure that all students have access to rigorous, grade-level curriculum because *all* students can engage in (and benefit from) rigorous, grade-level text-based learning. We call the process of supporting readers as they access and engage with grade-level texts *scaffolding*.

We define *scaffolding* as any temporary instructional support that helps students eventually achieve a learning goal on their own or to learn more fully than they otherwise would without the scaffold (Pea, 2004; Wood et al., 1976). This includes *planned scaffolding*, which is designed before the learning experience; and *scaffolding in action*, which refers to the in-the-moment choices teachers make while the students are in the midst of reading and learning from texts (Athanases & de Oliveira, 2014; Hammond & Gibbons, 2005).

HOW TO USE THIS BOOK

There are many ways you can use this book. One way is to read it cover to cover. Reading it this way will help you understand the bigger picture of how to scaffold and build your overall knowledge about various factors influencing students' ability to learn from texts. We don't think supporting reading consists of just tossing a graphic organizer or a reading strategy at a text—or worse, simply reading everything out loud to students or simplifying everything into a slide deck. Rather, scaffolding takes place at every step of the planning process, and we have organized this book to support teachers along the way. First, teachers must build their own understanding of what comprehension is really about (covered in this chapter) and what makes texts tough (Chapter 2). Next, we explain how to uncover and leverage students' strengths to support their emerging comprehension of those tough texts (Chapter 3). A discussion about supporting readers is not complete without considering how to design purposeful activities that support readers' learning from texts (Chapter 4). We also think that scaffolding can occur in the text selection process so that we can use texts themselves as supports (Chapter 5). We continue to show how to address specific challenges students face in the text, including how to support students in interpreting texts dense with complex ideas and meaning (Chapter 6), understanding texts with high background knowledge demands (Chapter 7), and supporting comprehension of texts that have complex text structure (Chapter 8) or unfamiliar vocabulary (Chapter 9). We also include ideas for helping students who can't sound out the words in the text (Chapter 10). Lastly, we end with how to put it all into action and support students in the moment while teaching (Chapter 11).

However, if you don't want to read the whole book, you can also just jump in at any point. Perhaps you want to simply look for scaffolds that address a particular challenge your students face in the text? Well, dive right into the chapter about that challenge.

In this chapter we will begin by describing the process of comprehension and how you can teach it. We will then explore how comprehension practices vary across content areas.

WHAT IS COMPREHENSION?

While we have spent time with teachers in schools, we have often observed the myths that comprehension is either (1) a black-and-white process—you either do or don't comprehend—or (2) oversimplified to a set of skills related to the standards. For example, we have observed lessons with the objective of finding the main idea of a text or identifying supporting details or the author's purpose. Often these lessons are disconnected to the experience of *learning from* a text, and these standards are seen as the goal of comprehension. But comprehension is so much more. In order for teachers to understand how to support their readers and help them truly learn from a text, all teachers need to have a deep understanding of the comprehension process and what happens in students' brains as they make sense of texts (Lupo et al., 2022).

Research shows that *comprehension* is a dynamic literacy process that happens in three layers (Kintsch, 1986, 2013). Figure 1.1 shows how these three layers work. The first is the literal layer of comprehension, which includes the readers' ability to recall key facts or details from a text. For example, in the textbook excerpt below from a history textbook chapter entitled *The First Americans: The Olmec*, readers can literally understand that Mesoamerican cultures existed from present-day north Panama to central Mexico, believed in multiple gods, and made jewelry out of jade.

> Mesoamerica is the geographic area stretching from north of Panama up to the desert of central Mexico. Although marked by great topographic, linguistic, and cultural diversity, this region cradled a number of civilizations with similar characteristics. Mesoamericans were polytheistic; their gods possessed both male and female traits and demanded blood sacrifices of enemies taken in battle or ritual bloodletting. Corn, or maize, domesticated by 5000 BCE, formed the basis of their diet. They developed a mathematical system, built huge edifices, and devised a calendar that accurately predicted eclipses and solstices and that priest-astronomers used to direct the planting and harvesting of crops. Most important for our knowledge of these peoples, they created the only known written language in the Western Hemisphere; researchers have made much progress in interpreting the inscriptions on their temples and pyramids. Though the area had no overarching political structure, trade over long distances helped diffuse culture. Weapons made of obsidian, jewelry crafted from jade, feathers woven into clothing and ornaments, and cacao beans that were whipped into a chocolate drink formed the basis of commerce. The mother of Mesoamerican cultures was the Olmec civilization (OpenStax, n.d.).

Next is the *inferential* layer of comprehension, which we think of as "reading between the lines." This layer gets a lot of attention in schools. Several state literacy standards, including those specific to science and social studies, highlight important aspects of

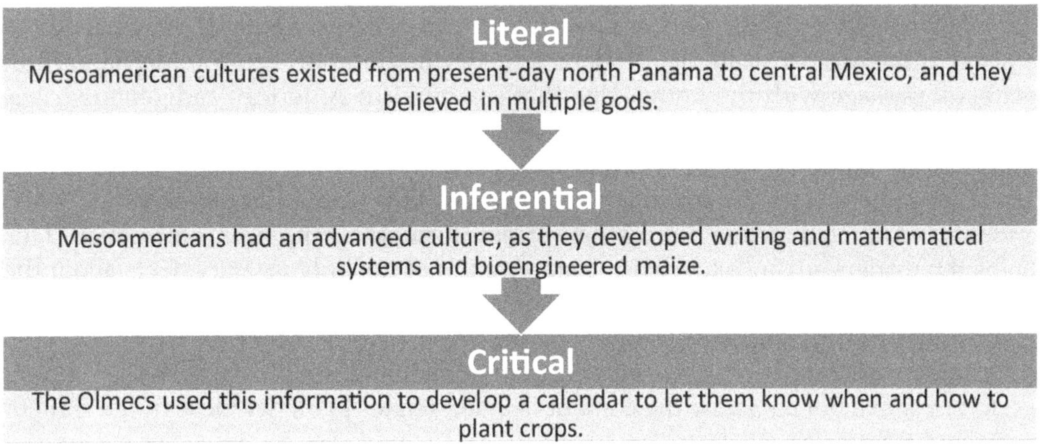

Literal

Mesoamerican cultures existed from present-day north Panama to central Mexico, and they believed in multiple gods.

Inferential

Mesoamericans had an advanced culture, as they developed writing and mathematical systems and bioengineered maize.

Critical

The Olmecs used this information to develop a calendar to let them know when and how to plant crops.

FIGURE 1.1. Layers of comprehension.

this process. For example, one state standard indicates that students should learn to "identify aspects of a text that reveal an author's point of view or purpose" (National Governors Association Center for Best Practices & Council of Chief State School Officers, 2010). Similarly, another standard states that sixth graders should learn to be able to "explain the relationships . . . between two or more individuals, events, ideas, or concepts in a historical . . . text" (National Governors Association Center for Best Practices & Council of Chief State School Officers, 2010). At this layer, students are able to use their background knowledge to infer things about the texts that the author did not directly say. For example, from the Olmec excerpt above, a reader may infer that the Mesoamericans had an advanced culture, as they developed writing and mathematical systems, bioengineered maize, and created a complex calendar to predict seasons for planting and harvesting their crops.

However, inference and analysis of a single text are not enough to support students' learning from texts. We need the critical layer of comprehension in which readers go beyond making inferences and are able to critically and thoughtfully evaluate a text to determine if what the author is saying is true, or whether it is complete. They are also able to look across multiple texts and synthesize information, deal with conflicting information, and make sense of that information as they synthesize what they're learning across text sources. For example, a student reading this textbook excerpt about the Olmec excerpt might also read *Before Columbus: The Americas of 1491* by Charles Mann (2009) and synthesize ideas across both works. Students can compare texts to see that *Before Columbus* discusses not only particular technological advances of Mesoamerican culture similar to the previous text, but also how that knowledge contrasts with popular stereotypes about Indigenous persons as simple bands of people with unsophisticated societies.

Most importantly, at the critical layer of comprehension, readers *integrate* the knowledge they are learning in a text with their own knowledge to grow their knowledge base. This integration process allows readers to apply this knowledge to a novel situation. For example, perhaps a reader might approach the Mesoamerican textbook passage with the knowledge that some North American Indigenous tribes planted corn, beans, and squash together as a regular agricultural practice (knowledge that is often taught to U.S. children during initial explorations about Thanksgiving). Then, from the text they learn that the Olmec calendar would have determined when and what to plant, thus integrating their prior information with new information. This helps the readers advance toward the larger goals of not only learning facts about the Olmecs, but also deeper understandings of the precise and calendar-driven scientific and agricultural practices of Indigenous peoples of North America. Ultimately, the critical layer of comprehension helps readers understand not only what's said or suggested in a text, but also how the content of a text relates to bigger ideas in the content areas and the world.

So, what does all this mean for teachers? It means that as we use texts as a tool for learning content, the goal is to help students achieve a critical level of textual understanding. As displayed in Figure 1.2, to achieve this goal, students must read multiple texts about a topic, including different *genres*, or kinds of texts, and also read various perspectives on a topic. Also, when necessary, they should read texts that provide conflicting information so that they can learn to synthesize information across texts and evaluate sources for the quality and reliability of their information.

Along these lines, the *quality* of the text is crucial. We need texts that have interesting and engaging ideas that are worthy of students' time. We also need texts that align with learning goals and that convey accurate information in engaging and interesting ways. For example, Sarah's children's history textbook includes accurate and relevant information in which the author has integrated stories to depict the historical

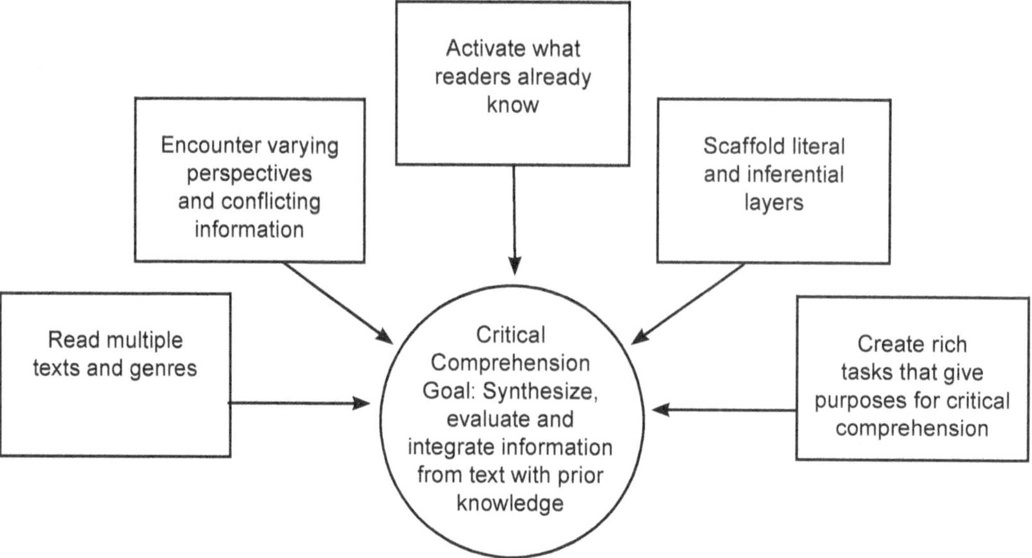

FIGURE 1.2. Key elements of instruction.

information in a way that children enjoy. It's a far cry from the dry history textbook that puts its readers to sleep—or worse—a textbook with incomplete or inaccurate information that support myths and misconceptions.

Additionally, to foster knowledge integration, it is essential for teachers to activate what students already know about the topic (more on this in Chapter 7). Lastly, instruction around content-area texts must include tasks that allow students to recall what they are reading to help them store the information in their memory, evaluate and synthesize information across texts, and, when possible, apply what they are learning to a novel situation (more on this in Chapter 4). For example, students might read about a contemporary debate about Indigenous and U.S. government law (such as recent Supreme Court decisions in *McGirt v. Oklahoma* in 2020, *Oklahoma v. Castro-Huerta* in 2022, and *Haaland v. Brackeen* in 2023) and consider how historical perceptions of Indigenous peoples are shaping contemporary public and judicial opinions.

WHAT ABOUT LITERACY STANDARDS?

You may notice that although this book centers on building students' literacy skills, we do not begin with the literacy standards. Do the standards even matter? To that question we answer a resounding "yes!" However, we view the standards in literacy differently from the standards in science or social studies (as many of the authors of the standards have assured us they did, too). Although many English teachers—often under the tutelage of the administrators who guide them—treat the literacy standards as the *goal* of reading, we view the standards instead as the *vehicle* to comprehension. For example, using the text excerpt above, perhaps a teacher might consider the goal of reading to learn key information about the Olmec people in order to better understand their cultural practices. Thus, the teacher may then select the standard "determine two or more main ideas of a text and explain how they are supported by key details" as a focus standard for the lesson. By helping students identify the main ideas of a text using supporting details, the students would better *learn* the information about the Olmec people. If students stop at the literal layer of comprehension—as in a lesson focused on just finding the main idea of a single passage—students might only recite some facts about the Olmec. But students who are guided to the critical layer of comprehension will have deeper and more lasting understanding of Indigenous history.

ANOTHER WAY TO UNDERSTAND COMPREHENSION

An educator once described understanding texts as a field of daisies (Wix, 1927). One reader may walk through the field and pick one daisy. Another may pick a handful of daisies. A third may come out with a bunch of daisies. All three of these readers understood the text. But they took away different—and differing amounts of—information. This view of comprehension emphasizes *what* students understand rather than whether they do or don't. The teacher's role, then, is to provide scaffolds to help readers pick their own daisies. Teaching comprehension is about teaching students what and how to pay attention to texts as they read. It's not mastering strategies (although strategies that help students pay attention while reading have been shown to help) or standards.

CAN SOME ADOLESCENTS REALLY NOT READ?

We have also seen readers' abilities often pinned to a particular "grade level," with the misunderstanding that readers who "read at a fifth-grade level" cannot comprehend texts at the ninth-grade level without simplified texts or only lectures with bullet-point slides. This is a myth about reading and learning from texts. Remember the daisy metaphor? Children who pick one daisy, rather than a bunch, still understood the text, even if they did not take away as much information as students who collected a bunch of daisies. Comprehension is not black and white. And picking one daisy from a quality, but complex, grade-appropriate text is a stepping stone to being able to pick a bunch of flowers and building a beautiful bouquet.

Why is it a myth that some adolescents "can't read"? It boils down to a misunderstanding about how to read test scores. When students take a norm-based test, such as the Northwest Evaluation Association (NWEA) MAP assessment or the Woodcock-Johnson, the test will produce a grade-equivalent (GE) score. GE scores are not reading levels. This score does not indicate that students will struggle with *content* at that particular grade band. Rather, GE scores simply show that a student *reads* similarly to others at that grade level. For example, John, an eighth grader, took a norm-based comprehension assessment and his GE score was 12th grade. In other words, although he is 13 years old, his reading skills are similar to those of 12th graders. Does that mean he can tackle the mature content of the texts an 18-year-old might read? The reading test doesn't measure that skill, but we can assume not, based on the developmental level of a typical middle-schooler. On the other hand, Alice, an 11th grader, received a GE score of fifth grade, thus indicating that her reading skills are more similar to those of fifth graders. This does not mean that she cannot read texts typical for 11th graders. Rather, the GE score Alice received is an indicator that she may need *significant* support to read texts typical for her grade level.

What is key is identifying *why* grade-appropriate texts are so challenging for Alice and providing supports that will help her overcome those specific challenges. In this book, you will learn how to analyze texts for the challenges they present and how to understand your students so that you know what might be difficult for them. This will allow you to adequately support their understanding of the text, even if their GE scores are far below their current grade. This will ultimately help students be able to pay better attention and pick more daisies.

WHAT DOES THE RESEARCH SAY ABOUT HOW TO TEACH ADOLESCENTS TO BE BETTER READERS?

Before we dive into "the research" on comprehension, let's define what we mean by *research*. We wrote this book in part to quench educators' thirst for teaching approaches grounded in research and evidence. However, we have noticed that the word "research" has been used so much in education that it has nearly lost its meaning. We have also noticed that it means different things to different people.

What Is Research?

We define educational research as the scientific body of evidence that has examined the processes or efficacy of teaching approaches. We draw on many kinds of research for this book. We value both quantitative studies, which use statistical methods to determine what works, and qualitative studies, which rely on narratives, interviews, observations, or other data to systematically explore how and when and under what conditions certain teaching approaches have worked. Drawing from both quantitative and qualitative studies *humanizes* research by highlighting what it looked like *with real people.* In addition to empirical studies, we rely on theoretical papers, and all of the research we cite has been published in peer-reviewed journals, which means that they have undergone a review by experts in that area and have been deemed trustworthy. Periodically, we will also refer to other types of research, which include policy or foundation reports or meta-analyses that sum up previously conducted studies, because they can tell us what the research says about certain approaches across multiple studies. We also draw from another body of research that we refer to as *practitioner pieces,* which are books or journal articles that share teaching approaches specifically for an audience of teachers, rather than researchers. However, we read and choose practitioner pieces carefully to ensure that the approaches shared are grounded in relevant studies and theories. And, as always, we make sure they have been peer-reviewed.

We believe that all of these works are necessary to provide you with the most complete picture of how to support adolescents in reading challenging texts. Additionally, we primarily draw from research conducted with adolescents because we know that research conducted with younger students does not always work for older readers.

A Research Model for Understanding Scaffolding

Understanding the dynamic nature of comprehension, and what happens in readers' heads as they read, is the first step in understanding how to *support* students. A great model for helping teachers understand *how* to scaffold readers' comprehension is called the RAND model (RAND Reading Study Group [RRSG], 2002), which explains that reading is an interaction between three key factors: the text, the reader, and the activity, which are situated within the context of the instructional environment.

Text. We define *texts* broadly to include "[a]ny representational resource or object that people intentionally imbue with meaning" (Siebert et al., 2016). These can be traditional written texts, as well as pictures, maps, videos, or even games (more on games in Chapter 5). As we mentioned earlier, the quality of the texts matter too, and may play an influential role on readers' long-term comprehension ability. Texts that contain rich and precise language, complex syntax structures, and interesting, challenging, and engaging ideas are more likely to provide the necessary exposure to elements of challenge that readers need to grow their literacy skills.

Furthermore, text types can vary across subjects. For example, in science students may need to read research articles, material lists, or detailed procedures for an experiment. In social studies, students may read primary source documents, such as letters from historical figures, journal entries, as well as secondary source accounts, such as textbooks. ELA texts are broader, but may include poems, short stories, scripts, and various subgenres of novellas and novels as well as nonfiction texts, such as biographies, articles, and narrative nonfiction.

Activity. The *activity* in an academic setting includes tasks that the teacher creates in order to successfully comprehend and learn from the text(s). These tasks include summative or culminating assessments that occur at the end of a unit, as well as the smaller daily activities that occur throughout the unit. For example, in a unit on Mesoamerican cultures, one large task may be for students to read across several texts to construct a timeline. This summative assessment is a purposeful task that will align with the overarching goals of the unit. The teacher may also plan several smaller tasks for students to complete as they read each individual text. These smaller tasks may include *scaffolds* that the teacher might put in place, such as small-group or whole-class discussions and brief writing opportunities—for example, journaling to connect prior knowledge to what they are learning; and other formative assessments. In Chapter 4 we present an in-depth description of the tasks teachers create to give their readers purposes for reading.

Reader. This element of the RAND model includes everything that the person reading the text brings to the reading experience: notably, their background knowledge and experiences that relate to the topic of the text, their motivation (or lack thereof) to read, the purpose they have set for reading that particular text, their skills for reading various types of texts, the vocabulary words they know, and much, much more. We will discuss a strengths-based approach for leveraging these assets students bring to the reading experience in Chapter 3.

Reading is situated in a particular context. As you can see from this model, reading comprehension is a dynamic process, meaning that these three elements (text, activity, and reader) *interact* to influence readers' comprehension within the larger *context* in which the reading experience is happening. The context refers to the literacy beliefs and practices of the classroom, as well as to how literacy is valued in the school and local community. This means that the environment and context for learning matter. Throughout this book we will provide examples of how to ensure that the context for learning supports students' ability to learn from texts in your classroom.

What we love about the RAND model is that it demonstrates how much power teachers have to facilitate successful reading experiences. While you can't change what your readers bring to the text, you *can* select the texts, activities, and tasks (including scaffolds), and create a classroom environment conducive to reading. As a result of the positive reading successes of these interactions, over time the reader can develop more literacy skills and with them, perhaps a more positive attitude toward reading that may lead to . . . more reading! We believe this challenging work is the powerful art and craft of creating great content-area and literacy learning.

Thus, the RAND model supports the idea that scaffolding is key to helping readers understand texts. As we mentioned earlier, scaffolds are instructional techniques that teachers can employ to support students in their efforts to better understand a text and should help students attain the critical level of comprehension. As such, scaffolding should consider all elements of the interaction: the reader, the text, and the task.

Consequently, scaffolding is not just "simplifying" the text or lowering the bar of the learning goals. Nor is scaffolding popcorn reading (teacher calling on one student at a time to read aloud for the class), simply reading the text aloud, or removing reading from the curriculum by covering everything with lecture slides and videos. While occasional read-alouds can be useful, the task of reading must eventually be turned over to students. We caution that it is certainly possible to *over-scaffold* (Daniel et al., 2016). For example, if the teacher does too much of the reading, then the students are not reading. If the teacher is directing every point of a class discussion, students are not responding to each other's ideas. If the teacher creates a graphic organizer for every reading, students never have to discern the structure of the text. We cannot emphasize enough that for students to become better readers (and writers) they must be doing the work of reading and thinking about what they have read.

DOES READING ABILITY MATTER IN SUBJECTS OTHER THAN ELA?

One thing we hear a lot is, "I don't need to teach reading because I am teaching science or social studies." That mindset raises the question, "Does reading ability really matter across different subjects?" To help illustrate why comprehension matters, we want to explore what this looks like in a real classroom. Read below as we introduce you to a science teacher, Dr. Perch. As you read, consider whether or not reading ability matters in his science classroom.

Dr. Perch is a 10th-grade biology teacher in a rural northern Ohio district, serving 75% white students and 25% Latinx immigrant students. Next week he begins his third year of teaching biology; however, prior to teaching he was a scientist for nearly two decades. During the past two years, Dr. Perch has struggled to engage his students in the subject matter and has found vocabulary a particular challenge. Additionally, many of his students seem to struggle with reading and writing in general. At times, Dr. Perch wanted to use his textbook to help students build knowledge about a topic before beginning an inquiry-driven lab investigation. But his quizzes revealed that his students hadn't mastered the concepts after reading a section of the textbook.

As a result, many of his students performed poorly on their end-of-course state biology assessment, which, unfortunately, is a requirement for graduation. Dr. Perch is at a loss. He wonders what he is missing that will help him engage his students. He also wonders why his students struggle to read the texts he presents them or engage in the writing tasks and what his role should be in helping them develop their literacy skills. Overall, as a biology teacher, he feels unprepared to support his students' immense literacy needs.

Dr. Perch decided to meet with his school's reading specialist. In that meeting, the reading specialist presented data about students' comprehension abilities that changed how he viewed their literacy skills. Three times a year, all students in the school take a standardized benchmark comprehension assessment, which produces a norm-based reading level for each student indicating how they perform related to other students at that grade level.

Additionally, every year Dr. Perch's students take the required state biology assessment, which consists of multiple-choice questions that gauge students' grasp of various aspects of biology such as evolution, heredity, cell structure, and ecology. Dr. Perch often felt confused when he saw his students' test results because some of his students whom he *knew* had mastered a great deal of the content in his course performed poorly, while others, whom he knew did not master as much biology material scored well. When the reading specialist at his school shared the results of the comprehension assessment alongside his end-of-year biology assessment (see Figure 1.3), a lightbulb went off.

Dr. Perch saw how many of his students who had grasped the science content during class discussions were unable to show what they learned on his biology assessment. For example, Caleb has a deep knowledge of, and passion for, biology. He knew more about how genetics, cell mutation and cell reproduction processes

Name	**Benchmark Reading Level**	**Percent Correct on Year-end Standardized Biology Assessment**
Huda	2.9	*35% (not passing)*
Jesus	4.9	*45% (not passing)*
Nasli	4.1	*46% (not passing)*
Ena	3.9	*51% (not passing)*
Caleb	5.7	*58% (not passing)*
Arthur	4.9	*63% (not passing)*
Susan	6.2	65% (passing)
Patience	7.1	68% (passing)
Xavier	9.1	70% (passing)
Aysa	5.9	75% (passing)
Celia	6.2	76% (passing)
Jeff	6.9	85% (passing)
Alex	8.1	88% (passing)
William	7.1	89% (passing)
Anastasia	10.5	90% (pass advanced)
Annabelle	9.4	91% (pass advanced)
Jacob	11.2	93% (pass advanced)
Nasli	12.1	95% (pass advanced)
Oliver	11.5	100% (pass advanced)
Clara	12.1	100% (pass advanced)

FIGURE 1.3. Dr. Perch's reading comprehension and biology assessment data.

than anyone else in his class. However, he did not receive a passing grade (58%) on the state test.

Dr. Perch also observed how a few of his students who had not necessarily grasped the biology content, but who were strong readers, were able to score well despite their lack of science knowledge. For example, Xavier had exhibited poor attendance throughout the year, and when he did come to class, he was often unengaged. Xavier is a strong reader, however, and was able to eke out a passing grade on the assessment, despite his limited knowledge of biology.

So, did reading ability matter in Dr. Perch's classroom? We resoundingly say "YES!" His students' reading skills were preventing them from being able to accurately show what they knew on the assessments and for Dr. Perch to draw from the full repertoire of teaching tools he needed to help students learn biology content. Reading and writing are critical for learning information, and without access to these two learning modes, Dr. Perch's teaching repertoire was limited. Thus, we believe that even though Dr. Perch is a biology teacher, he needs to understand—and support—reading comprehension to enable his students' learning success.

YES, STUDENTS CAN READ DIFFICULT TEXTS . . . WITH SMART SCAFFOLDING

Teachers have powerful influence over whether their students can comprehend texts in their subject, regardless of the skills and attitudes of the readers entering their classrooms. An essential key to supporting readers is to believe that *all* students are capable of reading and engaging with texts across the disciplines—when provided with appropriate support. This book is designed to help you scaffold text-based instruction to support your readers to *learn* from texts in your discipline. It is our hope that by deepening your understanding of how to scaffold text-based learning, you will increase your students' content knowledge and literacy skills in your subject.

CHAPTER 2

What Makes Texts Tough?

GUIDING QUESTIONS

1. What makes a text hard or easy?
2. How can teachers determine the challenges presented in the text?
3. Can a text be too challenging?
4. How can teachers determine which scaffolds they need to provide?

"My students are having a difficult time making sense of the texts I give them, but I don't know why they are having trouble, and I don't know what to do about it."

This is something that middle and high school teachers across the country have shared with us. One thing that every secondary teacher seems to agree upon is that content-area texts are *tough* for some students—in some cases, *really* tough. The key to helping students make meaning from these challenging, academic, vocabulary-rich texts is to figure out what *exactly* is difficult about them so that teachers can find a way to support readers. In this chapter we will explore what the research says about what actually makes a text difficult and discuss what to do when a text may be too challenging. We will also provide a text analysis tool to help teachers determine the types of scaffolds they need to provide to help students comprehend—and learn from—texts across the disciplines.

WHAT MAKES A TEXT HARD OR EASY?

Understanding the challenges that texts present involves understanding the process of comprehension. As we discussed in Chapter 1, comprehension of texts is an interaction between the text, the reader, and the activity (or task) that the teacher engages in. The *difficulty* of a text plays an important role in this interaction. Of course, the reader is part of the equation as well, as some texts will be difficult for some students, while the same text may be less difficult for other students based on their level of skill and background knowledge (more on what readers bring to texts in the next chapter).

But how can we understand what challenges our readers actually face in a particular text? Scarborough's Reading Rope is a model of the reading process, which names the challenges people face while reading (see Table 2.1). In the rope, reading comprehension is broken into strands that weave together to form a rope of *skilled reading*, which is defined as "fluent execution and coordination of word recognition and text comprehension" (Scarborough, 2001).

The rope consists of two bundles of strands labeled word recognition and language comprehension. *Word recognition* is essentially students' ability to sound out the words on the page. This includes readers' *phonological awareness*, *fluency*, and *decoding* abilities, which influence whether or not readers can automatically read the words aloud in a text. (For more on what these processes mean, see Chapter 10.)

Language comprehension refers to readers' understanding of the meaning of the text. These five strands (background knowledge, vocabulary, language structures, inferencing and interpretation skills, and literacy knowledge) will influence how well readers can learn from a particular text. Table 2.1 provides a description of each strand.

To better understand how the aspects of Scarborough's Reading Rope influence comprehension, let's do an activity. Read the following text and answer the three questions that follow.

Possible Hak for the High Number of Yasli Ugrasmis Okuganlar

One can only attempt to sort out the possible hak for this alarming situation. Social scientists have examined societal factors that might contribute to some yasli ugrasmis okuganlar lack of okumak. Some see the increasing numbers of fakir cocuklar as a major contributing hak. Others believe that cocuklar who are transient and are exposed to inconsistent pedagogical approaches to okumak as they move from school to school are more likely to ugras in okumak. For many, lack of a consistent, well-organized, research-based okumak program—one that provides for early intervention and individual help—might be the reason behind this crisis in okumak. Other hak that affect the success of ugrasmis yasli okuganlar include teacher competence and variations in school funding. For example, in California, the number of kitaplar per child in school libraries has declined from thirteen to just three in the last decade (Klein, 1999). In addition, per-pupil expenditures, teacher salaries, and class sizes differ from school to school. (Adapted from Schifini, 1999)

Comprehension Questions

1. What are the haklar that yasli okunlar okugmakila ugrasiyorlar?
2. What does California's example tell us about yasli ugrasmis okunlar?
3. Yasli ugrasmis okunlar have been a problem for decades. Why has this only recently reached the level of an "alarming situation"?

TABLE 2.1. Strands of Reading Comprehension

	Strand	Description
Language Comprehension Strands	Background Knowledge	Facts or experiences relevant to the text topic
	Vocabulary	Breadth and depth of familiarity with the words in the text
	Language Structures	Understanding of syntax, semantics, text organization
	Inferencing and Interpretation Skills	The ability to understand metaphors or inferences in a text, interpret the text, understand multiple meanings
	General Literacy Knowledge	Understanding of genres and modalities, disciplinary reading skills, reading strategies, purposes for reading
Word Recognition Strands	Phonological Awareness	Understanding of the patterns in words, syllables, and phonemes
	Decoding	The ability to sound out the words in a text based on phonics and alphabet knowledge
	Fluency	The ability to read words automatically (without sounding them out) with good expression and appropriate intonation

Note. Based on Scarborough's Reading Rope (Scarborough, 2001).

After you have read the passage, consider:

- How did you feel trying to answer these questions?
- What aspects of Scarborough's Rope were impacted by the strange words?
- What could a teacher do to help you understand this passage?

How Did You Feel Reading This Passage?

You were able to read 87% of the words in this passage. Thirteen percent of the words in the passage were replaced with Turkish words (using the English alphabet). I (Sarah) have done this activity with thousands of teachers over the last decade. Teachers' experiences vary quite a bit. Some teachers are eager to try to "figure out" the words using the context and have gone so far as to create a glossary of words and their meaning to help them make sense of the text. In contrast, other teachers shut down once they realize how difficult the task is. In fact, in a study Dan conducted with some colleagues (Pendergrass et al., 2018), master's level education students were presented with engineering texts on the first day of class. Some of them quickly gave up, doodled, or cried, while others even tried to cheat to find the answers. The researchers found it was actually quite easy to turn expert readers into struggling readers by giving them a task outside of their expertise.

These varying reactions reflect the experiences of many adolescents as they are presented with challenging texts all day long in middle and high schools. Like the adults Sarah and Dan worked with, many adolescents have strong reading skills, but when presented with the challenges common in content-area texts in secondary settings, they struggle to comprehend.

What Strands of the Rope Were Impacted?

During your reading of the passage, you encountered some challenges, but also because you are likely a proficient reader you had some strengths that helped you make meaning of the text. Now, go back to Scarborough's Reading Rope (see Table 2.1) and consider which strands of the rope made the text *easier* for you and which strands made it tougher.

While experiences in reading this text vary from person to person, many people report that vocabulary is a challenge in this text. However, your background knowledge may have been a *strength* for you because this text is about education, and as teachers, we suspect you know a lot about education. In this way, your background knowledge *helped* you understand the text, and even figure out some of the unfamiliar words from the context.

Similarly, language structure and literacy knowledge (understanding the genre, grammar, and the way print works) may have been relative strengths for you as well. For example, you understand the basic *syntax*, or grammar, of the English language that was used in this passage. You are also familiar with how informational texts such as this news article are organized. Knowledge of that *text structure* may also have helped you figure out some unknown words.

Alternatively, because of your unfamiliarity with many of the key words, it may have been more difficult to make inferences or understand nuances presented by the author. This shows how a weakness in one strand (vocabulary) may have weakened another strand (inferencing and interpretation skills). An important takeaway here is that you may have strong inference and interpretation skills overall, but for *this text* those skills were weakened. Thus, making overall claims about students' ability to "make an inference" (i.e., saying they can't do it) wouldn't make sense because this skill may vary from text to text.

Lastly, many people report that they struggled to sound out the words that do not use typical English patterns, and as a result, they had trouble reading this text fluently. This problem is related to the decoding and fluency strands of the rope. It's important to note that you do not necessarily need decoding or fluency instruction to help you read this passage. You need vocabulary scaffolds. (For examples of vocabulary scaffolds, see Chapter 9.) We have observed adolescent readers being diagnosed with decoding and fluency issues when, in fact, they simply need to learn more words.

Along these lines, an often-used scaffold for understanding challenging texts that we have observed in schools is that teachers read everything out loud to students. However, that "scaffold" wouldn't help you here because you don't know the *meaning* of these words. In fact, reading aloud perhaps could make understanding this passage even more difficult for you. Think about how you used context clues to figure out word meaning; that could have been much harder had you been listening to the text and not reading it yourself. This is why it is so critical to understand the challenges presented in a text before designing scaffolds. Understanding that your issue here is related to vocabulary rather than fluency is key to providing the scaffolding you need to understand this text.

Now, if you want to read the original version of the text to see how close you were in understanding it, you can read the full text (in English) in Appendix 2.A at the end of this chapter.

HOW CAN TEACHERS DETERMINE WHAT IS HARD OR EASY ABOUT A TEXT?

So, how do teachers figure out what is tricky in a text so they can develop appropriate scaffolds? We turn back to the research: Remember Scarborough's Reading Rope? The challenges presented in the text are related to the strands of the rope. In Figure 2.1, we have boiled this down to five categories of challenges that teachers can target and support.

First, one challenge is that the ideas in the text may be *dense,* and as a result, they may be difficult for readers to interpret. This text challenge relates to two strands of the rope: inference and interpretation skills and general literacy skills, which include readers' ability to interpret and analyze a text to understand its deeper meaning. This challenge may include interpreting sophisticated themes or making sense of ambiguous ideas. It also can include multiple possible layers of meaning—or even multiple meanings—of a text, such as those in a poem or short story. Dense texts also tend to have abstract concepts or ideas that are not easily visualized or may be counterintuitive, such as the process of photosynthesis or the laws of gravity. In addition, texts

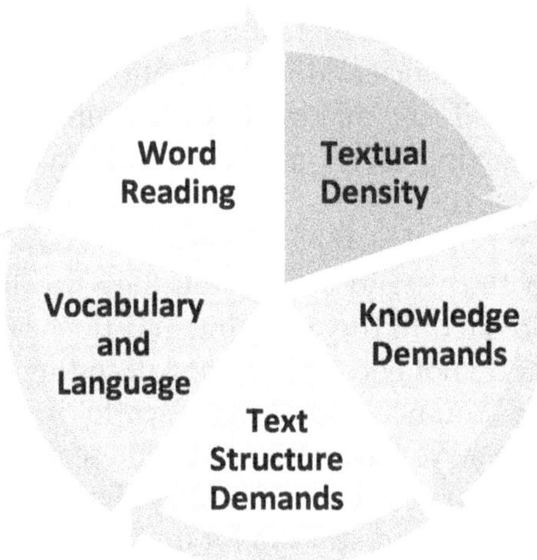

FIGURE 2.1. Text challenges.

with dense ideas may require specific skills, such as the ability to source or corroborate ideas in historical texts, evaluate the trustworthiness of scientific information to understand science reports, or synthesize information across texts. In Chapter 6 we will dig deep to understand this challenge as well as present scaffolds to help readers understand dense texts.

Knowledge is another challenge that readers face related to the background knowledge strand of the rope. We also discussed in Chapter 1 the relationship between comprehension and knowledge, particularly the idea that the critical layer of comprehension requires that readers integrate the new knowledge they are reading with existing knowledge. In this way, both building and activating knowledge are important considerations for teachers to address when scaffolding knowledge demands. We scaffold this challenge in two different ways. First, we *activate* readers' knowledge or relevant experiences to help them integrate what they are learning with what they already know or have lived. Then, we help readers *build* any necessary knowledge they need to understand a text, focusing on building knowledge that the author has *assumed* readers know, but they may not actually know. In addition, we surface any knowledge students have that may conflict with what they are going to read, such as misunderstandings or misconceptions about the topic, so we can help scaffold their text understanding. Chapter 7 addresses scaffolds for both activating and building readers' knowledge as well as how to address potential misconceptions.

The third challenge, the *structure* of texts, refers to how the content of the text is organized. For example, authors may organize expository texts in familiar ways, such as describing a problem and then its solution, or using chronological order. Readers' familiarity with text structure and ability to identify the clues that authors provide about the text structures can influence their comprehension. Additionally, authors may use cohesive devices, such as connectives ("but," "as," "because"), to clue the reader in on how ideas across a text are related to each other—or aren't. Authors also use anaphoric references, which include (but are not limited to) pronouns that refer back to earlier mentions of words, and these can be easy or difficult to understand. When pronoun use is difficult, it can be hard for readers to connect ideas across sentences. In Chapter 8 we will share techniques for scaffolding these and other text structure challenges by showing readers how to identify and use the clues the author has provided to understand how ideas are connected across a passage.

A key aspect of understanding a text is knowing the words that an author uses. This brings us to the fourth challenge, the *vocabulary and language* in the text—a common challenge for adolescents and one you likely experienced earlier while reading the Turkish text. Language challenges occur across all the content areas. For example, when reading science texts, adolescents are often unfamiliar with the challenging technical and scientific vocabulary. In social studies, readers particularly struggle with reading primary source documents. These documents often contain language that we no longer use today (and often alongside text structures that are unfamiliar, making this language even more challenging). Another aspect of language is syntax, which refers to how easily readers can interpret complex sentence structures. Students can also struggle with general academic language, which crosses content areas. For example, words such as *infer* or *conclude* can be difficult for students but may not be taught directly because they are not content-specific words. (We discuss how to support adolescents in understanding text with unfamiliar vocabulary and language in Chapter 9.)

Lastly, some readers will need scaffolds to support their *word reading*. As Scarborough's Reading Rope demonstrates (see Table 2.1), word reading comprises a number of skills, including the ability to segment and blend sounds, knowledge of phonics patterns and the sounds associated with those patterns, and the ability to read texts smoothly and easily with good expression and intonation. At the secondary level, students' understanding of complex sentence structure also influences their ability to read texts fluently—and to understand the meaning of those longer and more complex sentences. While many of these so-called foundational skills are first taught in grades K–2, we include them here for two reasons: First, some students arrive in secondary school without having completely mastered those skills; and second, the echoes of issues with those skills linger as students learn to read, pronounce, and understand the complex words and sentences necessary for learning with texts across subjects.

Fortunately, disciplinary teachers do not need to know how to teach phonics patterns or how to segment and blend sounds. However, secondary teachers *do* need a good toolbox of techniques to support readers who are unable to read passages smoothly, accurately, and with appropriate expression and intonation. We share these easy-to-use techniques in Chapter 10.

So, a key step in supporting adolescents in reading texts across subjects is to identify the challenges in the text while considering the ability of your particular readers. Skipping this step can lead teachers to provide vague or unhelpful scaffolds, such as reading everything out loud to students (Remember, this won't help your students if they are unfamiliar with the words in a text.) or providing generic graphic organizers that don't actually support readers in overcoming the challenges in texts. For example, have you ever used Cornell notes? These are great! But if you have a truly challenging text (which we recommend), your students may need *additional scaffolds* to overcome what is tricky about that text and successfully complete the Cornell notes. Thus, identifying what is challenging about the text must come first.

To engage in text analysis, you will need the text and the organizer presented in Form 2.1. To begin, you should read through the entire text once. Then, as you go through each of the five steps presented below, you will *skim* the text again to look for particular challenges. When engaging in a text analysis, it is important to reflect on your students and have their needs in mind as you analyze the text, as challenges are specific to readers. This means considering their level of skill, as well as their background knowledge and relevant experiences.

To practice, we are going to visit a teacher named Mr. Douglass and explore his planning process for his Advanced Placement (AP) U.S. History class. He has chosen a difficult text, a chapter from *1491* by Charles Mann (2011). This is the second edition of the book, intended for adult readers. In Chapter 1, we mentioned *Before Columbus* (Mann, 2009), which adapted the first edition's content for adolescents. Let's explore the excerpt from *1491* that Mr. Douglass is planning to use with his AP U.S. History

FORM 2.1. Text Analysis Tool

Text Feature	Guiding Questions	Challenges in the Text
Density	• Does the passage contain dense ideas, multiple or layers of meaning, or complex themes? • Does the passage include abstract ideas or concepts that are complicated to understand and do students have those skills?	
Knowledge	• What knowledge does the reader have about this topic that will help them understand this text? • What background knowledge does the author assume that the reader has? • Does the reader have the knowledge that the author has assumed they have? • Is there any information in the text that conflicts with what readers already know about this topic?	
Structure	• What clues has the author provided to show how the text is organized, and what help will your students need to use those clues to help them understand the text? • Does the author use a lot of cohesive devices, and are your students familiar with words and how they connect ideas? • Does the author use a lot of pronouns or other grammatical clues that connect ideas across sentences that will be difficult for your students to understand?	
Vocabulary and Language	• Are your students familiar with most of the words in the text, including vocabulary specific to your content area? • Is there academic language such as words like infer or conclude that is unfamiliar to your students? • Is there complex figurative language or older language use (think about primary source documents), or a dialect or format of English that is particularly challenging?	
Word Reading	• Will students be able to sound out complex words, or do they struggle to identify chunks or patterns in words? • If asked to read out loud, are students able to read the text with smoothness, using appropriate intonation and expression?	

class. Read the following passage and then follow along as we show you how to analyze it.

> **_1491_ Excerpt: "Laying the Land"**
>
> Erickson and Balée belong to a cohort of scholars that in recent years has radically challenged conventional notions of what the Western Hemisphere was like before Columbus. When I went to high school, in the 1970s, I was taught that Indians came to the Americas across the Bering Strait about thirteen thousand years ago, that they lived for the most part in small, isolated groups, and that they had so little impact on their environment that even after millennia of habitation the continents remained mostly wilderness. Schools still impart the same ideas today. One way to summarize the views of people like Erickson and Balée would be to say that they regard this picture of Indian life as wrong in almost every aspect. Indians were here far longer than previously thought, these researchers believe, and in much greater numbers. And they were so successful at imposing their will on the landscape that in 1492 Columbus set foot in a hemisphere thoroughly marked by humankind. (Mann, 2011, p. 4)

Step 1: Assess the Density of the Text

When assessing the density of the text, teachers should consider how difficult it will be to understand the concepts, layers of meanings, and themes in the text as well as what specific skills students will need to interpret the text. Thus, consider the following questions as you read through the text:

- Does the passage contain dense ideas, multiple layers of meaning, or complex themes?
- Does the passage include abstract ideas or concepts that are complicated to understand?
- Are there specific skills that students will need to be able to understand this passage and do students have those skills?

As Mr. Douglass reviews the text, he determines that the text contains a dense idea; namely, that stereotypes of Indigenous populations permeate U.S. culture. For students to understand this dense idea, they will need to synthesize conflicting information across sources to make sense of this text.

> **IS TEXT ANALYSIS TOO TIME CONSUMING?**
>
> While text analysis is a time-consuming process, particularly the first few times you do it, we find that it starts to go relatively quickly after we have practiced it. When you begin to analyze texts, take your time. As you learn how to do it, you may not need to use the organizer, and you'll find that you can complete many of the steps instantaneously in your head as you read through the text. However, if text analysis is an unfamiliar process for you, we recommend spending time to do this slowly to learn the process.

Step 2: Analyze the Knowledge Demands of the Text and Consider Readers' Knowledge

Determining the knowledge demands of the text is twofold: This means we have to consider the knowledge demands of the text as well as the knowledge that students bring to the reading experience. To do this, consider the following questions:

- What background knowledge does the author assume readers have? Do readers have the knowledge that the author has assumed they have?
- Is there any information in the text that conflicts with what readers already know about this topic?

As Mr. Douglass reads through the text, he realizes that his students have built extensive background knowledge about the landscape of early America and natural resources and the story of Columbus's journey. However, some of what his students read here may conflict with what they have previously learned in other history courses about Indigenous populations. For example, Mr. Douglass realizes that information in *1491* conflicts with typical narratives that draw simplistic and misguided pictures of Indigenous populations, reinforcing stereotypes in our society. This text may be difficult for students to grasp if they believe that history textbooks are infallible and are not subject to challenge or revision when new evidence comes to light. Thus, Mr. Douglass realizes that he will need to provide knowledge scaffolds to both help students use what they know to make sense of the text, and also to question their own knowledge as they synthesize conflicting ideas across sources.

Step 3: Assess the Text Structure Demands of the Text

The next step in text analysis is to explore what clues the author has provided to show readers how the text is organized and to consider how well your students will be able to use those clues to make sense of the text. This step includes considering the overall organization of the text as well as how the author has connected ideas across sentences. Thus, we suggest considering the following as you read the text:

- Does the author use a lot of cohesive devices (however, therefore, but), and are your students familiar with them and how they connect ideas?
- Does the author use a lot of pronouns or other grammatical clues that connect ideas across sentences that will be difficult for your students to understand?

Mr. Douglass notices that the text is structured in a straightforward, descriptive way, and, as such, his students won't need much support to use clues about text organization, cohesive devices, or pronoun use to connect ideas across sentences.

Step 4: Assess the Vocabulary and Language Demands of the Text

When considering the vocabulary demands of a text, we want to consider whether the students are familiar with words and language, including the syntax (or sentence structure) that the author has used. We suggest that teachers read the text to consider the following questions:

- Are your students familiar with most of the words in the text, including vocabulary specific to your content area?
- Is there general academic language, such as words like *infer* or *conclude*, that your students are unfamiliar with?
- Is there a great deal of complex figurative language or older language use (think about primary source documents), or a dialect of English that is particularly challenging?
- Is the syntax, or structure of the sentences, familiar to students?

Mr. Douglass notes that there are several vocabulary words that are used in history texts that his students may not be familiar with, such as *habitation* and *conventional*. He also noticed general academic language not specific to history, such as *regard*, *cohort*, and *imposing*. He believes that his AP students are likely familiar with these words and do not need specific vocabulary scaffolds to support their text understanding. However, Mr. Douglass also observes that the author has used complex sentence structures, often with multiple phrases or clauses in a sentence, which may require scaffolding.

Step 5: Assess the Word-Reading Demands of the Text and Consider Readers' Skill

The last challenge sits with the reader rather than with the text. When assessing for this challenge, teachers should consider their readers' ability to read this particular text accurately and smoothly. Thus, teachers should consider the following:

- Will students be able to sound out complex words, or will they struggle to read letter patterns or parts of the words?
- If asked to read out loud, are students able to read the text with smoothness, using appropriate intonation and expression?

Mr. Douglass notes that the text contains many multisyllabic words and long sentences (as noted earlier). However, he does not have any students in this class who have trouble with fluency or word recognition, so he determines that he does not need to scaffold this text challenge.

After analyzing his text, Mr. Douglass has a clear understanding of its challenges and can begin to design scaffolds to support his students in understanding and learning from this text (see Appendix 2.B for a summary of his text analysis). While the example we show in this chapter is from social studies, text analysis is useful in all the disciplines. See Appendix 2.C for an example of text analysis in ELA.

CAN A TEXT BE TOO CHALLENGING?

Teachers often wonder if a text could ever be so difficult that even with scaffolds, students may not be able to make sense of it. We believe that most adolescents can read most texts, even really difficult ones, across all of their classes, with appropriate scaffolds. We also believe (and research supports it) that the best way to grow readers' skill is to provide them with experiences in reading texts that are challenging in each of the ways we describe in this book (meaning, knowledge, vocabulary, text structure, and word reading). We believe that struggle is not a bad word (for more on this research on this topic read Lupo et al., 2019). With scaffolding, students can productively struggle (with adequate teacher support) and learn how to be better readers of texts that contain these challenges.

That said, we consider a few things as we explore the appropriateness of our texts. First, we look for texts that present some challenges in the areas we describe above, but we try to avoid texts that present all of the challenges in the same text, when possible. For example, we can scaffold students' understanding of a text that contains many unfamiliar vocabulary words that are hard to sound out—when provided with strong vocabulary and fluency scaffolds. However, if a text has challenges in all five areas, it would require an extensive amount of scaffolds—and likely take a lot of time for us to read that text with students in a way that truly supports their comprehension.

If that happens, we then consider whether this text is worthy of the time it will take to scaffold and support readers, or if there is another text that we can use instead that fulfills the same learning goals. Sometimes there is no other text, and we may deem the really tough text worth our time. In those instances, we read the text slowly and carefully with students while providing extensive scaffolding to support their text understanding. In other instances, we might find that another text provides the same information or fulfills the same learning goals, but perhaps with less effort, and we will swap out that text instead.

HOW CAN TEACHERS DETERMINE WHICH SCAFFOLDS THEY NEED TO PROVIDE?

Now comes the fun part and the purpose of our book. Once a teacher has determined the types of challenges that readers may face in the text, they can look for scaffolds that will help readers overcome those specific challenges. We have written one chapter showing how to scaffold for each challenge. See Table 2.2 for a list of all of the scaffolding techniques for each challenge in this book.

What do these scaffolds look like within the classroom? Throughout this book, we will join several classrooms to see how these scaffolds can be used. Let's return to Mr. Douglass and his challenging text *1491* to see an overview.

Mr. Douglass determined that, for his AP students, the main challenges in the text *1491* are density (questioning the authority of a textbook, being able to synthesize information across sources) and language (complex and unfamiliar sentence structure). Additionally, Mr. Douglass noted that his students have extensive background

TABLE 2.2. Scaffolding Techniques to Address Challenges of Complex Texts

Chapter 6: Density	Chapter 7: Knowledge	Chapter 8: Text Structure	Chapter 9: Vocabulary	Chapter 10: Word Reading
Chunking	KWL	SQ3R	List–Group–Label	Morphology Posters
Visualizing Abstract Ideas	KEWLS	Summary Fiction: Somebody Wants But So	Graphic Organizers Frayer model	Morphology Frayer Model
Multiple Readings for Different Purposes	Pre-Post Journal	Summary Sentences (A-B-C) nonfiction	Concept Mapping	Badd Spelling Protocol
Notice and Wonder	Driving Question Board (DQB)	Teaching Connectives	Concept of Definition	Chunking Words
Think Aloud	Carousel Brainstorm	Annotate Anaphoric References	Probable Passage	Scaffolded Partner Reading
Perspective Journal	Double Entry Journal	Unscrambling Texts	Semantic Feature Analysis	Radio Reading
Sentence Paraphrasing	Anticipation Guide		Make It Fit	Say it like a Character
Reading Guide	Free Writing Journal			Emotions Reading Game
Fishbowl				Etymology
				Word Wall

knowledge of early America that he wants to help his students activate and use to help them understand the chapter as well as to help them address misconceptions they have about Indigenous populations as they read. He then needs to select at least one scaffold that will help support his readers to overcome each of those particular challenges in this text while leveraging the background knowledge students bring to the text.

To learn more about leveraging students' strengths during the reading experience, see Chapter 3. In Chapter 4 we will show you how you can develop disciplinary goals that will support your students to want to learn from texts, and in Chapter 5 we will show you how to select companion texts to help readers better understand the disciplinary goals you set for your units (thus using texts themselves as scaffolds).

KNOWING WHAT MAKES TEXTS TOUGH ENABLES STRONG SCAFFOLDING

In this chapter, we answer the question "What makes texts tough?" by revealing text challenges, including evaluating how dense the ideas in the text are, considering vocabulary, knowledge demands, and text structure demands as well as how well students will be able to read the words. Text analysis is a key step in learning how to scaffold reading to support all readers in engaging with tough texts. Once teachers identify what is difficult about the text, they can thoughtfully scaffold those challenges and support all students in learning from tough texts.

APPENDIX 2.A. Original Passage from Reading Activity

One can only attempt to sort out the possible reasons for this alarming situation. Social scientists have examined societal factors that might contribute to some students' lack of literacy attainment. Some see the increasing numbers of youngsters living in poverty as a major contributing factor. Others believe that students who are transient and are exposed to inconsistent pedagogical approaches to reading as they move from school to school are more likely to struggle in reading achievement. For many, lack of a consistent, well-organized, research-based reading program—one that provides for early intervention and individual help—might be the reason behind this crisis in reading. Other factors that affect the success of struggling older readers include teacher competence and variations in school funding. For example, in California, the number of books per child in school libraries has declined from thirteen to just three in the last decade (Klein, 1999). In addition, per-pupil expenditures, teacher salaries, and class sizes differ from school to school.

From Schifini (1999). Reprinted with permission from PREL.

APPENDIX 2.B. History Text Analysis Example, *1491* Excerpt, Mr. Douglass's AP U.S. History Class

Text Feature	Guiding Questions	Challenges in the Text
Density	• Are there dense ideas, multiple layers of meaning, or complex themes in this passage? • Are there abstract ideas or concepts that are complicated to understand? • Are there specific skills that students will need to be able to understand this passage?	The text contains a dense idea that the typical narrative of Indigenous populations that permeates U.S. culture is woefully inaccurate. Understanding this text will require students to synthesize multiple sources.
Knowledge	• What knowledge does the reader have about this topic that will help them understand this text? • What background knowledge does the author assume that the reader has? Does the reader have the knowledge that the author has assumed they have? • Is there any information in the text that conflicts with what readers already know about this topic?	Students know a lot about the landscape of early America and natural resources, which they can use to help them understand this text; thus, they need activating-knowledge scaffolds to support them in using this knowledge to understand this text. However, what they are learning in this text may conflict with their existing knowledge, so the teacher may need to scaffold students' misconceptions.
Structure	• What clues has the author provided to show how the text is organized, and will your students need support to use those clues to understand the text? • Does the author use a lot of cohesive devices, and are your students familiar with words and how they connect ideas? • Does the author use a lot of pronouns or other grammatical clues that connect ideas across sentences that will be difficult for your students to understand?	The author has organized the passage in a simple descriptive manner, and students should not need any scaffolds to use cohesive devices or understand pronoun use to connect ideas across the passage.
Vocabulary and Language	• Are your students familiar with most of the words in the text, including its discipline-specific vocabulary? • Is there general academic language, such as words like "infer" or "conclude," that your students are unfamiliar with? • Is there a great deal of complex figurative language or older language use (think about primary source documents) or a dialect of English that is particularly challenging? • Is the syntax or structure of the sentences familiar to students?	Although the text contains many advanced vocabulary words, students are familiar with these words and do not need additional vocabulary scaffolds. However, the author has used complex sentence structure, often with multiple phrases or clauses in a sentence, and that may need scaffolding.
Word Reading	• If asked to read out loud, are students able to read the text with smoothness using appropriate intonation and expression? • Will students be able to sound out complex words, or do they struggle to identify chunks or patterns in words?	Although the text contains many multisyllabic words and long sentences, students in this class do not have fluency or word recognition issues, and they do not need fluency scaffolds.

APPENDIX 2.C. ELA Text Analysis

Text Sample to Analyze from *The Tempest* by William Shakespeare

SCENE 1

A tempestuous noise of thunder and lightning heard. Enter a Shipmaster and a Boatswain.

MASTER: Boatswain!

BOATSWAIN: Here, master. What cheer?

MASTER: Good, speak to th' mariners. Fall to 't yarely, or we run ourselves aground. Bestir, bestir!

He exits. Enter Mariners.

BOATSWAIN: Heigh, my hearts! Cheerly, cheerly, my hearts! Yare, yare! Take in the topsail. Tend to th' Master's whistle.—Blow till thou burst thy wind, if room enough!

Enter Alonso, Sebastian, Antonio, Ferdinand, Gonzalo, and others.

ALONSO: Good boatswain, have care. Where's the Master? Play the men.

BOATSWAIN: I pray now, keep below.

ANTONIO: Where is the Master, boatswain?

BOATSWAIN: Do you not hear him? You mar our labor. Keep your cabins. You do assist the storm.

GONZALO: Nay, good, be patient.

BOATSWAIN: When the sea is. Hence! What cares these roarers for the name of king? To cabin! Silence! Trouble us not.

GONZALO: Good, yet remember whom thou hast aboard.

BOATSWAIN: None that I more love than myself. You are a councillor; if you can command these elements to silence, and work the peace of the present, we will not hand a rope more. Use your authority. If you cannot, give thanks you have lived so long, and make yourself ready in your cabin for the mischance of the hour, if it so hap.—Cheerly, good hearts!—Out of our way, I say!

He exits.

GONZALO: I have great comfort from this fellow. Methinks he hath no drowning mark upon him. His complexion is perfect gallows. Stand fast, good Fate, to his hanging. Make the rope of his destiny our cable, for our own doth little advantage. If he be not born to be hanged, our case is miserable.

He exits with Alonso, Sebastian, and the other courtiers. Enter Boatswain.

BOATSWAIN: Down with the topmast! Yare! Lower, lower!

Bring her to try wi' th' main course. *(A cry within.)*

A plague upon this howling! They are louder than the weather or our office.

Enter Sebastian, Antonio, and Gonzalo.

Yet again? What do you here? Shall we give o'er and drown? Have you a mind to sink?

SEBASTION: A pox o' your throat, you bawling, blasphemous, incharitable dog!

BOATSWAIN: Work you, then.

ANTONIO: Hang, cur, hang, you whoreson, insolent noisemaker! We are less afraid to be drowned than thou art.

(continued)

ELA TEXT ANALYSIS EXAMPLE, MRS. BARTLEBY, 12TH GRADE BRITISH LITERATURE

Text Feature	Guiding Questions	Challenges in the Text
Density	• Are there dense ideas, multiple layers of meaning, or complex themes in this passage? • Are there abstract ideas or concepts that are complicated to understand? • Are there specific skills that students will need to be able to understand this passage?	There are multiple layers of meaning: First, the text simultaneously describes a physical conflict (the storm) and a social class conflict between the nobles and the sailors. Second, imagining the text acted out on a stage is also challenging: readers have to mentally envision the stage and scene as there are few stage directions.
Knowledge	• What knowledge does the reader have about this topic that will help them understand this text? • What background knowledge does the author assume that the reader has? Does the reader have the knowledge that the author has assumed they have? • Is there any information in the text that conflicts with what readers already know about this topic?	Students may have knowledge that relates to the theme of the passage that they can draw on to help them understand the text; in particular, they have experienced betrayal or revenge, and as such, the teacher may activate that knowledge to support their text understanding. Students may need some knowledge built around the difference between noblemen and sailors to understand themes of class differences.
Structure	• What clues has the author provided to show how the text is organized, and will your students need support to use those clues to understand the text? • Does the author use a lot of cohesive devices, and are your students familiar with words and how they connect ideas? • Does the author use a lot of pronouns or other grammatical clues that connect ideas across sentences that will be difficult for your students to understand?	The text is structured in a standard way for plays and tells us who is talking and when. The author uses a lot of pronouns, which may require some scaffolding to help students track across sentences.
Vocabulary and Language	• Are your students familiar with most of the words in the text, including its discipline-specific vocabulary? • Is there general academic language, such as words like "infer" or "conclude," that your students are unfamiliar with? • Is there a great deal of complex figurative language or older language use (think about primary source documents) or a dialect of English that is particularly challenging? • Is the syntax, or structure of the sentences, familiar to students?	The archaic language, nautical terminology, figurative language, and unfamiliar sentence structure may make this a difficult read for students. They will need scaffolds to understand the language.
Word Reading	• If asked to read out loud, are students able to read the text with smoothness, and appropriate intonation and expression? • Will students be able to sound out complex words, or do they struggle to identify chunks or patterns in words?	Mrs. Bartelby notes that she has a few students who have fluency struggles in her class and that the complex syntax of the text may make fluency difficult for other students as well. As such, she plans to add a fluency scaffold to support students.

CHAPTER 3

What Do Adolescents Bring to Texts?

GUIDING QUESTIONS

1. How can we use readers' strengths to support their literacy learning?
2. How can teachers learn about their students' strengths and identities?
3. What does the research say about how to leverage adolescents' strengths and identities to support literacy and learning from texts?

"I love Shakespeare, but my students just can't connect. If it's not on their phone, they aren't interested."

We know firsthand how problematic it can be to help students connect to some of the texts they encounter in schools, especially, as we mentioned in the previous chapter, when those texts are difficult. In Chapter 1 we identified the process of comprehension as one in which the reader, text, and task interact. In this chapter we shift focus to the reader to consider what strengths students bring to the reading experience so that teachers can leverage what students know to help students learn from texts.

HOW CAN WE USE READERS' STRENGTHS TO LEVERAGE THEIR LITERACY LEARNING?

In our approach to supporting students' reading skills, we draw from *culturally sustaining pedagogy,* which promotes valuing the cultural and linguistic strengths that students bring to the reading experience while building students' school-based literacies (Paris, 2012). Our goal is not simply to honor or celebrate our students' identities, knowledge, and out-of-school linguistic practices, but to *sustain* their out-of-school linguistic skills alongside academic literacies, integrating them into the fabric of curriculum and instruction. Thus, a *strengths-based approach* to literacy scaffolding begins with understanding that students lead rich lives outside of our classrooms and that those strengths can be *leveraged* to support learning.

A terrific example of leveraging students' strengths comes from the research by Moll and colleagues (1992) who studied *funds of knowledge*—topics or areas that students and their families know a lot about but aren't necessarily represented in school curricula. They studied Mexican American households to see how families' funds of knowledge could connect to schooling experiences. After studying the Lopez family's work and the school's curriculum, the teacher and researcher collaborators discovered that a fifth grader, Carlos, ran a schoolyard business reselling candy he acquired in Mexico to his classmates in Tucson, Arizona. The teacher then used this information to implement a relevant economics unit addressing important aspects of Carlos's business, such as cross-border economics, currency exchange procedures, and possible bulk discounts. By learning about Carlos's background, the teacher was able to increase his engagement in an interdisciplinary unit and as such, improve the whole class's knowledge of economics.

Thus, we propose using a strengths-based framework to scaffold literacy (see Figure 3.1). What does this mean? To begin, teachers *recognize* the knowledge, experiences, linguistic resources, and aspects of students' identities that they bring to the reading experience. This means *valuing* students' background knowledge as well as their experiences and connections in their communities.

After recognizing student strengths, teachers then *leverage* those strengths and relevant aspects of their identities through purposeful learning experiences (more on this in Chapter 4), thoughtful text selection (more on that in Chapter 5), and targeted scaffolds (Chapters 6–11). Finally, teachers *support* students by providing scaffolded and relevant practice and instruction with literacy skills. In this way, teachers can use students' strengths as levers for learning from texts to provide transformative learning experiences that support students' identities alongside their learning (Martinez et al., 2017).

A strengths-based framework to literacy learning is key to maintaining equity

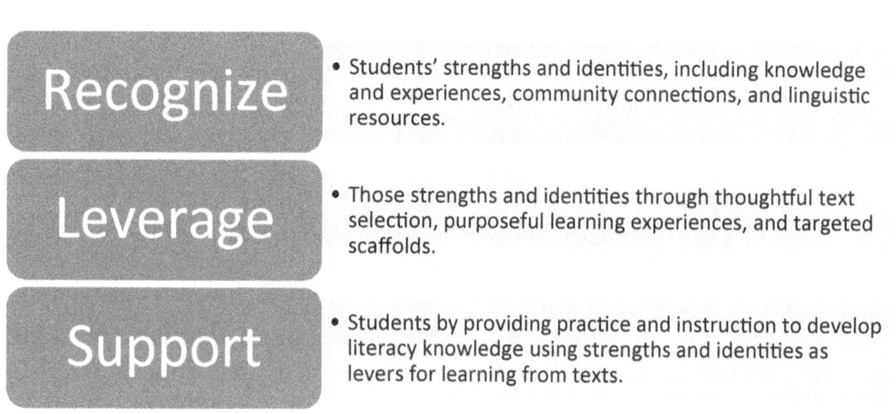

FIGURE 3.1. A strengths-based framework for scaffold literacy.

in literacy activities so that we can make learning about science, literature, and history relevant, but also support students' identities as learners. This process begins by learning about our students' strengths and identities.

HOW CAN TEACHERS LEARN ABOUT THEIR STUDENTS' STRENGTHS AND IDENTITIES?

We have found that one of the most rewarding aspects of teaching is getting to know students from different backgrounds. But how can middle and high school teachers with 100 or more students each year uncover what each student knows and can do?

A good place to start is getting involved in students' communities. Attending sporting events, going to proms, eating with students in the lunchroom, inviting students to chat with you, and engaging in discussions with parents and guardians are all helpful ways to learn more about students and their communities. Additionally, providing opportunities for students to write—and make connections with their knowledge and experiences in that writing—is a great way to continue to get to know students throughout the year. For further discussion on that topic, see Chapters 6 and 7.

Another way that teachers can get to know students is through a survey. Surveys help teachers to be systematic and connect with *every* student, not just those who attend school events. But first, let's look critically at the typical "get to know you" survey that many teachers hand out in the first week of class. Many teachers, if they do this at all, ask surface-level questions such as "What is your favorite book?" or "What is your favorite food?" While such questions are a start, they do not provide teachers with enough information to truly learn about–and leverage—what students bring to the reading experience.

We suggest giving students an opportunity to share more of their identities (if they feel comfortable). For example, teachers can connect learning with students' backgrounds, the languages they use, or the cultural holidays or religious beliefs they observe. We note some of these questions might be seen as more direct than those most teachers usually ask. However, learning about students' identities is beneficial, and we always encourage students to share only those things they are comfortable sharing.

For students, these questions (1) signal to students that teachers care about who they are; (2) empower them to share their background on their own terms; and (3) develop a sense of belonging in a classroom where they will be seen. For teachers, we are able to use this information to better understand the geographic, cultural, and sociopolitical contexts of students' lives and use that information to select meaningful texts, develop smart scaffolds that build on students' existing literacy habits and experiences. Let's explore what this can look like in practice by visiting Ms. Anthony in her classroom.

Meet Ms. Anthony and Her Students

Ms. Anthony, a first-year teacher, is teaching eighth-grade U.S. history at a public school. Her school is located in a small city that has a large refugee population. Most of her students were born and had most of their education in refugee camps after being displaced from countries such as Somalia, Nepal, and Myanmar. Many of her students are learning English, learning how to read, and learning about the history of the United States all at the same time.

Ms. Anthony creates the following survey on a digital form that she can use to sort their information and even potentially form flexible groupings based on interests later on:

- What name and pronouns do you prefer?
- If you feel comfortable sharing, with what race and/or ethnic background do you identify?
- What languages do you and your family (parents, guardians, grandparents, cousins) use, even a little?
- If you feel comfortable sharing, what are some important aspects of your identity that you want to share with me? This could include hobbies you engage in, cultural holidays that you observe, religious traditions that you participate in, sports you play, etc.?
- Who are some of your favorite authors and other creators—musicians, actors, directors, YouTubers, and so on?

When she received the results, she was disappointed to find that 30% of her students said they didn't have a favorite author, but 65% followed the same YouTube accounts that she had never heard of before. After some internet sleuthing, she found that the same account did cheeky short videos about current events that she would be able to include as a way of hooking her students into an upcoming unit.

Ms. Anthony's classroom includes students at various literacy abilities and languages, so she invited students who were not as proficient in English to share some of their responses verbally with peers, who communicated them to Ms. Anthony with the student's permission. By asking students where they lived, and where their family was from (including extended family), as well as about their religious practices, Ms. Anthony learned some heartbreaking stories as well as valuable information about what was important to her students. For example, one student, who likes to be called Mai, grew up in Myanmar with her extended family, all of whom were practicing Muslims. Mai grew up in a refugee camp and has heard family stories of violence that led to many of her extended family dying because of their religious beliefs.

Ms. Anthony considered her next unit in her U.S. History class about the American West, particularly the experiences of Indigenous populations during the United States' expansion in the 19th century. Initially, she wondered how her refugee students would be able to connect to learning about Indigenous populations in the United States, but she has since realized how much some of her students' might relate to these experiences of displacement. She wondered how she could connect her students' experiences and knowledge about standing up for religious freedom to support their learning in this unit, while remaining cautious about triggering some of the trauma her students had experienced.

OUR EXPERIENCES LEARNING ABOUT OUR STUDENTS

Dan's Experiences

While I have taught at schools with diverse student populations in four states throughout my career, I continue to recognize how the richness of students' cultures, languages, and communities can inform my curriculum. Last year. I taught a reading class at an Ohio high school serving mostly Black students, which helped me see new aspects of their racial and linguistic identities, such as the way students repurposed words in their everyday talk and the ways they negotiated between Black English and Standard English in school. Now, as a teacher educator, I work to help my students see how their own histories shape their teaching visions, and I try to help them see new possibilities in students' racial, linguistic, and cultural backgrounds. This includes activities such as finding new young adult literature texts featuring racially and culturally diverse characters and studying classroom discussions to understand how high school students' language and identities shape their learning.

Sarah's Experiences

I spent most of my K-12 teaching career primarily teaching students whose backgrounds differed from my own. As I sat with my uncertainty, I looked for ways to connect with my students and seek out our similarities. For example, I'm a frequent migraine sufferer, and so was one of my students, a refugee from Myanmar. She shared with me some natural remedies for migraines that she used in her home culture that were helpful, and my interest showed her how I valued her knowledge and cultural background.

However, showing my students (and their families) how much I valued their cultural backgrounds didn't always come easily. At one school, I fell into the trap of taking up the popular stance that *some* parents just "don't care" about their children. In one parent meeting, after we finally got the parent to come in for a meeting after an extended period of trying, a parent shared her lack of participation was due to her own negative experiences in school. Because of her own experiences, she did not feel comfortable in school spaces and had been nervous to meet with us. I never again touted the phrase that some parents "don't care," and instead was careful to ensure that parents felt welcomed and encouraged during my interactions with them.

Christine's Experiences

I'll share here an example of how teaching backfires when we don't take student learning into account: I was charged with assessing the "literacy levels" of a group of sixth graders in the wonderful city of Houston. Some of these students were from the area, and others were immigrants from rural Mexico. Almost none had ever seen snow. So when I asked them to read a selection about tobogganing, students could easily decode the passage, but scored atypically poorly on the comprehension questions. Could they really not read the passage? Or did they simply not have background knowledge of winter games?

WHAT DOES THE RESEARCH SAY ABOUT LEVERAGING ADOLESCENTS' STRENGTHS AND IDENTITIES TO SUPPORT LEARNING FROM TEXTS?

Connect to Students' Out-of-School Identities to Support Learning

As we mentioned previously with the example of Carlos and his school-yard economics unit, research has documented the benefits of connecting students' identities and out-of-school experiences with what they learn in the classroom. Other research has also shown such benefits of leveraging students' home-related knowledge to increase literacy and content-area learning. For example, Moje and colleagues (2004) have documented how students' knowledge of family agricultural practices can be linked to scientific literacies in biology. I (Sarah) and my collaborators similarly demonstrated that my rural students' agricultural knowledge could be leveraged to support science learning in an interdisciplinary unit exploring water quality (see Lupo et al., 2023). Everyday knowledge can be a strong foundation for instruction if teachers can recognize the possible connections.

Religion is another deep, yet often untapped, aspect of students' identities that teachers can connect to support literacy and even content learning. Almost 4 million students in the United States attend religiously affiliated schools (National Center for Education Statistics in 2015), and 60% of U.S. teens said that religion was either "very important" or "somewhat important" to their lives (Pew Research Center, 2020). Public school teachers are often understandably cautious about incorporating religious identities into classroom instruction. Guidance from the U.S. Department of Education does prohibit, according to the First Amendment, public schools and teachers in their official capacities from endorsing or favoring religions. However, that does *not* mean that religion is a forbidden topic in classrooms. See U.S. Department of Education (2023) for guidance on constitutional issues involving religion in public schools.

In both religious and secular settings, teachers can connect religious texts to learning by having students consider both their religious literacy practices and the purposes for reading religious texts (Rackley, 2014; Skerrett, 2014). For example, Sutton and colleagues (2023) propose ideas for how students can explore social justice issues in a Catholic school setting. The authors suggest that students read stories about Black teenagers' experiences (such as *The Hate U Give*), while critically reading several U.S. Catholic bishops' statements about racism in the 20th century. They further suggest that students could discuss the Church's call for justice and eradicating racism, while also interrogating the Church's inconsistent history of action against racism. Whether in public or religious school settings, when exploring religious identities with students, we encourage teachers to work with their administrators and families to be clear about the learning objectives of the instruction.

Let's explore another example in the classroom. Ms. Anthony considers the knowledge and experiences that her students bring wonders how she can leverage that knowledge to support learning. She considers her upcoming unit, which explores Indigenous populations in the United States, and she observes the contrast between the typical stories (and stereotypes) and the actual stories of Indigenous peoples. She thinks the unit may feel disconnected for those of her students who did not grow up in the United States. But she also thinks about how some of her students may have experiences and knowledge about losing land and about standing up for their religious beliefs that they can leverage to help them understand and learn the material. As such, she decides to build in specific scaffolds to activate her students' prior knowledge, particularly considering their experiences with being displaced. She also decides to do so cautiously, knowing that some of the readings about Indigenous populations may be triggering for her students. In Chapter 7 we describe the scaffolds that she adds to support her readers, using their knowledge and experiences to learn from texts about Indigenous populations.

Make Community Connections to Increase Literacy Learning

Another way teachers can leverage adolescents' out-of-school identities is to help them make connections with their local community. For example, Athanases and de Oliveira (2014) compared two kinds of scaffolding in a California high school serving mostly Latino students. One teacher directly engaged students in social justice topics such as whether the government was responsible for providing economic aid to low-income communities and how community activism could improve Latino voter turnout. This teacher observed students taking ownership of the content-area literacy tasks. In contrast, the other teacher focused her scaffolding on routines—providing sentence stems for developing academic language or graphic organizers for structuring essays—but she was frustrated that her students struggled to write without the scaffolds. Thus, Athanases and de Oliveira demonstrated the power of connecting learning to the local community.

Connecting with the community can also provide an opportunity for students to show pride in their culture while learning about local history. For example, students in Pittsburgh examined the history of the Hill District, a historically Black neighborhood that suffered dramatic economic decline after failed urban renewal projects (Kucan et al., 2018). In this study, the teachers and researchers designed a unit that would bring students' knowledge of and personal connections to the Hill District neighborhood to help them advocate for change. Students then studied maps, primary and secondary sources, and digital history archives that told the story of the Hill District as a cultural center, but also demonstrated its subsequent economic decline. After engaging with those sources, the students gave final presentations, which were organized around the question, "What should the city do with the Hill District today?" In those presentations, the teachers and researchers found that students displayed cultural pride and knowledge of local history, as well as displayed traits of "citizens who can advocate for change" (Kucan et al., 2018, p. 24).

Similarly, de los Ríos and Molina (2020) found that connecting to community issues strengthened literacy instruction. In this study, the authors supported students in reenvisioning Mexican American cultural and religious practices such as Las Posadas—as both a march for justice for immigrants to the United States and as an opportunity to develop critical literacies and community awareness. Students wrote letters to local businesses inviting them to participate, made posters highlighting the little-known taxes paid by undocumented immigrants, and wrote reflective essays.

Creating rich tasks like these was an inherent form of scaffolding, helping students transform their existing racial, cultural, and religious knowledge into a purpose for learning.

Let's explore another example in the classroom. Do you remember Dr. Perch, the 10th-grade biology teacher, from Chapter 1? Let's revisit his planning as he looks at his next unit on ecosystems and considers how to engage his rural students, who appear to be apathetic to learning about biology. He conducted a survey similar to what we describe above, and he learned that his students love going to the beaches on the Great Lakes not far from where they live in rural Ohio. He remembers a recent article in the paper that reported how some of the beaches were closed due to poor water quality, and another article about invasive species that were threatening the aquatic balance in the Great Lakes. He decides to center his ecology unit on the local community issue of controlling invasive species and managing water quality in the Great Lakes. Here again, the community connection is a driver for learning in addition to a rich fund of knowledge.

Support Adolescents' Multilingualism

More than one fifth of U.S. children speak a language other than English at home (Annie E. Casey Foundation, 2022). Research clearly shows that encouraging students to use all of their languages in the classroom supports both content learning and literacy development (Goldenberg, 2020). This is a powerful way to leverage students' multilingual knowledge and affirm their linguistic identities. In fact, one study showed that teachers who learned about the practice of translanguaging reduced their students' anxiety (Cenoz et al., 2022). This approach can be eye-opening for monolingual teachers, and it can make a meaningful difference for multilingual students. How can teachers, even those who do not speak a language other than English, incorporate students' home languages into the classroom? First, simply taking the time to learn just a few words of a student's language can help break down barriers and support youth. For example, Stewart and colleagues (2022) worked with monolingual high school teachers across content areas who wanted to better support their English learners, or ELs. They taught teachers how to incorporate translation devices into instruction and how to provide key texts in multiple languages. They also showed teachers how to invite students to use their home languages (even though teachers did not know those languages) and create multilingual word walls. It was often an uncertain experience, but this community of teachers ultimately succeeded in breaking down language barriers in their school.

Let's visit another teacher, Ms. Astrid, who teaches sixth-grade science, to explore what it looks like to incorporate students' home language practices into instruction. She has been teaching at a Catholic school in a small city for the last 12 years. Her students are mostly Latino, and even though they are attending a private school, many of them qualify for free and reduced-price lunch. Ms. Astrid conducts her getting-to-know-you survey and learns that many of her students speak Spanish at home and are generally more comfortable speaking Spanish than English. This surprised Ms. Astrid, given that most students seem to demonstrate a strong command of English.

She also learns that many of her students' parents and other relatives (many of whom live with them) do not speak English at all, which explains why her students' out-of-school lives are conducted mostly in Spanish.

Ms. Astrid considers her next science unit on space exploration, and in particular, understanding universal gravitation and its effect on planets, moons, stars, spaceships, and satellites. Although all of her texts are in English, she decides she wants to incorporate more opportunities for her students to speak in Spanish, if they prefer, to process the information. She also wonders if there is a way for her students to create a final product in Spanish, in which they could describe what they had learned. This may enable her students to share their learnings more easily and fluidly with their parents and caregivers.

Value Students' Linguistic Resources to Develop Critical Literacy Skills

Linguistic resources are the knowledge of structures and practices around language that readers know and bring to a reading situation. In school, much of the language practices are academic in nature and may be rooted in standardized English. However, *all* students bring rich knowledge of language and practices to school, although those practices are often not valued (Baker-Bell, 2020). We believe that affirming students' language knowledge and practices in order to amplify students' thinking is the best way to value students' rich language (Uccelli et al., 2020).

For example, Lee (1995) showed how high school English classes could teach Black students to unpack the complexities of figures of speech in the African American oral tradition. For example, students learned about "signifying," which is a form of wordplay in Black English with contrasting meanings, often humorous as in "Yo Mama" jokes. Analyzing the richness of Black English helped students understand the literal and metaphorical aspects of their own speech tradition and to develop more complex literary interpretations of Black authors' works such as Alice Walker's *The Color Purple.* In this way, students' learning in ELA was enriched by helping them understand the richness of their own language practices.

This is also true in science and history class. Brown (2021) recommends that teachers start lessons by listening to students' everyday explanations of scientific phenomena (such as what it means to exercise), and then expand on that language to build vocabulary and complex conceptual understandings of specific science phenomena (e.g., metabolism). Similarly, Uccelli and colleagues (2020) showed how skilled teachers invite students of U.S. history to explain their existing understandings, and then the teachers re-voice, which means to repeat back to them their own emerging thinking, and in doing so, scaffold them toward more precise understandings. In both of these models of instruction, students' language is both a foundational asset and a springboard toward achieving a deeper conceptual understanding of science and history.

Similarly, Orellana (2003) documented ways in which bilingual adolescents who were more confident in their English than their parents served as interpreters for their parents in both official and unofficial ways. One fascinating aspect of this research shows that students are often "language brokers" in quite sophisticated ways, leveraging their funds of knowledge of English to support their parents and their families. These language strengths are often unnoticed by teachers and in the curriculum. However, we want to make sure that teachers don't view students' multilingual skill as a reason not to provide a professional translator: The role of the school is to ensure strong communication directly between educators and parents. Students' linguistic resources are better channeled toward their learning opportunities, but this research shows just how valuable, multifaceted, and powerful students' linguistic potential can be.

Let's go back to Ms. Astrid's sixth-grade science class to explore how valuing students' linguistic resources can develop critical literacy skills. Ms. Astrid knows many of her students speak Spanish, although she herself does not. Wanting to leverage their knowledge as she plans her unit, she looks up key conceptual words in Spanish. She discovers that some words, like *luna* (moon), are distinct in Spanish and English, but that many academic words are cognates: *planeta* (planet), *gravedad* (gravity), *satélite* (satellite), and *orbita* (orbit). The Latin roots in much of science- and history-specific language often show this overlap for students of Romance languages, including Spanish, French, and Portuguese. She posts these words in both languages to make a multilingual word wall, and she intersperses both the English and Spanish versions in her explanations. In this way, she encourages her students to use both languages in discussions.

Develop Students' Critical Rhetorical Flexibility

Valuing students' linguistic resources can seem daunting if students speak a variety of English typically not used in their school. A popular approach involves encouraging students whose everyday English is seen as nonstandardized to "codeswitch," or use certain varieties or registers of language with certain audiences. Essentially, teachers tell students to talk "their English" at home or on the playground but to use "school English" in class. While this approach is well-intended, it is also steeped in discrimination because in the United States white students are almost never asked to codeswitch, whereas Black students often are. So what should we do?

Instead, we encourage teachers to support students in *critical rhetorical flexibility*, or flexibly adapting language to their contexts and audiences (Uccelli et al., 2020). It is imperative to teach students the critical awareness that certain types of language have been discouraged, silenced, or even systematically destroyed (that's the *critical* part), and that experiences of language discrimination have been associated with negative educational outcomes (Benner & Graham, 2011; Gatlin-Nash & Wanzek, 2015). Many students—especially speakers of nonstandardized varieties—are already sensitive to the social, class, and racial assumptions concerning language. For example, middle-school students are well aware that varieties of English really do matter both in school and in life, and they understand the ways their language presents themselves in and out of school (Uccelli & Phillips Galloway, 2017).

Fortunately, teachers can teach critical rhetorical flexibility with a positive approach. For example, teachers of Latino students may allow students to flexibly move between English and Spanish as they try to explain new complex ideas in social studies. This also means that teachers can connect language and history. For example, Baker-Bell (2020) documents how her Black high school students were not aware that enslavers in the antebellum South systematically separated enslaved Africans by the language they spoke because groups speaking the same languages would be better able to coordinate resistance. By teaching students that language varieties are subject to discrimination and have their own histories, teachers can more deeply and fully show how English is and has been used in the United States. Critical rhetorical flexibility helps students transfer their understanding of complex ideas and language across contexts in and out of school.

Let's explore what it looks like to develop students' critical rhetorical flexibility with a new teacher that we have not yet introduced. Mrs. Bartleby teaches 12th-grade English in her urban charter school, where about 70% of students are Black. Her district requires that she teach a Shakespeare play, and she is concerned about how to make this relevant for her students. She also knows that many of her students use Black English, but also that all of her students need opportunities to critically analyze the power associated with different forms of English—from Shakespearean English, to Black English, to standardized English. She considers placing Shakespeare alongside a contemporary work that shows the legacies of colonialism through global varieties of English, spoken by Black Americans, African immigrants to the United States, white Britons, and white Americans. This range of English varieties, alongside Shakespearean English, will give her opportunities to discuss how each of these varieties of English is laden with historical and contemporary power associations.

STUDENTS BRING THEIR KNOWLEDGE, LANGUAGE, AND IDENTITY TO READING EXPERIENCES

With knowledge of students, families, and communities, teachers can design relevant scaffolding that leads to comprehension success. In the next two chapters, we'll show how teachers can use this knowledge to create tasks and build text sets that both meet students where they are and aim for ambitious goals for their reading and learning in English, history, and science.

CHAPTER 4

Why Should Students Read?

GUIDING QUESTIONS

1. Why is it important to read for a purpose?
2. How can teachers develop purposeful reading experiences?
3. How can purposeful reading experiences support specific content-area goals in ELA, history, and science?

"Why do we have to read this?"

If you have ever been in a classroom, you have heard this phrase. As a teacher, it can be maddening (we know the text is important), but as a student, it's a rational concern: Faced with the time-consuming prospect of tackling a tough text, students want to ensure that their efforts are necessary and will be fruitful.

So, why *are* you assigning reading in your class? In this chapter, we will consider the specific learning goals in ELA, history, and science, and show how to use purposeful, scaffolded reading experiences to achieve those goals and motivate students to read.

WHY IS IT IMPORTANT TO READ FOR A PURPOSE?

In the previous chapters, we examined how reading comprehension success is partly dependent on which strengths students bring to understand complex texts. In this chapter, we consider how the task, or activity that is associated with reading can influence reading success. A reading *task* is what the reader will actually do with the text. Tasks include the big goals of a unit (for example, crafting a comprehensive report), as well as the quick scaffolds to help students process the reading in the moment (small-group discussion). The reading task should help students process, comprehend, and learn from the text.

So, how can the task influence reading? Let's compare these two examples: Mrs. Bartleby, a 12th-grade English teacher, might assign her first period to write a literary analysis essay on the themes of power in *The Tempest.* In contrast, her fifth period must memorize and perform the final scene of *The Tempest.* How might readers approach the same text differently based on these two different tasks? In the first example, students will need to read the text closely and make connections and draw conclusions across several scenes through the lens of a theoretical framework. They will need to fully comprehend the text itself as well as make evaluative and critical judgments. In the second example, students will need to read the text closely and also perform it, demonstrating comprehension of individual key scenes.

Are both assignments equally valid, or is one "better" than the other? To answer this question, we must first consider the goals of the subject.

We know that content-area texts can be difficult for students. Strategically planning the reading tasks, including the scaffolds, is a key method for ensuring reading success. Scaffolding text learning can seem overwhelming when there are often *so* many challenges to overcome in a text (as we described in Chapter 2). However, we have found that zeroing in on the goals for content learning is crucial for teachers to help them figure out *which* scaffolds to focus on and when.

So then, what *are* the goals of the content areas? What are the key concepts, skills, and knowledge that students need to achieve in ELA, history, and science, and how do teachers figure out these goals? Standards are often a good place to start when considering content-area literacy objectives, but they are not the end goal. We often hear teachers discuss how lesson planning has to "start with standards." We agree . . . sort of. Let's explain: Whether you use state standards or national frameworks, such as the C3 Standards from the National Council for the Social Studies (NCSS) or the Next Generation Science Standards (NGSS), learning standards help to highlight the specific benchmarks students are mandated to master for each grade level. Embedded within the standards are various literacy practices that are specific to each content area. These practices represent subject-specific ways of reading and writing (Siebert et al., 2016). For example, in ELA teachers may engage students in close reading of texts, whereas in history, evaluation of sources for historical accuracy is of critical importance. See Table 4.1 for more on disciplinary literacy practices.

However, standards alone should not drive the content learning or literacy goals of a unit. For example, is the ultimate goal of English class really just to, as one standard puts it, *use context to determine the meaning of a word or phrase?* We encourage teachers to think bigger than the narrow—albeit important—standards within their subjects. To do this, it's helpful to consider the underlying epistemologies of their content areas. By epistemology, we mean what counts as knowledge in a subject. For example, quotes from a poem or a personal experience might be judged as evidence to build literary knowledge, but the natural sciences don't consider personal experience or mere words to be valid evidence for scientific knowledge. For that, scientists typically expect carefully observed and measured data as evidence to build new scientific advances.

We challenge simplistic assumptions about epistemologies and disciplinary literacy practices. Literature is not merely an artistic interpretation of dusty canonical works: it's the way a community of writers and readers unearth moral, cultural, and personal

TABLE 4.1. Disciplinary Literacy Practices and Texts

Literacy practice across subjects	ELA-specific literacy practice	History-specific literacy practice	Science-specific literacy practice
Consider the true **nature of the work** in discipline. But what does this look like?	Students should not be attempting to regurgitate a teacher-determined meaning but rather learning to use ELA tools approaches and doing their own literary interpretation within a community	Students should not be merely memorizing names and dates but rather conducting historical inquiries to address competing questions and possible narratives into the best possible narrative given the evidence	Students should not be merely memorizing vocabulary or concepts but rather seeing science as ways to solve problems given the best available evolving evidence, and engineer solutions
Close reading. But **what texts** are read closely?	Poetry (lyric and epic) Narrative or nonfiction short stories, novels, or novellas Essays, memoirs Fables, myths, legends Plays and drama Secondary sources—texts *about* literary texts—scholarly interpretations or popular interpretations (e.g. SparkNotes)	Primary sources: historical artifacts from time periods Letters, journal entries, maps, carvings in rock, newsclips, photos, or video footage Quantitative data Secondary sources *about* primary sources Historical summaries Analyses of primary sources History textbooks	Primary sources: science texts themselves Research articles Steps of an experiment Results of an experiment Secondary sources: sources *about* primary science text Explanatory text Diagrams and models of science phenomena Science textbooks
Making claims with evidence. But **what kind of evidence?**	Quotes from literary texts, connections to personal experience, moral and ethical frameworks	Quotes or visuals from primary sources, with context provided from secondary sources	Data collected either from hands-on experiments, or from interpreting secondary data collected by others
Use criteria to judge claims. But **what criteria?**	Literary aesthetics, literary craft and devices, literary lenses on reading (e.g., postcolonialism)	Historical contexts, social structure frameworks, historical thinking frameworks (e.g., those defined by NCSS)	Cross-cutting goals or frameworks (e.g., those defined by NGSS)
Create claims in disciplinary forms. But **what are those forms?**	Literary interpretations based on textual evidence	Historical narratives and arguments informed by sources	Explanatory models informed by data and scientific principles

Note. Adapted from Goldman et al. (2016) and Project READi's work on defining how disciplinary epistemologies shape content area literacy.

questions of who we are. History is not simply a collection of names and dates of leaders and battles, but a constantly evolving set of stories about who human beings are and how our history shapes us today. Science is not merely a list of vocabulary words and concepts to remember, but a way of seeing and knowing how the natural world works and how humans live within it—and shape it. Framed this way, the academic work of reading and learning with disciplinary texts is ultimately about who humans are, who we have been, and how we live in the natural world—or even the natural universe. From this perspective, we can see how Mrs. Bartleby's *Tempest* example from the beginning of this chapter pushes students to master disciplinary goals. When she is designing her reading task (acting out the scene or writing the essay), she must weigh how each task communicates to her students the goals and purposes of literary study.

HOW CAN TEACHERS DEVELOP PURPOSEFUL READING EXPERIENCES?

How do we move from these lofty content-area goals and year-long standards-based learning goals to meaningful text-specific reading tasks? We believe that *essential questions* are key for shaping units to motivate learning and reading aligned to broader content-area goals. Essential questions are important, timeless, inexhaustible questions. These questions are both central to the work of a discipline and accessible even to novice learners (for more information on essential questions and unit design see Wiggins & McTighe, 2005). Ultimately, essential questions should motivate kids to want to engage in rich reading tasks. After all, why should we read Shakespeare? Why does 500+ year-old Indigenous history matter? What will we have to do to protect the stability and balance of the Great Lakes for the next generation of beachgoers and fishermen? These inexhaustible questions can be the source of deep knowledge and inquiry for both students and scholars in these fields.

Thus, when we are considering content-area learning goals, there is a lot to think about. Let's put all this together to explore content-specific texts and practices in Ms. Anthony's eighth-grade history class. As you read the case study, consider how she thinks about her students, how she frames the work of her student historians, and how she engages them in disciplinary practices in history.

Case Study: Ms. Anthony

Ms. Anthony, an eighth-grade history teacher, is a first-year teacher in a small city, and many of her students are newcomers to the United States from a multitude of national, racial, and linguistic backgrounds. She's excited to work with just this population of students, and she would like them to participate in reading texts that engage with complex ideas in U.S. history and government. But her fellow teachers have warned her that their students are not strong readers, and she fears that her ambitious plans might be derailed if she can't figure out how to help the students read complex texts. She hopes to prepare them for rigorous high school social studies coursework, but she's not quite sure how to handle the literacy demands. One practice that Ms. Anthony has to teach is how to evaluate historical sources for accuracy. To do this, she would like students to examine a popular version of the story of Rosa Parks, which describes Parks as worn out after a day of work from her job sewing and simply too tired to give up her seat on a bus to a white person. Some elementary social studies textbooks omit Rosa's training as an activist, ignore her deep connection to a Black community grassroots movement, or do not mention that she was not the first Black woman to defy the bus segregation law (read more about Claudette Colvin if you want to know that part of the story). These versions of Rosa Parks's story make it sound like individual heroism is all that is needed to counter systematic racial injustice. While Ms. Anthony has a general idea of what to cover and the skills she wants students to have, she is puzzled about what this can look like in the everyday classroom.

Ms. Anthony is on the right track—engaging with content-area texts can help even middle-school students avoid these overly simplistic stories. To properly evaluate the accuracy of this account, students can read additional accounts of the time period, including primary source accounts, in order to compare what occurred in that textbook account with additional sources. Carefully curating text sets can help students build these critical skills.

Figure 4.1 contains two primary source accounts regarding the bus incident, in the form of letters (Robinson, 1954). The first is a letter from JoAnn Robinson, who was president of an organization called the Women's Political Council. Her letter reveals that the Women's Political Council had been fighting to eliminate racial injustice on Montgomery buses for years before Rosa Parks was arrested, and demonstrates that the Mayor had not acted on their requests. It also hints at the plans for what would become the year-long bus boycott of 1955–1956.

Additionally, a second letter from Virginia Foster Durr to Miles and Zilphia (Durr, 1956), demonstrates that Rosa Parks's training at the Highlander Folk School prepared her for her role as an activist. This letter is dated January 30, 1956, which reveals that Ms. Parks received extensive training to be an activist prior to the bus incident of December 1, 1955. These accounts reveal that Rosa Parks was not simply tired and that her refusal to get up from the bus that day was part of a coordinated effort of African Americans collectively working together, along with white allies, to create intentional and necessary change in U.S. society. But it also mentions that Rosa Parks was a "quiet and retiring person," which might be the source of the myth that she was not an activist. Ultimately, viewing these letters alongside a traditional account of Rosa Parks as a tired seamstress helps challenge the historical inaccuracies that discount the larger efforts of the African American community, the stories of the allies, and the ultimate nature of the civil rights movement as a social phenomenon. Understanding the true nature of the community efforts needed to challenge racism will better prepare students to do that work themselves today. And the students, in engaging in this work with primary sources, are not merely memorizing names and dates, but are truly acting as historical detectives—almost mythbusters—to establish a more accurate historical narrative based solidly on primary source evidence. These learning activities are stronger examples of content-area literacy in history than merely reading and summarizing a passage about Ms. Parks.

In the case of Rosa Parks and so many more activists, texts matter across the disciplines, as do teaching specific disciplinary literacy practices. For example, students can't appeal to personal experience (as they might be able to in ELA) to justify an argument about the true story of Rosa Parks. Instead, they have to appeal to historical context and corroborate across sources. However, reading and interpreting these primary source documents, as well as other discipline-specific texts, can often be challenging for adolescents, particularly those who experience difficulty with academic texts. We will discuss more about how to select and sequence texts to support disciplinary learning goals in Chapter 5.

HOW CAN PURPOSEFUL READING EXPERIENCES SUPPORT SPECIFIC LEARNING GOALS IN ELA, HISTORY, AND SCIENCE?

When designing purposeful reading tasks, we remind teachers that unit planning is an iterative process and that this process looks different across content areas. We believe that identifying learning goals and essential questions can guide teachers to consider what texts to choose. Without considering the deep learning goals of the unit, the texts may not facilitate learning.

However, as former ELA teachers, we know this is often not the way it works in ELA. Sometimes, instead of beginning with the standards, we start with the texts that will form the backbone of our curriculum. We do this for many reasons. First, we may select our core texts because we know they are deeply connected to critical aspects of our students' identities. Alternatively, we choose them because they are rich literary works that can be subjected to multiple inquiries and tasks. So after we select some of those texts, we organize them to fit a curriculum design. As such, for ELA teachers, considering texts alongside learning goals is critical.

On the other hand, in history and science courses, specific content is often prescribed. These teachers often start with their content standards, then build tasks, and only then do they select specific texts. We think this makes perfect sense: The content in those courses must drive the text selection, not the other way around. Engaging students in the literacy work in a particular content area must be accountable to the specific content of that discipline. Let's explore what developing purposeful reading tasks looks like across different subjects.

Developing a Purposeful Reading Experience in ELA

Let's revisit an English teacher you met in an earlier chapter, Mrs. Bartleby, as she plans her next unit for her 12th graders. She teaches in an urban charter school that serves a majority of Black students and is required to teach Shakespeare, something that she knows her students struggled to connect to during her first few years teaching at this school. This year, she wants to think more about how to develop a purposeful reading experience for her students. Because she knows her students bring a range of language varieties to her classroom, including varieties of Black English, and is aware of the power associated with different variations, she sees an opportunity to connect Shakespeare and contemporary texts that showcase the intersections of colonial

Letter 1: Letter from JoAnn Robinson, a Black activist, to W. Gayle, White Mayor of Montgomery, AL, May 21, 1954	Letter 2: Letter from Virginia Foster Durr, a white activist, to Myles and Zilphia Horton, White Directors of The Highlander School, January 30, 1956
Dear Sir: The Women's Political Council is very grateful to you and the City Commissioners for the hearing you allowed our representative during the month of March, 1954, when the "city-bus-fare-increase case" was being reviewed. There were several things the Council asked for: 1. A city law that would make it possible for Negroes to sit from back toward front, and whites from front toward back until all the seats are taken. 2. That Negroes not be asked or forced to pay fare at front and go to the rear of the bus to enter. 3. That busses stop at every corner in residential sections occupied by Negroes as they do in communities where whites reside. We are happy to report that busses have begun stopping at more corners now in some sections where Negroes live than previously. However, the same practices in seating and boarding the bus continue. Mayor Gayle, three-fourths of the riders of these public conveyances are Negroes. If Negroes did not patronize them, they could not possibly operate. More and more of our people are already arranging with neighbors and friends to ride to keep from being insulted and humiliated by bus drivers. There has been talk from twenty-five or more local organizations of planning a city-wide boycott of busses. We, sir, do not feel that forceful measures are necessary in bargaining for a convenience which is right for all bus passengers. . . . Please consider this plea, and if possible, act favorably upon it, for even now plans are being made to ride less, or not at all, on our busses. We do not want this. Respectfully yours, The Women's Political Council Jo Ann Robinson, President	Dear Myles and Zilphia; I just received a communication from there giving a summary of the past year's activities and I think you should add how much you had to do with the Montgomery Bus Boycott which is really making history and is of the deepest significance. LIFE, TIME, CBS, NBC, and countless other papers have been down here covering it. I think it is the first time that a whole Negro community has ever stuck together this way and for so long and I think they are going to win it. But how your part comes in is through the effect the school had on Mrs. Parks. When she came back she was so happy and felt so liberated and then as time went on she said the discrimination got worse and worse to bear AFTER having, for the first time in her life, been free of it at Highlander. I am sure that had a lot to do with her daring to risk arrest as she is naturally a very quiet and retiring person although she has a fierce sense of pride and is, in my opinion, a really noble woman. But you and Zilphia should certainly take pride in what you did for her and what she is doing. . . . Lots of love to all, come and see for yourself. VA

FIGURE 4.1. Primary source accounts to challenge simplistic Rosa Parks myths.

histories and the English language. In this case, Shakespeare's very "different" English, normally a barrier to students, can be reframed as the purpose for reading. By focusing on language and power (and not solely on the plot of the play, the history of Elizabethan England, or analyzing literary devices), her approach to the unit both leverages students' strengths and identities and gives them a reason to read.

As such, Mrs. Bartleby decides to explore some deeper questions in her unit to make Shakespeare relevant for her students. In particular, she asks her students to consider, "Whose stories get told? How can postcolonial perspectives help readers see historical and modern intersections of race and power?" These questions will guide her high school readers in interpreting texts in ELA through a particular theoretical lens (i.e., a postcolonial perspective) to see how race and power work. She also knows that she can develop a text set *around* Shakespeare that places his work in contemporary discussions about race, language, power, and colonial histories—the very topics her students enjoy discussing. These ideas and questions drive the *learning* she wants to take place in her unit: analyzing a point of view.

Now that she has established learning goals, she decides on a task for her students to drive the learning. She wants her students to show how a postcolonial perspective helps the reader see new aspects of race and power. As such, she decides that students will, after reading Shakespeare alongside contemporary texts, choose a text of their own that tells a story of race and power.

Developing a Purposeful Reading Experience in History

To explore purposeful reading experiences in history, let's go back to Ms. Anthony's eighth-grade class. Ms. Anthony is planning her next unit on Indigenous history in the United States. She considers her students, some of whom have experienced discrimination where classmates or neighbors have essentialized their experiences as refugees into stereotypical assumptions about their nationalities or religion. She also considers her learning goals, outlined by her state, that she is required to teach. In particular, Ms. Anthony needs to teach her students to analyze how relationships between humans and their environment extend or contract patterns of settlement and movement. They also must analyze how peoples' perspectives shape their historical sources and must do so through Ohio's U.S. history content standards.

As a result, she decides to explore the following essential question in her unit: "How do we sort truth from stereotype in uncovering Indigenous history?" This question is key to the work of historians: telling the truest possible story through genuine historical work. This requires pushing past the cultural stereotypes that have distorted American history and popular culture. For Ms. Anthony's eighth graders, this interrogation gives purpose to reading texts about Indigenous history. Typically, students in middle school have already learned simplified narratives of U.S. history from both elementary teachers and popular culture. But contemporary scholarship about Indigenous people in the Americas has challenged many of the assumptions about these narratives. Ultimately, we want students to wonder: What was Indigenous life before European colonization like, and why does an accurate answer to that question matter today?

Next, Ms. Anthony considers how to create a purposeful learning experience. She designs a unit task in which students will identify a current text about Indigenous peoples—such as a Wikipedia article, a government website, or a news article—and rewrite it using the knowledge and perspectives gained from the unit. Students will draw upon both the historical knowledge gained throughout the unit and the critical perspectives that interrogate stereotypes of Indigenous peoples. For example, reading about how Indigenous people reshaped their ecological environments will directly support students in analyzing how relationships between humans and environment extended or contracted spatial patterns of settlement and movement. These are foundational skills in historical thinking.

Rewriting contemporary texts will directly address an additional learning goal about analyzing how peoples' perspectives shape their historical sources as well as how to help students write informative texts to narrate historical events. We believe—and research supports—the idea that deep integration between content and literacy enriches long-term retention of historical information, develops their historical thinking skills, and even grows their reading comprehension (Nokes et al., 2007; Reisman, 2012).

Developing a Purposeful Reading Experience in Science

Dr. Perch, like most science teachers, also wants to start with the NGSS standards for life science—the LS2 standards—and improve his unit on interdependent relationships in ecosystems. He has also noticed that his own family has sometimes been unable to swim in Lake Erie beaches because of water quality alerts. The local community has had difficulty balancing the needs of farmers who fertilize their fields, recreational swimmers affected by runoff, and recreational fishermen who enjoy catching trout and salmon. Even some of his own students have talked about their love of swimming, fishing, and boating, but have also been frustrated by water quality issues. He sees an opportunity to teach about ecosystems not just as an abstract idea, but as central to the authentic disciplinary work of scientists who learn about ecosystems not just to pursue knowledge or pass a test, but to inform important public policy decisions.

Having this knowledge, Dr. Perch wants to design his unit around the essential question, "How can scientists design systems to protect the stability and balance of Great Lakes biodiversity?" This will require students to build knowledge about the food and energy webs in the Great Lakes, learn about the watersheds that bring water (and ships and invasive species) into the Great Lakes, consider the human impacts on the lakes (both intentional and unintentional), and design public policy that manages the lakes' treasures. He also knows that good science and public policy can work together to serve the public interest while also considering the needs of specific groups like farmers, fishermen, and swimmers. His final task, then, will be for students to redesign a board game that popularizes these concepts for a general public and adapt it to the local water quality issues.

To accomplish this task, Dr. Perch considers that students will have to build knowledge about how humans have shaped the Great Lakes, how water moves through the Great Lakes and its watershed, and how energy moves from sunlight to phytoplankton and through the invertebrates and fish in the lake. At the same time, they will develop scientific practices: engaging in argumentation from evidence, constructing explanations for why the Great Lakes ecological challenges have happened, and propose possible solutions to those challenges.

While that sounds like a daunting challenge for a teacher, Dr. Perch also thinks that the connection to local beaches and water quality will be a strong motivational factor for his students. When they read a watershed map, they'll see their own town on it. When they read about food webs in a lake, they'll be seeing the fish species that they catch in it. When they propose a solution to an ecological challenge in their board game, they will have to be accountable to the different interests in their own community. These motivational factors can help Dr. Perch support his students toward these ambitious goals.

Table 4.2 links the essential questions of each of our teachers' units to their disciplinary goals, their purposeful reading tasks, and their learning standards. Essentially, these ideas and concepts are the very backbone of their instruction: the text selection, the sequence of texts in a unit, and the scaffolding designs all flow logically from these decisions. We encourage teachers to think about these as the heart of each unit of literacy-rich instruction. If these units are well designed, the students will more easily see purposes for reading each text, make connections across texts, and utilize scaffolds toward the unit goals.

PURPOSEFUL READING FULFILLS DISCIPLINARY LEARNING GOALS

This chapter answers the question "why should adolescents read?" by exploring the various ways teachers can create purposeful reading experiences to fulfill learning goals. Now that Mrs. Bartleby, Ms. Anthony, and Dr. Perch have identified the goals of the unit and have developed purposeful reading experiences, their scaffolding will be much clearer as they can ensure that each student will achieve the end goals of their units. In Chapters 6–10, we will circle back to these task examples and explain how these teachers can develop specific scaffolds to support these learning objectives. In the next chapter, we focus specifically on the next step in designing scaffolding at the unit-planning level: selecting the specific texts that support learning.

TABLE 4.2. Purposeful Reading Experiences across the Content Areas

Subject and Topic	ELA Mrs. Bartleby's 12th-grade English	History Ms. Anthony's 8th-grade U.S. history	Science Dr. Perch's 10th-grade biology
Essential Questions	Whose stories get told? How can postcolonial perspectives help readers see historical and modern intersections of race and power?	How do we sort truth from stereotype in uncovering Indigenous history? How do we make amends for the ongoing treatment of Indigenous groups?	How can scientists design systems to protect the stability and balance of Great Lakes biodiversity?
Disciplinary Goals	Apply postcolonial perspectives across a variety of texts to show how race and power influence whose stories are told and how they are told	Read across primary and secondary sources to separate truth from stereotype in indigenous history, and use that knowledge to rewrite an inaccurate or incomplete source	Build knowledge of ecosystems and their complex interactions and use that knowledge to design public policy to protect the health of the lakes while still allowing for human use
Purposeful Reading Task	An essay that conveys an interpretation of a self-selected text with a postcolonial perspective	Rewritten version of a text from the unit using knowledge from the unit's readings to form a more complete picture of Indigenous life	Redesign a board game around the Great Lakes that illustrates solutions for the environmental and biodiversity challenges
Learning Standards	"Cite strong and thorough textual evidence to support analysis of what the text says explicitly as well as inferences drawn from the text, including determining where the text leaves matters uncertain" "Determine the meaning of words and phrases as they are used in the text, including figurative and connotative meanings; analyze the impact of specific word choices on meaning and tone, including words with multiple meanings or language that is particularly fresh, engaging, or beautiful" "Analyze multiple interpretations of a story, drama, or poem (e.g., recorded or live production of a play or recorded novel or poetry), evaluating how each version interprets the source text. Include at least one play by Shakespeare and one play by an American dramatist" (CCSSI, 2010).	"Analyze how relationships between humans and environments extend or contract spatial patterns of settlement and movement" "Analyze how people's perspectives influenced what information is available in the historical sources they created" (National Council for the Social Studies, 2013)	"Evaluate the claims, evidence, and reasoning that the complex interactions in ecosystems maintain relatively consistent numbers and types of organisms in stable conditions, but changing conditions may result in a new ecosystem" "Design, evaluate, and refine a solution for reducing the impacts of human activities on the environment and biodiversity" "Create or revise a simulation to test a solution to mitigate adverse impacts of human activity on biodiversity" (Next Generation Science Standards, 2013).

CHAPTER 5

What Should Students Read?

GUIDING QUESTIONS

1. How should teachers select texts to support content learning?
2. Why should teachers assign more than one text to teach about a topic?
3. How can teachers build a text set?

It's Sunday afternoon. Mrs. Bartleby, a 12th-grade English teacher, is reviewing her upcoming unit on Shakespeare and the district's standards that the unit is supposed to accomplish. Students need to

- *Analyze multiple interpretations of foundational works such as Shakespeare*
- *Analyze the impact of word choice on meaning and tone.*

Her 12th graders are getting ready to read The Tempest, *and in past years, she has suspected that only about a quarter of her students have typically done the reading before class. She knows they are not super-motivated to read a text with complicated language from four centuries ago. She is excited to try her new unit exploring colonialism and critiquing language structures. She searches for texts to accompany* The Tempest *that would be rich in perspectives about postcolonialism. But what should she pick?*

As former secondary teachers, we love exploring texts for students, but we also know how difficult and time-consuming selecting texts can be. Teachers often contend with multiple goals and student needs when selecting texts. For example, teachers must consider their learning goals, often outlined in the content standards. However, teachers also must consider other factors, such as how to make the content relevant for students and how to engage students with the topic. Teachers also need to know how to help students with a history of reading difficulties build essential background knowledge through texts and address relevant issues of justice and equity. Accomplishing all these goals in one text set is a challenging task.

Thus, in this chapter, we will address how to balance these various goals. We then present a framework for selecting texts to address a range of goals. No one text accomplishes all the unit's goals, but together they create richer learning experiences. Lastly, we share examples of three text sets for science, ELA, and history.

HOW SHOULD WE SELECT TEXTS TO SUPPORT CONTENT LEARNING?

Some teachers begin the text selection process from scratch, finding all of the texts on their own. Others may have a curriculum or textbook as a starting place, but this is increasingly rare in secondary settings. However, we have found that even if teachers are provided with some texts or a textbook as a starting place, it's helpful to understand the text selection process from scratch so that they can adapt the texts in their curriculum or textbook to meet their students' needs and address other important factors of instruction. As such, we suggest first reflecting on the learning goals you hope to achieve through the use of texts you have or plan to find. We use the following questions for reflection on text goals (a blank reflection template is offered in Form 5.1):

- *Essentiality:* How do the texts embody the core aspects of content knowledge?
- *Relevance:* How do the texts relate to issues in contemporary life?
- *Criticality:* How do the texts relate to issues of power, equity, and justice?
- *Curricular integration*: How do the texts build upon earlier knowledge on this topic and help students integrate additional topic knowledge?
- *Modality:* How do the texts leverage different media such as print, image, video, hypertext, sound, or memes?
- *Students:* How can the texts tap into students' funds of knowledge, connect to their interests, and affirm their identities?

Let's explore what this reflection process looks like in action. In Chapter 4, we noted that Mrs. Bartleby is going to teach students how to analyze a Shakespearean play (*The Tempest*) as required in her curriculum guide by her district. So, Mrs. Bartleby reflects on the above questions to help her decide how to select additional texts to support her students' learning across the unit (see Table 5.1). For example, when considering *relevance,* she acknowledges that Shakespearean plays can seem irrelevant to students. She wants to focus on teaching students to read *The Tempest* with a new lens, and so she is employing postcolonial perspectives in order to provide a different context for reading Shakespeare. Further, as she considers *criticality,* Mrs. Bartleby decides that since the students are exploring postcolonialism, she wants to support them in exploring whether interpretations and performances of the play reinforce or challenge the dominant master–slave colonialist narrative. These foci will help Mrs. Bartleby guide her students toward a deeper understanding of criticality and relevance rather

FORM 5.1. Text Goals Reflection Tool

Element	Question	Reflection
Essentiality	How do texts embody the core aspects of content knowledge?	
Relevance	How do the texts immediately relate to issues in contemporary life?	
Criticality	How do the texts relate to issues of power, equity, and justice?	
Curricular Integration	How do the texts build upon earlier knowledge on this topic and help students integrate additional later knowledge?	
Modality	How do the texts leverage different media such as print, image, video, hypertext, app, sound, or memes?	
Students	How can the texts tap into students' funds of knowledge, connect to their interests, and affirm their identities?	

than simply knowing the plot or identifying Shakespearean language devices. You can see Mrs. Bartleby's reflection on other elements (essentiality, modality, and curricular integration) in Table 5.1.

When selecting texts, we often hear teachers ask, "Some of my students read below grade level, so what if I choose a text that my students can't read?" Our answer to this question, in fact, is why we wrote this book. Our goal is to support teachers

TABLE 5.1. Mrs. Bartleby's Text Goals Reflection Tool

Element	Question	Reflection
Essentiality	How closely do the texts embody core aspects of content knowledge?	I am required to teach Shakespeare, and in particular, *The Tempest*. Specifically, I need to focus on teaching literary standards about the author's construction of plot and resolution, analyzing multiple interpretations of a literary work, and connecting to foundational works of British literature.
Relevance	How do the texts immediately relate to issues in contemporary life?	Reading *The Tempest* from a postcolonial perspective directly connects to current issues of racism, language, and injustice and their antecedents. Additionally, I want to look for other texts that capture both historical and modern experiences of colonialism.
Criticality	How do the texts relate to issues of power, equity, and justice?	Because we are focusing on postcolonialism, I want students to interrogate the master–slave colonialist narrative throughout this unit, and examine how those colonial legacies still affect contemporary people. Therefore, I need texts that will help us explore this.
Curricular Integration	How do the texts build upon earlier knowledge on this topic and help students integrate additional topic knowledge?	Students often study a Shakespeare play in previous grades, so they may have some exposure to his works. Students who have completed U.S. or World History can apply that knowledge to understanding colonial geographies and histories. These goals also prepare students for advanced literary work—not just reading Shakespeare, but also using critical literary perspectives across many texts.
Modality	How do the texts leverage different media such as print, image, video, hypertext, app, sound, or memes?	I want to make sure to provide visuals and texts across modalities to support students' learning in different ways. A TED talk or a video showing dramatic aspects of *The Tempest* may help students see the text not just as print but as enacted on the stage.
Students	How can texts tap into students' funds of knowledge, connect to their interests, and affirm their identities?	The racial diversity and the varieties of English in my class are a good place to start for examining race, power, and language.

in scaffolding readers of varying abilities to learn from texts, even challenging ones, across content areas. The research on text complexity is a helpful starting place for understanding how and why readers of all levels can and should read grade-level texts in science, social studies, and ELA textbooks and curricula. Teachers also wonder where they can find quality texts quickly. For that, Appendix 5.A at the end of this chapter provides a list of websites that are excellent resources for locating texts that support learning across science, history, ELA, and even other subjects.

You may notice that we do not recommend the popular method of simply using "reading levels" to match readers and texts. This method can seem deceptively simple: test the students' comprehension (often via standardized benchmarks) and then use the test data to assign them texts at the same reading level, such as a Lexile level. Seems logical, right? Unfortunately, this method is highly problematic, and we cannot support it as a research-based strategy. Here is a real-life example of how this method can hurt student learning:

Dr. Perch, the biology teacher you met in Chapter 1, receives the standardized reading data on his students and finds that many of his 10th-grade students read below grade level, including several who read at a fourth-grade level, so he assumes that his textbook, written for high school students,will be too difficult for them. He therefore assigns a series of science videos to explain the concepts instead of the chapters from the text. As a result, his students are never exposed to the essential vocabulary of science for 10th grade concepts level or to instruction for tackling these challenges. Could his students have successfully read that textbook? We say yes! With adequate scaffolding, even his supposed "fourth-grade level" readers could have been successful. Let's discuss why and how the text-matching approach is flawed.

First, it is important to know that the comprehension assessments teachers typically use to determine a student's reading level are not aligned with the algorithms that textbook companies use to level their texts (e.g., Hiebert, 2017). In fact, it's like comparing apples to oranges. For example, remember that in Chapter 1 we explained that many reading assessments are "norm-based" assessments, meaning that they tell us how children read compared to their grade-level peers (e.g., NWEA MAP assessment). This means that a student who is determined to be a "fourth-grade level reader" on a norm-based assessment reads similarly to other fourth graders. This type of test does not indicate that children can read texts *determined by a publisher* to be a "fourth-grade" text.

Publishers, in fact, use a completely different method for determining reading level of texts. They use an algorithm, or formula, to determine how difficult a text is, often based on word length, sentence length, word frequency, and other quantitative variables. These algorithms are based on the assumption that texts with longer words and sentences and fewer repeat appearances of words are more difficult than texts with shorter words and sentences and more frequent appearances of words.

To make matters even more confusing, publishers can use different algorithms so that there is no standard agreement in the field about what a "fourth-grade" level text is (for the research on this topic, read Hiebert & Tortorelli, 2022 or Powers, 2008). Muddying the waters even more, these types of measures often fail to take into account qualitative measures of what makes a text difficult. For example, *Beloved* by Toni

Morrison, has a Lexile of 825, which correlates approximately to fifth grade. However, the mature and complex themes of this book are more appropriate for students in high school, thus showing how unhelpful reading levels on their own can be when choosing texts for instruction.

It is no surprise then that there is no research that shows that "matching" students with texts at their "level" is beneficial. In fact, challenging texts, which are texts that are typical for a reader's grade level, or even above, have many benefits for readers. Perhaps surprisingly, challenging texts are more motivating and engaging, even for adolescents with reading difficulties (e.g., Fulmer et al., 2015). Challenging texts provide necessary exposure to more complex vocabulary and syntax and help readers learn to develop more sophisticated inferencing and analysis skills (e.g., Shanahan et al., 2016). The benefits of challenging texts far outweigh the benefits of easier texts. In fact, there is no evidence that an easier version of a science, social studies, or ELA text increases readers' comprehension, even for readers who read far below grade level (Lupo et al., 2019). This shows that adolescents can learn from texts that are not "on their level." Altogether, the research indicates that *struggle* is not a bad word, meaning that when readers have proper scaffolding and support, they can learn from challenging texts and these experiences are more likely to improve their overall comprehension (for a summary of this research, read Lupo et al., 2019).

WHY SHOULD WE ASSIGN MORE THAN ONE TEXT TO TEACH A TOPIC?

Given the multiple goals of instruction that drive teachers' curricular choices—such as building content knowledge, improving literacy skills, and developing a critical lens—teachers have a lot to consider when selecting texts. To help with this process, we recommend using a text set framework to organize and support learning objectives in your subject. Many teachers simply think of text sets as any group of texts on a topic. We define a *text set* as a collection of texts, including written but also visual or multimodal texts, that centers both content and literacy goals.

In this chapter, we compare aspects of three research-based approaches for building text sets (see Table 5.2). The *Quad Text Set* supports students in reading material that might be harder than they are used to reading (Lupo et al., 2018). Therefore, the goal of this type of text set aims to support students to learn from conceptually and linguistically challenging texts across different subjects.

In contrast, the *Critical Literacy Text Set* emphasizes developing justice- and equity-oriented mindsets (Dyches, 2018; Lechtenberg, 2018, Muhammad, 2020). This text set aims to disrupt dominant narratives and to help students read with criticality.

Finally, the *Disciplinary Reasoning Text Set* focuses on developing analytical skills of the specific content areas (Levine et al., 2018). These skills may include engaging in literary interpretation, contrasting historical perspectives, or evaluating scientific evidence, as discussed in Chapter 4. Table 5.2 describes the elements of these three different text selection frameworks.

TABLE 5.2. Different Approaches for Selecting Texts

Approach	Goal	Centering Text	Supporting Texts
Quad Text Set (Lewis et al., 2014; Lupo et al., 2019)	To read and learn from conceptually or linguistically complex texts	*Target* text is a linguistically and conceptually challenging text with difficult syntax and vocabulary	Easier visual and informational texts build knowledge and "hook" readers' interest
Critical Literacy Text Set (Dyches, 2018; Lechtenberg, 2018; Muhammad, 2020)	To read across different perspectives to support justice, equity, or social change	*Fulcrum* text illustrates tensions around dominant ideologies or beliefs	Context texts and texture texts provide counterstories and illustrate different facets of the fulcrum text
Disciplinary Reasoning Text Set (Levine et al., 2018)	To engage in discipline-specific reasoning around texts	*Focal* text exemplifies complex disciplinary characteristics (not necessarily linguistic complexity)	Gateway texts/ activities, cultural modeling texts, and background building texts provide practice disciplinary reasoning with less complex texts

Note. Based on Reynolds (2022).

HOW CAN TEACHERS BUILD A TEXT SET?

To create text sets, teachers begin by choosing one (or more) "centering" texts that align with learning objectives and drive the exploration of the essential questions in the unit (see Form 5.2 for a blank template to use). Centering texts are written texts that serve as a "goal" for the unit and need to do one or more of the following: provide a literacy challenge so students can read something difficult in the discipline, convey a dominant narrative that needs to be examined critically, and/or provide an opportunity for students to practice disciplinary reasoning or thinking skills. For ideas for where to find texts for your unit, see Sidebar 5.1 and Appendix 5.A.

After selecting the centering text, teachers will select supporting texts that will help students be able to read the centering texts. These texts may be multimodal, including pictures, videos, podcasts, or maps. They may also build specific knowledge necessary for comprehending the centering text. Together, supporting texts will help students build knowledge needed to understand the centering text, provide context for understanding the centering text, and/or provide counterstories that question the dominant narrative of the centering texts.

Lastly, we agree with research showing that motivation and engagement matter. As such, we suggest that teachers select at least one text that supports the relevance of the topic of the unit. This may include a fiction, nonfiction, or multimodal text or an activity that does one or more of the following: shows the relevance of the topic of the centering text, garners readers' interest and motivates them to want to read or learn in

WHERE CAN TEACHERS FIND QUALITY TEXTS?

Where do readers find quality texts and recommendations? From friends, from libraries, from news sources, and in social media feeds. But, first and foremost, you should be a reader in your subject area. Being a lifelong reader and learner in your area of expertise will invite texts into your world. If you have that habit, you're off to a great start. Once you really dive into the work of finding quality texts, here are some of our favorites to start with (see Appendix 5.B for full URLs for each organization and site):

- **Organizations that do real-world work in your discipline.** This includes the Library of Congress's education archives or Census data maps (for history teachers), government science agencies like NASA or the NOAA (for science teachers), or foundations like the Poetry Foundation (for ELA teachers).
- **Websites that curate and adapt texts for school use.** *CommonLit, ReadWorks, ActivelyLearn* are a few that work across subjects and operate on a freemium model. *Science Journal for Kids* and *Frontiers for Young Minds* are great for science research articles to be made kid-friendly. Many libraries already have subscriptions for teachers to use—ask about them.
- **Quality curriculum sources.** *Reading Like a Historian, WordGen,* and the *Big History Project* are published by nonprofit education research centers such as Stanford University and the Strategic Education Research partnership.
- **Nonprint resources from vetted sources.** Search your podcast provider for podcasts, streaming services for documentaries, your Spotify, and Audible account for audiobooks. Again, libraries often already carry expensive and valuable subscriptions (Hoopla, Libby, Flipster, Kanopy are a few) for all of these services.
- **Quality Open Education Resources.** We used free open-source versions of textbooks like CK12 and OpenStax for this project.

We also note here (and elsewhere) that the popular practice of replacing challenging texts by choosing online texts that provide different Lexile levels of a text is *not* supported by research, and we discourage the practice. Teachers must expose students to rich texts, language, and ideas. It is better to scaffold up to challenging texts than to dumb them down via an algorithm.

this unit, and/or engages students in a "gateway" activity that establishes a purpose for the unit.

Text Sets in Science

Let's explore what a disciplinary text set looks like in Dr. Perch's 10th-grade biology classroom. Dr. Perch wants to address the NGSS Standards on interdependent relationships in ecosystems (HS-LS2-6, 2-7, and 4-6). This requires students to build significant knowledge about how ecosystems work and to think critically about how human activity interacts with ecosystems. He designed the summative task that requires students to create scientifically feasible policy solutions to protect the stability of the Great Lakes in order to make the unit relevant to students' lives. He then decides to select the centering text *The Death and Life of the Great Lakes* by Dan Egan (2017) because it addresses issues of invasive species (e.g., zebra mussels, sea lampreys), shows how populations of different species have changed over time, and invites students to think as voters and policymakers about the trade-offs between agriculture, industry,

FORM 5.2. Text Set Framework Planning Template

Instructional Goals		Essential Questions	
Text Element	**Text Goals**	**Selections**	**Purpose for Reading**
Centering Text(s)	A textbook chapter, research, or other article, primary source document, or other written texts that does at least one of the following: • Provides linguistic or conceptual challenge • Illustrates counterstories that question the dominant narrative • Provides an opportunity for disciplinary reasoning		
Supporting Text(s)	Pictures, maps, videos, infographics, or other visuals that do at least one of the following: • Builds knowledge needed to understand the centering text • Provides context for understanding or critiquing the centering text • Conveys a dominant narrative that needs to be examined critically		
Relevance Text(s)	A fiction, nonfiction, or multimodal text that will garner students' interest and motivate them to want to read by doing at least one of the following: • Shows the relevance of the topic of the centering text • Provides a "gateway" activity that introduces the unit		

recreation, and ecosystem health. While this text has dense ideas and vocabulary, it's also written specifically to address policy issues, so students will be engaging with science in the public interest of their own communities, such as Dr. Perch's in rural northern Ohio.

But this text will likely require significant scaffolding to support his readers, so Dr. Perch selects a number of supporting texts to help his readers be able to learn from the centering text. For example, he decides to have his students use a map to help them visualize the Great Lakes watershed. The map will also help them understand one of the abstract ideas that makes the centering text so difficult: The routes into the Great Lakes for waterborne invasive species are crucial not because of the size of the waterway or lake, but because of their connection to other watersheds (such as the St. Lawrence Seaway connecting to the Atlantic Ocean). Dr. Perch also includes aerial photographs of Lake Erie showing the luminescent green algal blooms to help build knowledge about the Great Lakes watershed and provide an emotionally provocative picture of an ecosystem out of balance. The teacher also decides to include informational texts about invasive species such as zebra mussels and sea lampreys to help the students build knowledge before tackling the text.

Lastly, Dr. Perch searches for texts to help his students understand the relevance of this topic. He settles on a board game, the *Watershed Game*, developed by water ecology experts at the University of Minnesota (n.d.). This game invites students to start with a limited amount of resources, play different social roles (politician, farmer, industrial business owner, recreational swimmer, fisherman), and try to minimize water pollution with the resources they have. It's a great way to help students learn the bigger scientific principles while interacting with each other and to prepare them for the complex thinking they need to practice while engaging in the larger tasks of the unit: creating a simulation to test a solution to mitigate the adverse impacts of human activity on biodiversity and to evaluate the possible policy solutions explored in *The Death and Life of the Great Lakes*. This relevant text will also serve the final task of creating a board game based on the *Watershed Game* for the Great Lakes region. Students will use what they learned from the text set to create a version of the board game that brings in the specific local watersheds, the specific species (lampreys, trout, algae), and the specific community organizations that have a stake in the health of the Great Lakes. Dr. Perch's text set is summarized in Table 5.3. For middle school science teachers, an additional science text set example created by Ms. Astrid for her 6th graders and focusing on gravity can be found in Appendix 5.B.

Text Sets in Social Studies

Let's revisit a teacher we introduced in earlier chapters: Ms. Anthony, who teaches eighth-grade history. As she begins selecting texts, she considers her goals for the unit, which include learning about Indigenous populations and critiquing dominant narratives. In particular, she wants her students to analyze typical stereotypes of Indigenous populations and evaluate whether they are true. She also hopes that her unit will help her students better understand the wide-ranging stereotypes about Indigenous peoples—and the current research that challenges those historical biases.

TABLE 5.3. Dr. Perch's Great Lakes Ecosystems Unit Text Set for 10th-Grade Biology

Instructional Goals	Essential Questions
Create a model for protecting the Great Lakes from a human-induced threat (invasive species or algal blooms) to ensure its stability and balance. Read and evaluate claims about the balance of the Great Lakes ecosystem, considering the complex stakeholders (e.g., tourism, shipping, fishing, needs of local and state communities).	How can scientists design systems to protect the stability and balance of Great Lakes biodiversity?

Text Element	Text Goals	Selections	Purpose for Reading
Centering Text(s)	A textbook chapter, research, or other article, primary source document, or other written texts that does at least one of the following: • Provides linguistic or conceptual challenge • Provides an opportunity for scientific reasoning	Excerpts from the Introduction, Chapter 7, and Chapter 10 of *The Death and Life of the Great Lakes* (Egan, 2017)	Engage with a conceptually and linguistically challenging text that applies what students are learning in their ecology unit to a local scenario
Supporting Text(s)	Pictures, maps, videos, infographics, or other visuals that do at least one of the following: • Builds knowledge needed to understand the centering text	Great Lakes Watershed Map from the Introduction to *Death and Life of the Great Lakes* (Egan, 2017)	See geographical conduits for invasive species (the "front door" of the St. Lawrence Seaway and the "back door" or the Chicago Sanitary and Ship Canal) Recognize geographical constraints to any systems to protect Great Lakes ecosystem
		"NOAA, Partners Predict Large Harmful Algal Bloom for Western Lake Erie" article from the National Oceanographic and Atmospheric Administration website (NOAA, 2019)	Visualize colors of cyanobacteria showing the connections between runoff and lake water quality to increase knowledge and interest
		"Sea Lamprey Control in the Great Lakes: A remarkable success!" (Great Lakes Fishery Commission, n.d.)	Build informational text knowledge about lampreys and successful invasive species control. Prepares with knowledge to read the target text

(continued)

TABLE 5.3. *(continued)*

Text Element	Text Goals	Selections	Purpose for Reading
		"What Are Zebra Mussels and Why Should We Care About Them?" (U.S. Geological Survey, n.d.)	Provide a brief knowledge-builder about zebra mussels, a key Great Lakes invasive species discussed at length in the target text
Relevance Text(s)	A fiction, nonfiction, or multimodal text that will garner students' interest and motivate them to want to read by doing at least one of the following: • Shows the relevance of the topic of the centering text • Provides a "gateway" activity that introduces the unit	*The Watershed Game* (University of Minnesota, n.d.)	Engage students in simulation to tackle NGSS engineering practices: "students apply tools such as prevention, practices, plans, and policies to decrease water pollution while balancing financial resources"

Because one of her goals is to help students critique dominant narratives, Ms. Anthony looks for a centering text that provides a counterstory that will challenge popular beliefs about Indigenous populations in the United States. After some consideration, she selects *Before Columbus: The Americas of 1491* by Charles C. Mann (2009). This work, while written for kids, nevertheless presents historical evidence that challenges three assumptions:

- Indigenous peoples lived with low population density, in loosely organized societies or bands with little urban infrastructure.
- Indigenous technology was inherently inferior to that of Europeans, which led directly to European victories in armed conflicts.
- Indigenous peoples lived lightly on the land and did not engage in large-scale modification of the natural world, leading European settlers to encounter a largely pristine wilderness.

Next, Mrs. Anthony selects supporting texts. She first chooses a text that portrays the dominant narratives that her centering texts contradicts: a textbook chapter on the American West (CK-12, 2019). She knows that this text provides an incomplete picture, and chooses it so that her students can read it critically. She also selects several other texts that include relevant facts that are not in her centering text that will help students both understand the centering text and deepen their knowledge of Indigenous populations, including texts like *This Land*, a podcast hosted by Rebecca Nagle (2019) that illustrates how the historical systematic oppression of Indigenous peoples reverberates in U.S. law and culture today. Ms. Anthony also considers how a primary source map of Tenochtitlan before the Spanish conquest might supplement students' content knowledge when engaging with *Before Columbus* and also help both illustrate and support students to question dominant ideologies that reinforce incorrect assumptions about Indigenous people only living in loose rural bands. For example, the map shows Tenochtitlan as a sprawling metropolis built in a lake, with an elaborate system of human-made-canals, waterways, and aqueducts—all engineering marvels that challenge the stereotypes that Indigenous peoples did not have sophisticated engineering technologies, did not live in dense urban areas, and did not engage in large-scale environmental transformation.

Lastly, she considers how to make this text set relevant for her students, who live in Ohio, a state that has no federally recognized Indigenous reservations, which may make them feel disconnected from studying Indigenous populations. She chooses three relevance texts that contextualize the narratives in Ohio, such as the newspaper article "Ohio's Last Indian Tribe Was Forced out in 1843." Table 5.4 summarizes Ms. Anthony's text set.

Text Sets in ELA

Let's revisit Mrs. Bartleby, the 12th-grade ELA teacher, as she considers her unit's instructional goal: to engage students in complex literary reasoning with a complex Shakespearean text. She wants her students to not just read Shakespeare and comprehend the plot, or merely notice how he used literary devices, but rather to illustrate the process of reading through a theoretical lens, in this case, a postcolonial perspective. As a result, she decides to build in selections from Chimamanda Ngozi Adichie's novel *Americanah* to allow her students opportunities to compare and contrast language variations and to develop critical rhetorical flexibility (as we discussed in Chapter 3). Her supporting texts are designed around revisiting Shakespeare from a postcolonial perspective. She includes a text that explains the concept of postcolonialism, so that students can engage with the central concept directly.

She also wants to include contemporary interpretations such as summaries of *The Tempest* (n.d.) by SparkNotes and the Shakespeare's Birthplace Trust website. It may surprise you that we actually recommend using summaries to help readers through a complex text. You might ask, "If students can just look up the summary, how will I know they have read the real text?" We argue that placing the original text alongside a summary (even one generated by an AI chatbot) can give students a tool for comprehending the text and help them begin to interrogate the text. For example, the SparkNotes summary of Act V does not mention any resolution of the conflict between the enslaved Caliban and the master, Prospero. Is that summary accurate? When students read Act V for themselves, they can decide whether Caliban merely hides his resistance to Prospero's continued oppression. Thus, the supporting texts work with the central text to provide context and purpose (see Table 5.5). Reading the SparkNotes entry critically is also a way to build relevance and help students see that online summaries are also interpretations of literary works that decide what to include and exclude.

TABLE 5.4 Ms. Anthony's Indigenous Stereotypes Unit for Eighth-Grade U.S. History

Instructional Goals	Essential Questions
Analyze the relationships between Indigenous people and their environments, and how those relationships influence their settlement patterns. Analyze the perspectives and information of Indigenous people portrayed across various sources. Understand and question stereotypes of Indigenous populations based on evidence.	• How do we sort truth from stereotype in uncovering Indigenous history? • What was the relationship that Indigenous people had with nature and their environment, and how did that relationship influence their settlement patterns?

Text Element	Text Goal	Selections	Purpose for Reading
Centering Text(s)	A textbook chapter, research, primary source document, or other written text that does at least one of the following: • Provides linguistic or conceptual challenge • Illustrates counterstories that question the dominant narrative • Provides an opportunity for disciplinary reasoning	Excerpts from *Before Columbus: The Americas of 1491* (Mann, 2009)	To outline the central essential question about stereotypes of Indigenous history and see counterstories and counter-research that challenge those assumptions
Supporting Text(s)	Pictures, maps, videos, infographics, or other visuals that do at least one of the following: • Builds knowledge needed to understand the centering text • Provides context for understanding or critiquing the centering text • Conveys a dominant narrative that needs to be examined critically	Textbook chapter: *The American West* (CK12 Foundation, 2019)	To observe the dominant description of Indigenous populations and the story of how European Americans took their land
		Native Knowledge FAQs (Smithsonian National Museum of the American Indian, n.d.)	To show how many different names Indigenous groups have been given in comparison to how they refer to and view themselves

(continued)

TABLE 5.4 *(continued)*

Text Element	Text Goal	Selections	Purpose for Reading
		Chapter: The First Americans: The Olmecs and Map of Tenochtitlan (OpenStax textbook, n.d.)	To demonstrate the complexities and advanced technology of the Aztec people before the Spanish conquest
		This Land Podcast, episode 4 (Nagle, 2019)	To show how Indigenous groups have been systemically oppressed
Relevance Text(s)	A fiction, nonfiction, or multimodal text that will garner students' interest and motivate them to want to read by doing at least one of the following: • Shows the relevance of the topic of the centering text	Indian Removals in Ohio (Wikipedia, n.d.)	To give students the opportunity to identify accurate information and correct misinformation
	• Provide a "gateway" activity that introduces the unit	"The Forgotten History of Ohio's Indigenous Peoples," article in Walton, 2020	To give students alternative, and silenced, perspectives to consider while revising the above Wikipedia article
		Newspaper article from *Columbus Dispatch*: "Ohio's Last Indian Tribe Was Forced out in 1843" (Staff Writer, 2013)	

STUDENTS SHOULD READ A VARIETY OF TEXTS THAT SUPPORT LEARNING OBJECTIVES

Within this chapter we offered a practical framework to help teachers answer the question, "What should my students read?" We suggest that they should read a variety of texts that work to support strong unit objectives. As Mrs. Bartleby, Ms. Anthony, and Dr. Perch created their text sets, they considered the goals of their respective disciplines as they selected texts so that the readings truly became tools for learning. Now that our teachers have considered how to identify their students' strengths and relevant aspects of their identities, leverage these through thoughtful task and text selection, the next step is to scaffold the learning experiences they have designed. The rest of the book offers ideas for how to support students to read challenging texts, with each chapter addressing a different text challenge.

TABLE 5.5. Mrs. Bartleby's Postcolonialism Unit Text Set

Instructional Goals	Essential Questions
Apply postcolonial perspectives to compare and contrast the historical and present-day issues of racism, enslavement, and geography. Analyze the authors' word choice, including connotations of language use and how the words influence the tone in *The Tempest* and *Americanah*. Interpret the *Americanah* and *The Tempest* using textual evidence to support conclusions.	• How can postcolonial perspectives help readers see historical and modern intersections of race and power? • How can authors use language to exemplify issues of race and power?

Text element	Text Goals	Selections	Purpose for Reading
Centering Texts	A textbook chapter, research, primary source document, or other written texts that does at least one of the following: • Provides linguistic or conceptual challenge • Provides an opportunity for literary reasoning	*The Tempest* (Shakespeare, c. 1611)	Give meaning and purpose to required text through literary reasoning
Supporting Text(s)	Pictures, maps, videos, infographics, or other visuals that do at least one of the following: • Builds knowledge needed to understand the centering text • Provides context for understanding or critiquing the centering text	Shakespeare Birthplace Trust's summary of *The Tempest* (Shakespeare. org.uk, n.d.)	Introduce key concepts (postcolonial perspectives) from popular sources
		SparkNotes summary of *The Tempest* (SparkNotes, n.d.)	Read last two paragraphs to show that Caliban was left out entirely
		Chapters 35 and 37 of *Americanah* (Adichie, 2013)	Apply the postcolonial lens to a contemporary text, and act as a counterstory to Shakespeare's colonialist vision
		A webpage giving a definition of postcolonial lens (University of Washington, n.d.)	Build background on key concepts

(continued)

TABLE 5.5. *(continued)*

Text element	Text Goals	Selections	Purpose for Reading
Relevance Text(s)	A fiction, nonfiction, or multimodal text that will garner students' interest and motivate them to want to read by doing at least one of the following: • Shows the relevance of the topic of the centering text • Provides a "gateway" activity that introduces the unit	TED Talk: Dangers of a Single Story (Adichie, 2009)	Provide students a lens to think about whose stories are told and whose are left out and show relevance for exploring this topic in Shakespearean literature

APPENDIX 5.A. Text Resource Websites

- Library of Congress's Education archives: *www.loc.gov/programs/teachers/classroom-materials*
- Census data: *https://data.census.gov*
- NASA Education: *www.nasa.gov/hrp/education*
- NOAA Education: *www.noaa.gov/education*
- Poetry Foundation: *www.poetryfoundation.org*
- NewsELA: *www.poetryfoundation.org*
- CommonLit: *www.commonlit.org*
- ReadWorks: *www.readworks.org*
- ActivelyLearn: *www.activelylearn.com*
- Science Journal for Kids: *www.sciencejournalforkids.org*
- Frontiers for Young Minds: *https://kids.frontiersin.org*
- Reading Like a Historian: *https://sheg.stanford.edu/history-lessons*
- WordGen: *www.serpinstitute.org/wordgen-weekly*
- The Big History Project: *www.oerproject.com/Big-History*
- CK12: *www.ck12info.org/mission*
- OpenStax: *https://openstax.org*

APPENDIX 5.B. Gravity Text Set Example

Let's revisit Ms. Astrid and the unit she wanted to create about space: *Gravity and Orbits: How Would Human Life Be Reimagined in Space?* The following template provides an example of her goals, essential questions, and texts she selected for her unit.

Sixth-Grade Gravity Text Set Example

Instructional Goals	Essential Questions
Explain how universal gravitation works to cause observable orbits of planets, moons, satellites, and spaceships To apply knowledge of universal gravitation to explain the impacts of gravitation on a human spaceflight to Mars	• How does gravity cause the predictable orbits of planets, moons, satellites, and spaceships? • How would life aboard a Mars-bound spaceship reimagine human physical, mental, and social life?

Text Element	Text Goals	Selections	Purpose for Reading
Centering Text(s)	A textbook chapter, research, primary source document, or other written texts that does at least one of the following: • Provides linguistic or conceptual challenge • Provides an opportunity for disciplinary reasoning	Textbook chapter on gravity (CK-12, 2020)	To understand how the gravitational force of Earth pulls an object toward the planet's center
Supporting Text(s)	Pictures, maps, videos, infographics, or other visuals that do at least one of the following: • Builds knowledge needed to understand the centering text • Provides context for understanding or critiquing the centering text	PhEt simulation of gravitational pull and orbits in the solar system (Gravity and Orbits, 2023) Overview and 10 things to know about the solar system (NASA, 2023a)	To help readers visualize the idea of universal gravitation so they can better understand gravitational pull and the rotation of objects in our solar system. To help readers understand the various aspects of the solar system so they can understand the various gravitational pulls that cause gravity.
Relevance Text(s)	A fiction, nonfiction, or multimodal texts that will garner students' interest and motivate them to want to read by doing at least one of the following: • Show the relevance of the topic of the centering text • Conveys a dominant narrative that needs to be examined critically	Excerpts from Introduction and Chapter 1 ("Gravity Rules") from *Packing for Mars for Kids* (Roach, 2022)	To engage readers' interest in learning about gravity with an interesting text about spaceflight and the woes of zero-gravity.

CHAPTER 6

How Can Teachers Scaffold Dense Texts?

GUIDING QUESTIONS

1. How do we teach texts that are densely packed with challenging ideas and concepts?
2. How can teachers support students in breaking down dense texts?

Sir Isaac Newton famously declared the law of universal gravitation. He explained this law in his famous book, the Principia. *He wrote that "There is a power of gravity tending to all bodies, proportional to the several quantities of matter which they contain."*

Ms. Astrid stares at this paragraph from her science textbook, reading it multiple times as she wonders how to help her sixth-grade science students read this text and learn the concept within it. While there is some vocabulary here that students may find difficult, by and large they are more likely to struggle with the idea of universal gravitation, a nonintuitive concept that almost clashes with their everyday understanding of gravity as one-directional (an object falling) rather than universal (all objects exerting a pull on all other objects).

The core challenge of this text is that it is *dense* with meaning and the very concepts it conveys are difficult to understand. In particular, this text requires that the reader make inferences and interpret abstract concepts to understand universal gravitation. Other dense texts that require a high level of interpretative skills include narratives with layered, ambiguous, or multiple meanings, texts with sophisticated themes, or texts that require specific disciplinary literacy skills, such as corroboration or evaluation of scientific data. And sometimes, dense ideas are embedded into grammatically complex sentences, making the dense ideas even more difficult to understand.

HOW DO WE TEACH TEXTS THAT ARE DENSELY PACKED WITH CHALLENGING IDEAS AND CONCEPTS?

Let's start with a discussion about what makes a text "dense." As we mentioned earlier, dense texts are those that convey complex ideas, like laws of gravity, or texts with multiple meanings, such as literary satires with both literal and metaphorical meanings. For example, George Orwell's *Animal Farm* is an allegory and is not really about animals or a farm. Dense texts are often accompanied by sophisticated vocabulary that have abstract meanings and are hard to understand. Dense texts can also contain long, complex sentences that can make the text difficult to explain.

As secondary teachers, our job is to teach texts that contain the hardest concepts students have yet encountered in their academic careers. This is exciting. But it's also intimidating. Many students find that the generic reading skills they were able to use in previous grades, such as making connections or predictions, no longer work when reading about the technical, abstract concepts prevalent in secondary texts. To help students develop more effective interpretation skills, teachers need to evaluate the specific texts they are teaching and prepare students to engage with specific (not generic) skills for that text.

To support secondary readers in understanding dense texts, teachers need to identify which skills are needed to make sense of a text, and more importantly, they need texts and tasks that are difficult enough to require the use of those skills to make meaning of the text. This means considering your readers as well as their skills and knowledge.

In lieu of more generic thinking strategies, we suggest scaffolding and instruction for dense texts with three underlying assumptions. First, scaffolding to understand dense texts requires instruction that is *specific* to a particular text. Remember the gravity text we shared at the beginning of this chapter? That text will require students to understand concepts such as proportion and matter in order to understand that gravity is not just one-directional, but universal, meaning all objects in the universe are constantly exerting a pull on all other objects. These are specific concepts that need to be gleaned from this text, and to do so, students will need scaffolds specifically designed to support the learning of these concepts in place of generic graphic organizers or generic thinking skills.

Second, we argue that comprehension of one text does not happen in a void but is related to students' understanding of *other* texts on that topic. Remember the critical layer of comprehension we introduced in Chapter 1? To think deeply about texts, readers synthesize information across texts. For example, in Ms. Astrid's science text set, students read not only a direct explanation of the principles of gravity and its physical effects on all objects, but also a news article about its effects on human life in orbit. In this way, Ms. Astrid scaffolds students' understanding of gravity by helping them draw connections to *other texts they read.*

Third, as we mentioned in Chapter 4, we believe that scaffolding of dense texts requires challenging tasks that are aligned with essential questions and disciplinary learning goals. Without a task that requires students to learn from dense texts, why should they do it? As you consider your scaffolding, you need to make sure you have created a task for the text that actually requires students to engage in analyzing, interpreting, or understanding a dense idea.

One way to do this is to ask text-dependent questions, which are questions that require students to respond using textual evidence rather than solely relying on personal reflection or opinion. Text-dependent questions compel students to engage in close reading to figure out what the text says, how it works, what it means, and what it can inspire (Fisher & Frey, 2015).

Let's look at an example. Ms. Astrid wants her students to read a chapter on gravity (you read part of it at the beginning of the chapter). To develop a text-based question that serves as a task for the unit, Ms. Astrid first considers her unit learning goals and essential questions. She wants her students to learn how gravity works. In particular, she wants them to understand how gravity causes the moon to rotate around the Earth and the planets to orbit around the sun at a predictable rate. She then thinks about the text: What information does she want students to take away from this particular text to help them achieve the learning goals and answer the essential question? She realizes that this text describes a key element of understanding gravity—that it is universal. This is what makes it predictable in nature. So, she decides that she wants her students to answer the following text-based question "Why is gravity universal?" Now that she has a challenging task, she is ready to scaffold her students to be able to read this dense text.

One question we are often asked is how many text-dependent questions should students answer in a text? I (Sarah) have noticed that sometimes teachers write text-dependent questions for every single detail in the text that they want students to take away. I've seen teachers write as many as ten text-dependent questions for a two-page text. Remember what we learned about comprehension in Chapter 1: it's not a light switch. Successful comprehension relies on a complex process that requires students to do the work of making sense of the text in order to glean new information and integrate it into the web of knowledge they already possess. Our scaffolding should help them get there, but we need to ensure that we aren't "picking the daisies" (remember that metaphor from Chapter 1?) for students. As teachers, we can over-scaffold by asking too many really specific questions. Asking between one and three questions (depending on the length of the text) that keep students focused on the "big idea" of the passage is a good goal and will allow students space to pick their own daisies as they read.

HOW CAN TEACHERS SUPPORT STUDENTS IN BREAKING DOWN DENSE TEXTS?

In order to support students to interpret and understand abstract concepts and themes in dense texts, we need to show students how to break these texts into more manageable pieces. The following sections explore strategies inspired from reading research about how to do this.

Chunk the Text

Something we have noticed with adolescents that we have taught is that the length of the text can sometimes be overwhelming. This is especially true when the text is full of dense ideas. For this reason, an important first step in supporting readers to think deeply about texts is to **chunk the text.** This means breaking up texts into more manageable "bites." Chunks don't need to be of equal sizes. For example, sometimes short chunks (1–2 sentences) are the perfect amount of text for students to digest at once. In other instances, chunks may be several paragraphs or even a couple of pages.

We think of it like this: Where is the text super tricky, or where might students get lost or unable to interpret an abstract idea or miss a key piece of information that will allow them to understand multiple layers of meaning? Stop at those points, and make that the end of a chunk.

After chunking the text, you can support your students' thinking prior to reading the chunk by providing a direction to help them interpret the densest parts of the chunk. Then, at the end of the chunk, you can either write, draw, or discuss the dense ideas in the chunk. Additionally, many of the following techniques described in this chapter will begin by dividing the text into bite-size chunks or should be combined with text chunking.

What does this look like? Let's go back to the chunk of text at the beginning of the chapter that Ms. Astrid is reading with her students. Before reading, Ms. Astrid tells her students to look for how Isaac Newton defines universal gravitation in the chunk of the text. After reading, she asks her students to turn and talk to a partner and explain in their own words a definition of universal gravitation.

Help Students Visualize Abstract Ideas

One thing that makes dense texts challenging is that the ideas in the text are often abstract, which means they are hard to visualize. But visualization can support students in building comprehension (De Koning & van der Schoot, 2013; de Leur et al., 2020). Consider Ms. Astrid's passage about gravity. While gravity itself is something students see and experience every day when they jump and return to the ground, the idea of universal gravitation is much more abstract. Students can't, for example, see or feel that their bodies are also exerting a (tiny) gravitational force on the Earth. Thus, helping students figure out a way to form a picture of abstract ideas in dense texts can help their comprehension.

To help students visualize abstract ideas, teachers can include pictures or videos to illustrate a concept between chunks of the text. Remember when we told you that text understanding doesn't happen in a void? Ms. Astrid's gravity simulation takes the idea of universal gravitation and allows students to manipulate the masses of the objects, demonstrating that these manipulations change the orbit of planets. Ms. Astrid could use that simulation prior to reading the textbook chapter, and then show a screenshot of the simulation between chunks to help students visualize how gravity acts on two bodies proportional to their mass. Additionally, simply asking students to draw or map out ideas using digital apps is another way that teachers can help students visualize abstract ideas.

Read the Text Multiple Times for Different Purposes

Another way that we can help students interpret dense texts is by **reading texts multiple times** for different purposes. This reading can be done in many different ways. For example, Wineburg and colleagues (2012) propose that students first read a primary source for literal comprehension by simply finding out what the words on the page say. Then, they reread the text for deeper historical thinking—to source the primary source (i.e., to inquire about who wrote it and why) or to corroborate with other contemporaneous sources. This procedure builds on our definition of the layers of comprehension in Chapter 1 and also shows the value of multiple-text comprehension. By establishing the historical facts and the literal layer of comprehension first, the teacher can then scaffold toward the critical comprehension across texts in the set.

Another way we can incorporate multiple readings is to read a text for fluency, which means with smoothness, expression, and intonation, and then invite students to try more expressive or interpretive readings. This technique has a good research backing. For example, studies where students practice multiple oral readings of a text in preparation for a performance have shown that after students are more familiar with the text, they are better able to explore why the author included certain details or how the historical context shaped the text (Keehn et al., 2008; Young et al., 2019). In Chapter 10, we will share multiple scaffolds that support multiple readings that support both word reading and comprehension.

We do present using multiple readings with cautions, however. We have sometimes noticed (and been guilty of this ourselves) teachers asking students to read a text again simply because they didn't understand the first time. We have observed (and experienced) how unhelpful it can be for confused students to be asked to "just read it again." Thus, if we are asking students to read a text again, we need to make sure it's purposeful and that they are reading the text in a different way than they read it the first time. For example, if students read a portion of *Beowulf* to understand the plot, but were still confused, they can read the text a second time and focus on the characters' actions or emotions. This second read will help them focus on different aspects of the text that they didn't take away the first time. In contrast, we wouldn't recommend using class time to reread a text selection that students understood through the first reading. Multiple reads, or close reading, requires a text that is sophisticated and complex enough that students will have more to take away from the text during a second read.

Prompt Students to Notice and Wonder

Both chunking and multiple text readings lend themselves well to a common approach for helping students understand the dense ideas in a text: close reading. One close reading protocol that works well across subject areas is **notice and wonder** (Beers & Probst, 2013). In this technique, teachers create a simple noticing task that has an easy entry point to engage readers and learners but offers rich potential for complex thinking. Some call these "low-floor/high-ceiling" tasks, which means that we provide an entry point with an easy task (noticing) to help students engage with a more complex task (wondering about a deep content-area question). How does this work? First, we ask students to share what they *notice* about a text, and then we use this information to help them develop ideas about what they *wonder* (see Table 6.1 for directions).

What does this look like? Let's visit Dr. Perch, our 10th-grade biology teacher, as he conducts his unit about ecosystems of the Great Lakes. He asks his students to read a text by the National Oceanic and Atmospheric Administration (NOAA) about harmful algal blooms in Lake Erie (2019) and to look at the pictures in the text about the algal blooms, writing down what they notice. In particular, he prompts students to notice colors, water flow, and connections to cities. Dr. Perch then asks his students to share what they noticed with a partner. As he circulates around the room, he hears students share that they noticed a neon green color in the middle of a lake or that some blooms seemed to occur closer to the shore or near cities.

Next, Dr. Perch invites his students to read the first chunk of this dense text. As they read, he asks them to continue jotting down what they notice about the algal blooms, and also what they wonder about why the algal blooms are green or near cities. Here is the first chunk:

> Lake Erie blooms consist of cyanobacteria, also called blue-green algae, that are capable of producing the liver toxin microcystin that poses a risk to human and wildlife health. Such blooms may result in higher costs for cities and local governments that need to treat drinking water, prevent people from enjoying fishing, swimming, boating and visiting the shoreline, and harm the region's vital summer tourism economy. These effects will vary in location and severity due to winds that may concentrate or dissipate the bloom. (NOAA, 2019)

At the end of the chunk, he invites his students to share what they notice and wonder. One student wonders if the algal blooms will threaten Lake Erie cities' water supplies, while another student wonders about the geography of Lake Erie—in particular, whether the phosphorus-rich agricultural runoff from the Maumee River caused the algal blooms. Dr. Perch uses these noticings and wonderings to help his students interpret the dense ideas in this text.

Model *Your* Thinking

Conducting close reading using the noticing protocol is a really important way to help students do the thinking work required to understand dense texts. But what should we do if students don't know how to do that type of thinking? What if students need more than a scaffold to prompt them to think and notice and wonder about the dense ideas in the text? We have found that **think-alouds** are a fantastic way to teach students how to do the thinking work needed to comprehend dense texts. In fact, think-alouds can be used to teach students how to adopt many of the strategies we suggest in this book.

During think-alouds, the teacher displays or reads aloud a short portion of a text and literally "thinks aloud" to demonstrate how they made sense of a particularly dense or tricky part of a text (Ness, 2017). The beauty of this technique is that the teacher makes the invisible process of thinking about difficult texts visible for students. Teachers do so by revealing "insider" moves that an expert reader makes. This

TABLE 6.1. How to Notice and Wonder

Procedures	Recommendations
1. Select a text (or excerpt) that is dense with ideas.	If students keep a notebook for your class, have them write what they noticed in their notebooks.
2. Develop a prompt to help students notice something about what is happening in the text. The prompt should be simple but should lead students toward understanding your larger learning goals for your unit.	Different-colored flags can be used to notice different aspects of the text.
3. Ask students to read and notice. You may ask students to place flags at spots in the text where they notice something they want to share. You could also ask students to write what they notice.	
4. Invite students to share what they notice.	
5. Invite students to share what they wonder about the text, related to what they, or what other classmates, have noticed.	
6. Encourage them to expand on their wonderings to deepen text understanding.	

may include, but is not limited to, noticing text structures and features and how those helped them understand the text; modeling how they made sense of a tricky part of a text by rereading or monitoring comprehension; or demonstrating for readers how they figured out important but unfamiliar vocabulary using the context or relevant roots or affixes (Lapp et al., 2008).

To use think-alouds effectively, they must be planned fully in advance. We do not recommend doing them "on the fly," as it takes a lot of thought to show how we do an autonomous process. For example, as advanced readers, teachers often automatically understand these more complex ideas in texts. As such, it takes planning and forethought for teachers to figure out how to model that autonomous thinking effectively for their students.

To that end, we suggest considering which part of the text you will "think aloud" about first and then write a short script of what you will say ahead of time. Although I (Sarah) don't always use my script (and I never read verbatim), I have found that writing down my thinking ahead of time helps me figure out how to explain how I understood a dense idea or complex theme in a text. In this way, I am prepared to do the think-aloud when I'm teaching. See Table 6.2 for instruction on how to plan a think-aloud.

What does this look like? Let's visit Mrs. Bartleby's 12th-grade English class as her students read an excerpt from *Americanah* where Ifemelu, her boyfriend Blaine, and his sister Shan gather with friends on Election Day 2008 to celebrate the election of Barack Obama. In this part of the text, the characters in the book are discussing how the room they are in for the party does not represent how the world looks, noting that their space is safe and equal for everyone. Grace then suggests that Ifemelu, a Nigerian

TABLE 6.2. How to Plan a Think-Aloud

Procedures	Recommendations
1. Decide on a piece of text that is very complex that you can use to model your thinking. 2. Decide what is hard about that piece of text. What makes the text dense? 3. Figure out how you made sense of it. For example, did you use a clue in another sentence to understand this part of the sentence? Did you rely on a piece of knowledge to help you understand this? 4. Write down this thinking in a script. Edit your script to make sure your thinking is easy to follow. 5. Read aloud the part of text you want to think aloud about. 6. Read your script to students to model your thinking. 7. Find a place in the text for students to try a similar type of thinking with each other after you have modeled your thinking.	This strategy works well with really challenging passages. For easier passages, a think-aloud is not necessary.

woman, write a blog post about the election day party. Mrs. Bartleby decides that she wants to model for her students how to read Shan's response with a postcolonial perspective, which adds a layer of density to the interpretation of this text that is already difficult for students in other ways.

As you can see in Mrs. Bartleby's thinking displayed in Table 6.3, reading literature is partly about basic comprehension challenges—like remembering the relationships between the characters Ifemelu and Shan. But it's also about interpreting the text from a different lens—in this case, a postcolonial lens. Here, Mrs. Bartleby models how she interprets Shan's distinction between the experience of immigrant Africans living in the United States (like Ifemelu) and African Americans who have lived in the United States for all of their lives (like Shan), from a historical perspective. The think-aloud shows the teacher's ability to read with both layers and helps students realize that they should be simultaneously tracking plot and engaging in text interpretation from a postcolonial perspective.

Ness (2017) argues that although think-aloud scaffolds can be extremely powerful, teachers often forget to do them because they assume that the "insider" knowledge is already visible to students. We agree, but we also suggest caution in how we use think-alouds. As a general rule of thumb, we like to make sure that if we model some type of thinking or way to overcome tricky text, we then give students time to practice thinking aloud to each other with a different part of the text after we have modeled so they can practice the skill. During this time, we listen to students thinking aloud to each other so that we can provide feedback and support. Modeling is an important tool, but we do not want to overuse it to the point that we are doing all the

TABLE 6.3. Example of a Think-Aloud for Mrs. Bartleby's Postcolonialism Unit

Text excerpt from *Americanah* (Adichie, 2013, p. 418)	What will the teacher say?	What is the teacher modeling?
"You know why Ifemelu can write that blog, by the way?" Shan said. "Because she's African. She's writing from the outside. She doesn't really feel all the stuff she's writing about. It's all quaint and	When Shan says "outside," she might mean that Ifemelu hasn't experienced the racism that African Americans have experienced. Shan draws the distinction between African and African American.	Staying grounded in the plot.
curious to her. So she can write it and get all these accolades and get invited to give talks. If she were African American, she'd just be labeled angry and shunned."	Remember the definition of postcolonialism and how Nigeria and America have different colonial histories? Reading with a postcolonial lens helps me notice the distinction Shan draws.	Highlighting the colonial history differences—connecting to the postcolonialism explainer text.
"The room was, for a moment, swollen in silence.	Remember, they're supposed to be at a party. This accusation makes it really tense.	Keeping grounded in the setting.

Note. Text excerpt from Adichie (2013). Reprinted by permission of HarperCollins Publishers Ltd © (2013).

thinking (and reading) for students. If we do all the work, how will they ever learn to interpret dense texts on their own?

So, in her lesson Mrs. Bartleby asks her students to read the next two sentences in *Americanah* and then turn to their partner and think aloud using a postcolonial perspective:

> "I think that's fair enough," Ifemelu said, disliking Shan, and herself too, for bending to Shan's spell. It was true that race was not embroidered in the fabric of her history; it had not been etched on her soul. Still, she wished Shan had said this to her when they were alone, instead of saying it now, so jubilantly, in front of friends, and leaving Ifemelu with an embittered knot, like bereavement, in her chest. (Adichie, 2013, p. 418)

Prepared by her think-aloud, Mrs. Bartleby's class would then work toward noticing both how Ifemelu acknowledges the different colonial histories ("not been etched on her soul") and how that part of the story affects Ifemelu's character ("embittered knot"). This is challenging literary thinking, but good modeling can show students how to manage these demands.

Encourage Students to Write from a Different Perspective

Writing is an important tool that can help students unpack and understand dense texts. The integration of writing with reading tasks has a long history of helping support students' text understanding because writing helps students translate dense ideas into their own words (Pearson & Fielding, 1991). Daniels and colleagues (2007) refer to this process of translation as *writing to learn*, which they define as short, unplanned, informal writing that is unedited and unpolished. Writing can be used as a tool to examine the text from a different perspective to help students break down, or translate, dense ideas.

What does this look like? Let's visit our eighth-grade history teacher, Ms. Anthony, in her planning for the unit exploring stereotypes of Indigenous populations. She asks her students to read the text "Scientists Trace Corn Ancestry from Ancient Grass" from the National Science Foundation. In the following excerpt, the author explores where maize, an important food for Indigenous people, came from. This particular excerpt explores a theory that Indigenous populations bioengineered another plant (teosinte, pronounced "tA-O-'sin-tE") into maize. Researchers have identified corn genes that Native Americans selected during the plant's domestication from its grassy relative, teosinte, to the single-stalked, large-eared plant we know today.

> Understandably, a primary goal of teosinte domestication was to improve the ear and its kernels. A teosinte ear is only 2 to 3 inches long with five to 12 kernels—compare that to corn's 12-inch ear that boasts 500 or more kernels! Teosinte kernels are also encased in a hard coating, allowing them to survive the digestive tracts of birds and grazing mammals for better dispersal in the wild. But, for humans, the tooth-cracking coating was undesirable so it was selectively reduced . . . and reduced . . . and reduced . . . until all that remains is the annoying bit of paper-thin, translucent tissue that sometimes sticks between the teeth when one munches corn on the cob.
>
> Between 6,000 and 10,000 years ago, Native Americans living in what is now Mexico began domesticating teosinte, or the "grain of the gods," as the name has been interpreted to mean. Scientists cannot yet say how long this domestication process took, but they do know that around 4,500 years ago, a plant recognizable as today's corn was present across the Americas.
>
> So, thousands of years before Gregor Mendel suggested theories on genetics and heredity, indigenous Americans were breeding corn to select for desirable traits. By selectively breeding each generation, ancient farmers drastically changed teosinte's appearance, yield, grain quality and survivability—culminating in today's "corn." In fact, teosinte is so unlike modern corn, 19th century botanists did not even consider the two to be related.

Ms. Anthony keeps in mind her learning goals and essential questions (sorting truth from stereotype) as she considers a way for students to write in order to process the dense idea. She considers stereotypes about Indigenous populations (i.e., that they were simple or incapable of technological advances, or that they lived in harmony with nature without ever making any modifications to it). She thinks about how this passage challenges that idea. She also thinks about what makes this passage so dense. The challenge is that it is an abstract idea to consider how what we understand as corn today was actually genetically engineered hundreds of years ago without any present-day technology. Ms. Anthony decides to use writing to help her students process these complexities and challenge their assumptions about the "simplicity" of Indigenous populations.

TABLE 6.4. How to Plan and Implement a Perspective Journal

Procedures	Recommendations
1. Select a text, or excerpt of a text, that students will be able to learn from if they take another perspective. 2. Decide on a prompt to provide students so they can describe a portion of the text from a different perspective. This perspective need not be a human one. For example, students can write about the water cycle from the perspective of a drop of water. 3. Ask students to read the text. 4. After reading, provide the prompt and ask students to write. 5. Ask students to share their perspectives with each other to compare and contrast their ideas (think pair share, small group, whole group).	Carefully consider how you invite students to write from a perspective that is not their own, and avoid having students take on marginalized peoples' or oppressors' perspectives. Consider the disciplinary forms of the "journal": should they use first- or third-person pronouns when journaling about/as historical figures? How precise should their data (science) or quotations (ELA) be?

She settles on a **perspective journal** (see Table 6.4 for a description of how to do a perspective journal). This scaffold asks students to rewrite the concept or idea from a different perspective. This perspective can be from a different character or person in the text, but it doesn't have to be a human one. For example, students can write from the perspective of a drop of water in the water cycle.

In this case, Ms. Anthony decides to ask her eighth graders to write how maize was engineered from the perspectives of a ear of mutated teosinte. This would require them to consider the original source (teosinte), summarize its properties, and explain the process of selective breeding. By using writing to take another perspective, students can break down dense ideas and interpret them. As you can see from Bette's perspective journal in Figure 6.1, she was able to process the ideas in the text by putting them in her own words. She did this by imagining what it was like to be an ear of engineered teosinte.

Teach Students to Paraphrase Grammatically Dense Sentences

At this point, we've provided numerous ideas for how to tackle dense or abstract ideas. But what do we do when the sentences are grammatically dense? For example, try to read this sentence from the introduction to *1491: New Revelations of the Americas Before Columbus,* which Mr. Douglass wants to use in his 11th-grade AP U.S. History class:

> Much of the environmental movement is animated, consciously or not, by what William Denevan, a geographer at the University of Wisconsin, calls, polemically, "the pristine myth"—the belief that the Americas in 1491 were an almost unmarked, even Edenic land, "untrammeled by man," in the words of the Wilderness Act of 1964, a U.S. law that is one of the founding documents of the global environmental movement. (Mann, 2011, p. 4)

I am a seed of corn, but I'm sad because I'm different from all of my friends. I'm an ear of teosinte. Normally, teosinte has few very small kernels on it. This is unfortunate because it means we don't have much nutritional value. But I'm different! I have thicker and bigger kernels. Although I'm sad to be different, I show promise. It's possible, if someone can learn to grow more teosinte like me, that we could become more nutritious and feed people.

FIGURE 6.1. Bette's perspective journal around *Before Columbus*.

You may have found this sentence difficult to read, as did we! That is because there is a lot to digest in one sentence. William Denevan is identified as "a geographer at the University of Wisconsin"; "the pristine myth" is identified as the belief that the Americas were an untouched wilderness; and the Wilderness Act of 1964 is identified as a U.S. law that helped inspire the global environmental movement. In some ways, this is helpful information because many readers are likely unfamiliar with Wiliam Denevan, the pristine myth, or the Wilderness Act. But it also makes for a very dense sentence. In fact, it's hard to see the very heart of the sentence: that the environmental movement is inspired by the idea that nature was untouched before European settlement. So, how can we support students in unpacking these dense sentences?

Research supports teaching students how to break down longer and grammatically complex sentences that are impeding text comprehension (Goodwin et al., 2022; Shanahan, 2022). One way we can do this is through **sentence paraphrasing**. Dan used this strategy in a study where tutors guided students through unpacking dense sentences (Reynolds, 2021). In this study, the teacher preselected dense sentences that were critical to learning from the text and taught students how to paraphrase them. When teaching students to paraphrase, we suggest focusing on having students read the sentence, and then explain what the sentence means in their own words. This works best when students can paraphrase out loud with another person. The teacher can then prompt students to notice what their partner included in their paraphrase that they did not include. Table 6.5 gives step-by-step instructions for how to do this scaffold.

Let's go back to Mr. Douglass's class and see how his students can use sentence paraphrasing to help them unpack *1491*. Mr. Douglass asks students to read the sentence, paraphrase it, write it down, and share it with a peer. Before they share, he reminds them to check to make sure they are accurately portraying the authors' meaning and that they have included all parts of the sentence. While students share, Mr. Douglass circulates, listening. He hears the following conversation:

ETTA: A geographer named Mr. Denevan says that the myth that America was uninhabited in 1491 isn't true, but people think it is.

JACOB: You are missing the part about the Wilderness Act of 1964.

ETTA: Let me try again. A geographer named Mr. Denevan says that the myth that America was uninhabited in 1491 isn't true, but this myth started the environmental movement and influenced the Wilderness Act of 1964.

TABLE 6.5. How to Do a Sentence Paraphrasing Scaffold

Procedures	Recommendations
1. Select a text with syntactically rich sentences that will be challenging to unpack and paraphrase. 2. Contextualize the text you'll be working with, making sure students know the general gist before you start, so they can focus on the sentence paraphrasing. 3. Ask students to read the sentence and notice all the parts of the sentence. 4. Ask students to put the sentence into their own words. 5. Have students reread the sentence and make sure their paraphrase includes all of the parts of the sentence and accurately describes the authors' meaning. 6. Ask students to share and compare their paraphrase with a partner and see if they are missing any parts of the sentence or if they have accurately portrayed the authors' meaning. 7. The teacher listens as students share their paraphrases and selects one or two good examples to share with the class.	Use both short and long sentences to provide practice with different types of sentence structures, as some short sentences pack a lot of meaning (e.g., "Race is not genotype; race is phenotype"). Paraphrasing is a complex strategy to teach, and using think-alouds to model is a helpful way to teach students how to do this well.

Mr. Douglass jots down Etta's revised paraphrase and uses it as an example to share with the class.

Sentence paraphrasing can be especially helpful with Shakespeare. Mrs. Bartleby used sentence paraphrasing to help her 12th graders interpret dense sentences in *The Tempest*. For example, John paraphrased the following lines: "Sometimes a thousand twangling instruments/Will hum about mine ears," as "The island the characters are on has beautiful sounds that are not scary."

In this way, putting the dense language into their own words helped John understand the meaning of this line. Mrs. Bartleby also specifically chose lines for her students to paraphrase that would help her achieve her ultimate goal of the lesson to employ a postcolonial perspective. In the example above, she asks her students to consider what it means for an enslaved person to share this description.

Write Down Directions, Explanations, and Supports in a Reading Guide

Another important way we scaffold readers' thinking so that they can interpret dense text is by providing explicit written directions, supports, and explanations in a **reading guide**. In our work with teachers, we have noticed that the term *reading guide* has a lot of meanings for a lot of people. We often see its meaning boiled down to a set of comprehension questions that students could just as easily answer after reading, rather than during reading. As we mentioned previously, text-based questions are really important. Remember Ms. Astrid's text-based question above to help her students understand Newton's Law of Universal Gravitation?

However, adolescents often need *additional scaffolds* to be able to answer these questions, particularly when the passage is dense. Reading guides are helpful because they can help students figure out what to focus on while reading (which helps them answer the text-based question). In this way, reading guides help students be active rather than passive readers, meaning they are reading with purpose and are making meaning. Reading guides also help students foster independence. I (Sarah) have often found that my students can read just fine, with my help. Where they struggle is when I ask them to read independently. Reading guides are a great stepping stone toward developing independent readers. Additionally, reading guides can incorporate a lot of the techniques that we have previously described in this chapter. Table 6.6 describes guidelines for creating a reading guide.

So what else does Ms. Astrid need to do to support her students to answer her text-based question, and how can she create a guide for her students that contains all of these supports? First, Ms. Astrid considers what challenges her students will face in the text—specifically, what will prevent them from understanding that gravity is universal? Ms. Astrid notes that some of the key vocabulary, such as "exert" and "mass," from the text is unfamiliar. So, as you see in Figure 6.2, on the left side of this guide, Ms. Astrid has defined these terms using a clear and brief definition. We emphasize the brevity of definitions—and explanations—used in reading guides. The goal of the

TABLE 6.6. How to Create and Implement a Reading Guide

Procedures	Recommendations
1. Select a difficult text or excerpt that requires a high amount of scaffolding. 2. Read through the text and decide which parts of the text students will have trouble understanding. 3. Revisit each spot and decide exactly why this spot is difficult. 4. Create a scaffold for the difficult spots (define a word, provide a brief explanation, give a direction, ask students to draw a picture, insert a picture, ask a question, etc.). 5. Decide how to organize your scaffolds (separate document or alongside the text?) in a way that students will be able to use the guide as they read. 6. Ask students to read the text using the guide. Follow up with a discussion on key points of the text.	Use as few words as possible in your explanations, definitions, or directions so that the guide itself doesn't increase the burden of reading. You do not need to scaffold *every* text challenge: consider your learning objectives and focus your scaffolds on those. Do students need to write on the guide? Not necessarily. Only ask students to stop and write if you think that writing in this moment—during reading—will truly help them overcome a text challenge.

Note. Adapted from Lewis and Strong (2020).

Newton's Law of Universal Gravitation

Definitions		*Other Supports*
	Most of us think of gravity as the force that brings us back to the ground if we jump. But it's actually much more than that. Sir Isaac Newton famously formulated the **law of universal gravitation**. He explained this law in his famous book, the *Principia*. He wrote that "There is a power of gravity tending to all bodies, proportional to the several quantities of matter which they contain." What does that mean?	*Sir Isaac Newton was a famous scientist in the 1600s. He was such a great thinker that his ideas are still studied today!*
	First, he says the power tends to *all bodies*. By that, he means that a "body" is a physical object. A tiny molecule, a human being, the moon, the Earth, the sun, the stars—all objects.	*As you read the next section, think about what the phrase* all bodies *means.* *Write what the phrase* all bodies *means.*
Put forth effort to do something	And he then says the power is *proportional*, meaning that it depends on how much matter is in each body. So the sun's huge matter **exerts** more power on the smaller Earth, and the Earth **exerts** more power on smaller human beings.	*What does it mean that power is proportional?*
Anything that has mass and volume	The law works both ways: Every person is made of matter, and that **matter** exerts a tiny force on the much, much bigger Earth. That's also why astronauts on the moon, which is considerably smaller than Earth, can jump much more easily and higher than on Earth. There's less gravity on the moon than on Earth because it's smaller.	*Stop and draw a picture of the moon and the Earth. Show how proportional they are in size to one another.*
	The law can even explain why ocean tides exist: The moon isn't big enough to pull oceans off the Earth, but it does pull water in the oceans a little bit back and forth each day as the Earth rotates. Amazingly, Newton was the first to notice that every object exerts a force of gravity on every other object in the universe. That's why the law is *universal*.	*Add lines to your picture to show the pull of gravity between the earth and the moon.* Then, write: what does it mean that **gravity** is universal?

FIGURE 6.2. Example of Ms. Astrid's science reading guide.

reading guide scaffold is to ease the burden of reading, and adding too much text can increase the burden of reading, rather than decrease it.

Next, Ms. Astrid realizes that the density of the text may make it difficult for her students to see all of the author's clues that show them what universal gravitation means, such as the definition of "universal." So, she adds a direction in her guide to help her students notice key concepts that will help them understand the definition of this word, making it more likely that they will be able to use the definition to help them understand the text. For example, Ms. Astrid adds a support to direct her students to understand the concept of power as being proportional, so they can understand why gravity varies on the moon (a smaller object) compared to on earth (a larger object). Then, she realizes that this concept is abstract, so she adds a visual. She asks her students to draw the Earth and the moon proportionally; then, she asks them to draw proportional lines to show that gravity can exert its force in different directions simultaneously.

Another type of guide that can help students' thinking is an anticipation guide. We love anticipation guides as they help students to think about key ideas before they read, and then revisit those ideas after reading. As such, these serve to help students activate—and even build—knowledge before reading, and to help students integrate new knowledge gained in the text after reading. As such, we will discuss the power of anticipation guides in Chapter 7.

Use Discussion to Scaffold Dense Texts

An important way to help students unpack dense texts is to engage in purposeful discussions. However, discussion is often rare in secondary classrooms. While research does not identify clear reasons why discussions remain uncommon, many have speculated that discussions require students to be willing to share their ideas in front of peers and teachers to be willing to give up some control over the classroom. Additionally oral language skills are often overlooked in the classroom because they are difficult for students and are not assessed on state tests. Despite these challenges, discussions are critical for building the complex thinking and literacy skills needed to tackle dense texts.

But scheduling time for discussion alone is not enough: Teachers need to carefully plan for *and* teach students how to engage. Good discussions are unlikely to happen spontaneously, and simply walking into a classroom and posing a discussion question is unlikely to produce rich discussion that supports students in working through dense ideas in the text. We know that during a live discussion teachers need to be ready to support students, and in Chapter 11 we will address how to do this. But here we will focus on how to *plan* for and *teach* students how to engage in discussions that can support students in unpacking ideas in dense texts.

Planning for discussion with dense texts requires that teachers develop open-ended prompts grounded in the challenging texts that allow for interpretation, debate, and perspective taking. (For more information about crafting quality questions, see our earlier discussion in this chapter about writing text-dependent questions.) These discussion prompts are often variations on the unit's essential question(s). Planning for discussion means providing support for students to prepare their thinking, gather evidence, and try out ideas in less risky settings before discussing with the whole class.

Teaching students how to engage in rich discussion is a different part of the planning process. Tomes have been written about how to facilitate a good discussion, and we do not have the space in this book to cover all of it. We suggest that teachers consider which discussion skills their students need support with and focus on those specific skills. For example, are your students having trouble responding to each other's ideas, or are a few students monopolizing the floor? Are students having trouble keeping the discussion on topic? Select one or two skills, explain the skills to students, and include those skills as part of your discussion norms that you refer to before beginning discussion.

One way to facilitate productive discussion is to be explicit in what a good discussion looks like. This may include listing classroom discussion norms, which can include specific aspects of discussion that you are working on. For example, Ms. Astrid has a number of gregarious students who dominate conversations, and this doesn't allow her quieter students to participate. Her first two norms are "speak for an appropriate amount of time" and "encourage others to speak who haven't spoken yet." Additionally, she has been working with students on using text evidence to support answers and to build on others' ideas by restating what they have said, so she includes these as discussion norms, too.

MS. ASTRID'S DISCUSSION NORMS

- Speak for an appropriate amount of time.
- Encourage others to speak who haven't spoken yet.
- Use text evidence to support answers.
- Build on others' ideas by restating what someone else said first before stating own ideas.

In addition to explicitly stating discussion norms, teachers can add structure by using specific discussion protocols, such as a **fishbowl**. To do this, one group comes to the front of the class, and everyone observes that group engage in discussion. The rest of the class provides "glows" (what the group is doing well) and "grows" (what the group could do better) for the group in the *fishbowl*. All groups eventually get a turn "on stage," but they also have the opportunity to watch discussion and practice active listening. I (Sarah) have also asked groups to intentionally make mistakes so that the class has something to critique. This takes the pressure off of the group when receiving criticism because I can explain to the class that they made that mistake on purpose so we could talk about it.

Let's see another example. Ms. Astrid's class has just read their textbook chapter on Newton's Law of Universal Gravity, using the well-designed reading guide we shared above. Ms. Astrid focuses her discussion on the text-based question she embedded at the end of the reading guide: What does it mean that gravity is universal? She knows that her students are prepared for this discussion because she has scaffolded their understanding of dense ideas in this text with the reading guide, which students can also draw from during the discussion.

Ms. Astrid considers how to support her students in engaging in a good discussion. She reminds them of the discussion norms they have been using (see Sidebar 6.1), which include specific discussion skills they are working on, namely, building on each other's ideas and using text evidence to support responses. She has thoroughly taught them how to do both of these skills using fishbowls. Although her students are still moving toward proficiency of these skills, they have made much improvement in recent months.

TEACHING STUDENTS TO BREAK DOWN IDEAS IS KEY TO SCAFFOLDING DENSE TEXTS

This chapter provides a variety of suggestions to answer the question, "How can teachers scaffold dense texts?" The techniques shared here can help students break down texts that are packed with challenging ideas into meaningful chunks in order to process and interpret them through writing and discussion. But beyond that, the techniques described in this chapter give students a purpose for tackling the more challenging—yet also the most meaningful parts—of English, history, and science. These techniques provide a *why*: to understand that stories are more than plots, that history is more than names and dates, and science is more than theories. But even more vital, teaching students to tackle dense texts means teaching students how to be better *thinkers*, and what can be more rewarding than that?

CHAPTER 7

How Can Teachers Scaffold Knowledge Demands?

GUIDING QUESTIONS

1. How does a reader's prior knowledge affect what they will learn from a text?
2. How can we help students use what they know to understand a text?

So, a decade before Yuri Gagarin became the first person in space, long before John Glenn and Neil Armstrong, before Ham the astrochimp and Laika the space dog, before all of them, was Albert. Albert was a nine-pound rhesus monkey. In 1949, dressed in a gauze diaper, little red-haired Albert, one of five spacefaring monkeys named Albert, rode a V-2 rocket into space. He was the first mammal to go there. (Roach, 2022, pp. 9–10)

Ms. Astrid, a sixth-grade science teacher, stares at this paragraph in *Packing for Mars for Kids,* the text she is asking her students to read tomorrow. She wonders if her students know who John Glenn or Neil Armstrong are, or if they know about rhesus monkeys or V2 rockets, or that humans are mammals. She also wonders if they *need* to know these things to make sense of this text. She recently attended a teacher training session that reinforced the importance of knowledge on text understanding. She took away the message that kids can't comprehend texts if they don't have knowledge about the topic of the text. However, she doesn't know what to *do* about it.

Should Ms. Astrid focus on teaching her students about John Glenn, space mammals, and unfamiliar concepts before they read the text? In this chapter, we will answer her question by sharing what the research says about how a reader's prior knowledge influences their ability to learn from that text. We will also share techniques that help teachers build relevant knowledge and activate what readers already know to help understand and learn from texts.

HOW DOES A READER'S PRIOR KNOWLEDGE AFFECT WHAT THEY WILL LEARN FROM A TEXT?

The role that knowledge plays in comprehension is often misunderstood, which can lead to poor instructional practices that hinder the reader's ability to learn from texts across subject areas. To better understand the relationship between knowledge and comprehension, we must first understand the concept of *knowledge*.

Knowledge is the sum of what an individual knows, and it includes more than simply facts about science or social studies. As we discussed in Chapter 3, a person's knowledge includes linguistic structures, including dialects or different registers of speaking for different situations, as well as cultural and life experiences. Using this broad definition of knowledge can help teachers look for ways to support comprehension.

Extensive research has helped us better understand the relationship between knowledge and comprehension. As mentioned in Chapter 1, comprehension happens in layers (Kintsch, 2013; Kintsch & van Djik, 1978). The ultimate goal of comprehension, or the highest layer, is when a reader's existing knowledge is integrated with what they are reading. What does this mean? It means that readers learn something new in a text by connecting it with something they already know.

Does this mean that readers need to know things about a topic to be able to read? It depends. A reader's depth of knowledge about the topic is important because readers with greater knowledge of the topic may have a more nuanced understanding of the material (McCarthy & McNamara, 2021). Additionally, the *accuracy* of readers' knowledge of the topic influences comprehension and learning (McCarthy & McNamara, 2021). That means that teachers need to be aware not only of what readers know, but also of any misconceptions students may have about the topic. Addressing these inaccuracies prior to reading and letting students know that what they will read might be different from what they already know has been shown to improve students' text understanding (Hattan & Lupo, 2020). For example, Ms. Anthony, an eighth-grade history teacher, may address assumptions about the "first Thanksgiving" before asking students to read a text that builds a more robust picture of Indigenous populations. It is also important to distinguish between true misconceptions and differences of opinion or perspective.

However, knowledge of a topic is not a requirement for a student to be able to read and understand a text. We read about things that we don't know much about all the time. That is how we learn new things, and we're sure you do, too. The key to reading about an unfamiliar topic is whether the author has assumed that the reader knows anything about the topic. When authors write, they envision their audience and what that audience knows about the topic. If the author does not think their audience knows much about a topic, they will include explanations, pictures, and information to help the reader understand the topic.

Let's see what this looks like in a text. An excerpt from the NASA website (Figure 7.1) describes sun dust (it's a thing!). Here, the author did not assume that readers knew anything about sun dust, although they assumed that readers understood the general concept of dust. As such, the author explained how the dust got around the sun (it was surrounded by a disk of gas and dust early in its history) and provided a visual of what the dust rings look like. In this way, the text itself is a scaffold to better understand the concept, and so the reader is not required to bring much knowledge about sun dust to the reading experience in order to understand this text.

However, if the author has assumed that the reader knows quite a lot about a topic, they do not include these text scaffolds. But if the reader in fact *does not* know about this topic, it can impact their understanding of the text. Essentially, our prior knowledge about a topic shapes what we learn from a text rather than prevents it. This means that teachers don't need to activate all the possible knowledge in a text, just the knowledge aligned with the lesson's purpose. For example, let's go back to the text at the beginning of this chapter for Ms. Astrid's sixth-grade science class. In this text, students who don't know who John Glenn was can likely still infer that he was an early astronaut. Further, since the goal of Ms. Astrid's text set is to understand the effects of gravity on humans in space, it's not essential to know that Mr. Glenn was the first American to orbit the Earth. Thus, it's more important to scaffold the knowledge around NASA's animal tests and to consider that before the late 1940s, nobody knew if humans could even survive in space.

In this way, scaffolding knowledge requires paying equal attention to the text (what the author has assumed readers need to know) and your students (what they actually know that will be helpful in understanding the text). This means that scaffolding knowledge demands of a text requires both *activating* and *building* knowledge.

SUN DUST

The Sun would have been surrounded by a disk of gas and dust early in its history when the solar system was first forming 4.6 billion years ago. Some of that dust is still around today, in **several dust rings** that circle the Sun. They trace the orbits of planets, whose gravity tugs dust into place around the Sun.

FIGURE 7.1. Excerpt from Overview of the Sun from NASA website. Retrieved from *https://solarsystem.nasa.gov/solar-system/sun/overview.*

What does activating and building knowledge mean? Activating knowledge means bringing students' relevant knowledge to the forefront to make it more likely they will use that knowledge while reading. Building knowledge, on the other hand, means providing students with information about a topic that they do not already know so that it will help them better understand what they are reading. Building knowledge does not mean sharing information that is in the text prior to reading; rather it's providing information that the author has assumed students know but isn't in the text itself. For example, Ms. Astrid wants her students to read a textbook chapter on gravity that assumes they know what the solar system is and how it works but doesn't include information about the solar system in the text. Ms. Astrid realizes that some of her students know this information, but others do not, so she includes a brief reading about the solar system for students to read prior to reading the textbook chapter.

Although building relevant knowledge and activating existing knowledge are seen as different processes, the reality is that these processes often occur at the same time using the same techniques. For example, when teachers ask students to share what they know about a topic to activate their knowledge in a classroom discussion, they are simultaneously building essential topic knowledge for other students in the classroom. Or when students read a text or listen to a lecture to build knowledge about a topic prior to reading, their background knowledge on that topic is also activated while reading or listening. In the example above, Ms. Astrid knew some of her students already knew about the solar system, and as such the brief reading would activate what they knew, rather than build knowledge. Thus, we suggest approaching knowledge building and activating as two sides of the same coin, and most of the techniques we share below use both of these processes.

HOW CAN WE HELP STUDENTS USE WHAT THEY KNOW TO UNDERSTAND A TEXT?

In the following section, we show specific strategies for helping students activate and build knowledge. Both activating and building knowledge support students in integrating new knowledge about the subject with what they already know—a major goal of comprehension.

Use Other Texts to Build and Activate Knowledge

We have already introduced one of the most important ways we can help readers build and activate relevant knowledge to support their text understanding: have them read about the topic. In Chapter 5, we introduced the text set framework, using a *centering text* to anchor the unit, then finding *supporting texts*, which will help students understand and critically read the centering text, and *relevance texts*, which will serve to "hook" readers' interest. In this way, teachers can thoughtfully select texts that work together to support students' learning about disciplinary concepts.

For example, in Ms. Anthony's unit, her students read a text about stereotypes regarding Indigenous people set in their own state, "The Forgotten History of Ohio's

Indigenous Peoples" by Jessie Walton (2020). Students might learn some new things in this article, such as the fact that Ohio was an original Indian Territory location where Indigenous populations were initially forced into reservations. However, students will also be able to connect what they are learning in their unit to what they already know about Ohio. For example, the article describes some previous Ohio tribes, such as the Kickapoo, Shawnee, and Miami tribes. By eighth grade, many of Ms. Anthony's students are familiar with such tribes in Ohio. (They do a year-long Ohio history study in fourth grade.) As a result, the Walton article serves as a way to activate what they know by bringing this knowledge to the forefront of their mind to help them understand the text. Now, you may remember from previous chapters that several of Ms. Anthony's students who are refugees did not grow up in Ohio, so the same article might build relevant knowledge.

Use Activities to Build and Activate Knowledge

In addition to using texts to build and activate knowledge, teachers might use activities in this way too. In Chapter 5 we also introduced the idea of "gateway" activities that can help garner students' interest, as well as build knowledge about the topic. For example, in Dr. Perch's high school biology class, students engaged in the *Watershed Game*, a board game developed at the University of Minnesota to begin his unit on the impact of ecosystems of the Great Lakes. The game builds knowledge about different professionals whose work connects to watershed health, such as pollution specialists, reporters, and farmers, as well as the different kinds of pollution runoff (phosphorus and sediment) that affect watershed pollution. Students play different roles and scenarios to try to minimize water pollution on a fixed budget.

Other activities to build and activate knowledge might include an experiment or a demonstration. These types of activities have been shown to both build and activate what students know to help them understand a topic. For example, before reading a physics chapter about force and motion, students were asked to draw and describe the path a marble would take if it were shot off the table, then watch and see what happened when a marble was actually shot off the table (Alvermann & Hynd, 1989). In this way, they were able to activate what they knew about force and motion, and also build knowledge by observing the phenomena that the textbook chapter describes before reading.

Use Writing and Discussion to Activate Prior Knowledge

A tried-and-true method of helping children connect what they know to what they are learning is to simply prompt children to share ideas about what they know about a topic through writing and discussion. A well-known way of doing this is through the use of a **KWL chart** (short for Know–Want to Know–Learned) in which students think about what they know and want to learn about a topic prior to reading and what they learned after reading (Ogle, 1986). KWL charts are most effective when teachers can facilitate a strong discussion around each element (remember what we shared about discussion in Chapter 6—and we'll address discussion more in Chapter 11, too). The discussion should support students to elicit helpful knowledge and ask thoughtful questions prior to reading (Lupo et al., 2019). But further, teachers can use discussion to help students evaluate their knowledge or identify disagreements between students about the accuracy of the facts shared. These are great opportunities for teachers to help students formulate thoughtful text-based questions about what they want to learn in the passage. See Table 7.1 to learn how to plan for and implement a KWL chart that embeds thoughtful discussion and see Handout 7.1 for a blank template.

When teachers are conducting KWLs, it is imperative that they view all students as bringing some relevant knowledge to the situation, and work toward finding and drawing out that knowledge. In this way, teachers can take a strengths-based approach to knowledge and help their students recall knowledge that connects to the text. For example, in a classroom I (Sarah) observed, the teachers facilitated a discussion

TABLE 7.1. How to Plan for and Implement a KWL Chart

Procedures	Recommendations
1. The teacher identifies several topics that students may have knowledge about related to the topic and develops prompts to share with students to activate their knowledge. 2. The teacher first asks students to respond to the prompts in writing on their own KWL chart, then elicits ideas from the class to engage in a discussion around what the class knows. 3. As the class discusses, the teacher adds ideas about what students know on the whole class KWL chart. They may also note some areas of disagreement as well as help students evaluate their own knowledge and form questions about what they want to learn. 4. The teacher then prompts students to write additional questions about what they want to learn on their individual charts. 5. The teacher engages in a discussion about what students want to learn about the topic, writing more questions on the whole-class KWL chart and facilitating students to ask text-based questions that will guide their reading. 6. Students read the text. After reading, they add ideas into their "learned" column on their chart. 7. The teacher engages students in a discussion about what they learned. They review their Want to Learn questions, trying to answer each one.	This technique requires whole-group discussion to be effective. The teacher should continue to prompt students, going broader or switching topics, until they find something that students know about the topic. The teacher should provide guidance and support to help students ask strong questions that can be answered in the text.

around what students knew about Syria and the Holocaust to prepare them to read a text that compared immigration policies between Germany during the Holocaust and present-day Syria. The teacher began by asking students what they knew about Syria, and it was not very much. So, she switched topics and asked students what they knew about the Holocaust. The students had plenty to share about the Holocaust, and that knowledge helped them understand the text. What struck me the most was the teachers' assumption that all her students had knowledge, exemplifying a strengths-based approach to knowledge building.

Additionally, teacher facilitation can be used to help students generate text-based questions about what they want to read, which can help students set a purpose for reading. For example, in another ninth-grade classroom I observed (Lupo et al., 2021), students preparing to read a text about the ebola outbreak in New Guinea. The teacher asked them what they hoped to learn, and one student asked "Can newborn babies contract ebola?", which is not a question answered directly in the text. The teacher helped the student reshape the question to be more purposeful and relate to the text by adding, "I think you might be asking who can contract ebola or who is most impacted by the virus." This type of support is crucial in helping students develop good questioning skills.

Let's explore what this looks like in Ms. Anthony's eighth-grade class in her unit on Indigenous populations. Ms. Anthony considers how to support students in activating what they know before listening to the podcast *This Land* by Rebecca Nagel. Ms. Anthony knows that students have some misconceptions, or even stereotypes, that need to be addressed prior to reading. For example, her students might think that Indigenous people represent one big group, or they might not be able to recognize differences within Indigenous peoples. She also considers how to help all of her students draw on their background knowledge prior to listening to this text. She knows that she has students who might have been essentialized as larger groups of refugees, despite their own families' unique histories. So she includes one prebuilt note under the "W" in the middle column to help activate that connection to their identities and consider different viewpoints that states "Ms. Anthony's Wonder: How did the U.S. government view the Cherokees? As one group with one viewpoint? Or with multiple viewpoints?" Figure 7.2 shows a completed version of Ms. Anthony's KWL chart.

In science, **KLEWS** may be used instead of KWL (Hershberger & Zembal-Saul, 2015). As you can see in Table 7.2, KLEWS contains some elements of KWL, such as what do we know (K), what are we wondering about (W), and what are we learning (L), but adds exploring evidence for the claims and learning (E) and scientific principles (S). These additions can help science teachers connect their learning to evidence and scientific principles. See a blank KLEWS template in Handout 7.2.

What does KLEWS look like? Let's revisit Dr. Perch as he is planning to read the *Death and Life of the Great Lakes* during his unit on the Great Lakes ecosystems. Dr. Perch knows his students already enjoy Great Lakes recreation with swimming and fishing. The KLEWS procedure helps activate what students already know about the Great Lakes and name what they are learning while they read this passage. For example, Clara has indicated that she knows pollution is an issue (under column K) and wants to know what she can do to help (under column W). She is then able to connect this

K Know	W Want to Know	L Learned
• I know the Cherokee are an Indigenous tribe. • I know that the Cherokee were forced to travel west on the Trail of Tears. • I know that murder is illegal. I know that 1839 was a long time ago before the Civil War.	Ms. Anthony's Wonder: How did the U.S. government view the Cherokees? As one group with one viewpoint? Or with multiple viewpoints? Students' Wonder: • I want to know what the promise he made was. • I want to know why he was murdered and who murdered him. • I want to know what was in the treaty that made someone want to murder him.	• Americans migrated west earlier than I thought. • The Georgia military attacked the Cherokee nation after they made themselves a Constitution. • The Cherokee leaders had to sign a treaty to take land out west because President Jackson wasn't letting them keep their land in Georgia. • Other Cherokees killed the guys who signed the treaty because they didn't want to give up their land in Georgia.

FIGURE 7.2. Example from Ms. Anthony's KWL chart.

TABLE 7.2. How to Plan for and Implement KLEWS

Procedures	Recommendations
1. The teacher considers the text and students' knowledge and plans prompts to elicit what students know about the topic. 2. The teacher shares the prompts with students, asking them first to write their ideas under the "K" portion of the chart below, and then share out as a whole group. K—What do we think we know? L—What are we learning? E—What is our evidence? W—What do we still wonder about? S—What scientific principles help explain this phenomena? 3. After engaging in some learning, the teacher asks students to stop and jot down ideas about what they are learning under the "L" portion of their charts. 4. The teacher may ask students to jot down ideas about evidence and wonderings for that learning at the same time, or later in the lesson. 5. After the students have some information under learnings and evidence, the teacher asks students to consider what scientific principles help them understand this information. Here, the teacher should be ready to prompt students to go back to the text to name the scientific principles in action specifically. 6. Throughout the experiment, reading, or unit, the teacher continues to prompt students to add ideas to the organizer under each of the headings.	These prompts are not necessarily completed in order and can be done on different days throughout a unit.

learning to relevant scientific principles using key terms: She identifies that mussels are an invasive species because they disrupt the dynamics of the ecosystem (under S, see Figure 7.3). As Clara's example demonstrates, KLEWS is a great way for students to reinforce key science principles and vocabulary they are learning throughout this unit.

Another way teachers can use writing and discussion to activate students' prior knowledge is through a **pre–post journal.** A pre–post journal begins with the teacher providing a prompt for students to respond to before reading, and then asking students to revisit that prompt after reading to add ideas or adjust their thinking (see Table 7.3). In this way, students activate what they know prior to reading, making it more likely they will use that knowledge. In the end, they can see how their thinking had been changed or affirmed after reading.

Let's explore what this looks like. Ms. Anthony is considering how to help her students understand the text *Before Columbus* by Charles C. Mann (2011). She knows that her students have had exposure to pop culture views of Indigenous people that are often reflected in popular movies, and she wants to have her students explore their misconceptions in writing. As such, she asks them to reflect on the following question prior to reading:

> *What was life like for Indigenous people before European settlers arrived? Please consider how densely populated North America was (or wasn't), what kinds of technologies or advances Indigenous people were familiar with and used, as well as the relationship Indigenous people had with nature.*

K **What do we think we know?**	**L** **What are we learning?**	**E** **What is our evidence?**	**W** **What do we still wonder about?**	**S** **What scientific terms or principles explain this phenomenon?**
The Great Lakes used to be really polluted, and the rivers even caught fire, but now we've cleaned all that up. The Great Lakes are fun for swimming and fishing.	Freighters brought mussels and other species into the Great Lakes with the ballast water. The new species are devastating the Great Lakes ecology.	Trillions of mussels cover the lake floor of Lake Michigan from Michigan to Wisconsin. A total of 186 nonnative species live in the Great Lakes. Ballast water can be 10 swimming pools, so a lot of invasive species can be brought in with one ship.	This sounds really terrible. What can we do about it? Why didn't anyone stop the ballast water from being dumped in the lakes? Who else is affected by this damage?	**Invasive species:** This mussel is not just living in a lake, but it's disrupting the entire dynamic of the **ecosystem.** This relates to food webs because the mussels' filter feeding causes the lake to be unnaturally clear, affecting which plants grow on the lakebed.

FIGURE 7.3. Clara's KLEWS chart from Dr. Perch's Great Lakes ecosystems unit.

TABLE 7.3. How to Plan and Implement a Pre–Post Journal

Procedures	Recommendations
1. The teacher creates a prompt that students can write about both before and after reading that will activate relevant knowledge and provide opportunities for knowledge integration. 2. Students respond to the prompt before reading. 3. The teacher can provide opportunities for discussion to help students generate ideas with each other and activate more knowledge. 4. After reading, students add ideas to their original writing, or adjust what they wrote to have more precision and accuracy. 5. A follow-up discussion can help students further integrate what they are learning.	This technique works well when the text challenges students' existing viewpoints. Students can use different colors of writing utensils to show differences in their thinking before and after reading.

Let's explore one of Ms. Anthony's student's responses (see Figure 7.4). Notice how Mary's post-journal reflects how much her viewpoint has changed. For instance, Mary's pre-journal claims that "they would never hunt too much." But after reading the excerpt from *Before Columbus*, Mary shows a more developed sense of knowledge about Indigenous peoples. In the right column, she is unsure about whether Indigenous people left the land untouched ("this is a puzzling question") and considers that Indigenous people likely planted corn on larger scales ("they might plant a lot of corn"). By priming the student to integrate the knowledge from the passage, Ms. Anthony's scaffold helped her student to meet the larger unit goal.

Pre	Post
North Americans had a religious relationship with nature. They worshiped many different gods of nature, and they would never hunt too much. They may have harvested corn, if they worked and if it was harvesting season.	Did Native Americans leave the land untouched? This is a puzzling question, and I think it's a bit religious and a bit about population and a bit location wise. If a group of Native Americans worshiped a corn god hugely, they might plant a lot of corn. If there is a big group of Native Americans, they would plant more corn. Native Americans may have planted corn in meadows, but if they lived far away from any meadows, they may have cut down more trees to plant corn.

FIGURE 7.4. Mary's pre–post journal regarding indigenous peoples' relationship to nature.

Support Students to Integrate New and Prior Knowledge

To help students integrate new and prior knowledge, we suggest activities that may help students activate what they know prior to or even during reading, and then come back to that knowledge after reading to see how their ideas have been affirmed or changed.

One way you can do this is to use a **driving question board**. In this technique, teachers ask students to write ideas on a poster or sticky note related to the unit's essential questions throughout the unit (see Table 7.4 for more information). Students can write ideas on sticky notes or on the poster and then engage in discussion about those ideas. Essential questions can be broken down into sub-questions or subtopics to organize the driving question board into narrow topics.

What does this look like? Let's go back and visit Ms. Astrid as she begins her unit on gravity. She starts with her essential questions for the unit, "How would life aboard a Mars-bound spaceship reimagine human physical, mental, and social life?" She decides to break this question into subquestions to help her students activate what they know, such as "What do we know about traveling to space?" She also adds smaller questions to help her students integrate what they are learning about gravity with what they know, such as, "What challenges will people face in space travel?" She hopes that this question will let students take what they are learning about gravity and apply it. See an example of her driving question board in Figure 7.5.

Another way to help students integrate new and prior knowledge is through the use of a **carousel brainstorm** (Daniels et al., 2007). In a carousel brainstorm, which is similar to a driving question board, students share ideas to prompts on posters around the room, and then circulate so they can see others' ideas. After reading, students revisit their brainstorm posters and add or change ideas based on what they learned (see Table 7.5). The difference between driving question boards and carousel brainstorms is that instead of organizing ideas around the essential (or driving) question(s), students organize their new and prior knowledge around relevant topics.

TABLE 7.4. How to Create a Driving Question Board

Procedures	Recommendations
1. The teacher posts the essential question(s) for the unit on a wall of the classroom. This may include breaking down essential questions into smaller subquestions. 2. Near the beginning of the unit, students generate ideas and questions about the essential questions. 3. The teacher organizes these ideas into subquestions or categories, putting each idea onto the board. 4. The students add ideas and questions to the categories or subquestions as the unit develops.	Discussion pairs well with this technique. You can begin with subquestions, or develop additional questions as you learn more about the topic.

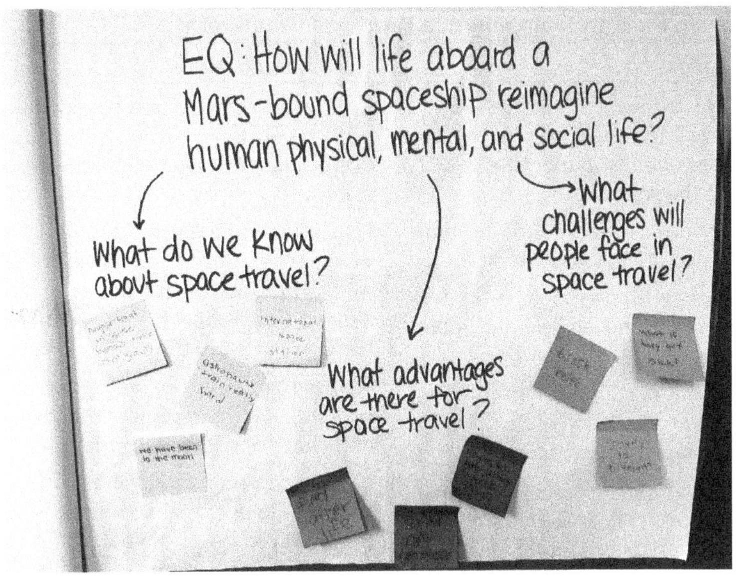

FIGURE 7.5. Example driving question board from Ms. Astrid's sixth-grade gravity unit.

For example, across the hall from Ms. Astrid is Ms. Bennett, who teaches sixth-grade ELA. Her students are currently engaged in a thematic unit exploring the complexities of family life. They are reading a number of texts, including the novel *The Evolution of Calpurnia Tate* by Jacqueline Kelly. There are thematic elements in this novel, such as complex families and gender roles, that are familiar to students but also complex enough for students to explore. As such, the carousel brainstorm is an ideal choice to activate knowledge about this book. Ms. Bennett decides to use several topics for her students to explore in a carousel brainstorm that they will revisit throughout reading the novel and other related texts in the unit:

- Ways that families can be complicated
- Impact of misconceptions about scientific knowledge
- Gender roles

Before reading, Ms. Bennet puts each topic on a poster. Students then rotate through each poster, spending 3 to 5 minutes jotting ideas down about the topic on a poster, drawing from their prior knowledge. At the last poster, Ms. Bennett asks students not to write, but to read others' responses and decide how to synthesize that topic for the class. Then, Ms. Bennett asks one volunteer in each group to provide a synthesis of the ideas for the class and engages the class in a discussion around the topics. Figure 7.6 shows students' initial responses to the prompt "Ways that family can be complicated."

Finally, at various points throughout the reading, Ms. Bennett asks her students to write some ideas about the topics on sticky notes and add them to the poster. For

TABLE 7.5. How to Plan and Implement a Carousel Brainstorm

Procedures	Recommendations
1. The teacher selects four to six topics that relate to the text and writes each of those topics on a piece of chart paper that gets posted around the room.	Each group can use a different color marker while writing on each poster, thus making it clear what each group has contributed to the topics.
2. The teacher divides the class into the same number of groups (4–6).	Use a timer to ensure that this activity moves along at an appropriate pace. It's helpful to provide more time for the first round and a shorter time for each subsequent round, as some ideas are already brainstormed.
3. Each group starts with one topic, discusses the topic as a group, and writes their ideas on the chart paper.	
4. After a set amount of time (2–5 minutes), the teacher asks students to rotate (like a carousel) to the next poster/topic.	Rather than have the last group write on the poster, have them review the ideas on the poster and share one idea with the class.
5. Students read the topic and the responses of the previous group(s), and then they discuss and add any new ideas.	Groups can then circle an additional time around the posters to come up with a list of unanswered questions.
6. Repeat until students have rotated through all the topics/posters.	
7. Briefly review/discuss what students have shared as a class.	
8. After reading, the teacher can have students write one idea on a sticky note to add to one of the posters.	

example, one student added, "Having six brothers is complicated," after reading that the main character is the only girl in a family of seven. Ms. Bennett also uses the ideas on the poster as a jumping-off point for discussion throughout the unit.

In a similar way, **double-entry journals** can help readers connect the new with the known by asking readers to select quotes and then reflect on those quotes as they read (Daniels et al., 2007). In this technique (see Table 7.6), students select relevant quotes from the text while reading, and then they reflect on those quotes to integrate what they are learning with what they already know.

What does this look like? Let's visit Mrs. Bartleby, a twelfth-grade ELA teacher, as she plans a lesson around the text "Dangers of a Single Story" for her postcolonialism unit. It's a video of a TED talk by Chimamanda Ngozi Adichie She thinks about her overall goals for the unit (reading Shakespeare with a postcolonial lens) and for this specific text (consider how there are more than one interpretation). She decides to focus students on looking for descriptions of stereotypes and asks them to write those in the left-hand column. Then, after watching the video, she asks students to reflect on those images that exemplify a single story in the right column. As you can see in the example in Figure 7.7, Teresa captures an idea about characters being white and blue-eyed, and reflects that many characters in childhood stories look the same. A blank journal template can be found in Handout 7.3.

Another great way to help students integrate new and prior knowledge, and in

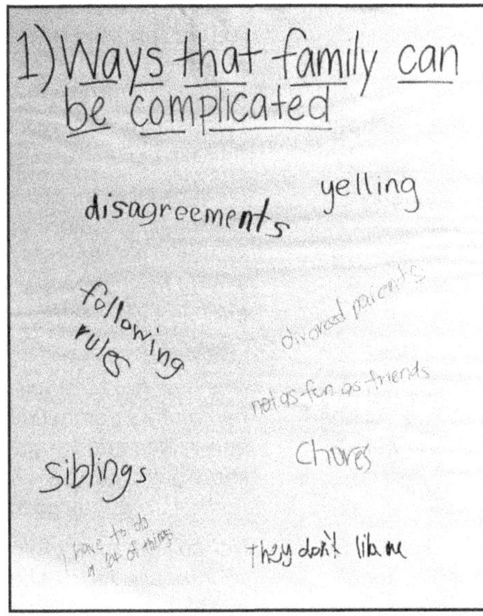

FIGURE 7.6. Example from Ms. Bennett's sixth-grade carousel brainstorm.

particular, address misconceptions students may have about the topic, is to use an **anticipation guide.** An anticipation guide (remember our mention of it in Chapter 6?) is a great way to tell students what to pay attention to before they read. In this technique, teachers provide statements that students agree or disagree with prior to reading. After reading, students can come back to these statements and see how their

TABLE 7.6. How to Plan and Implement a Double-Entry Journal

Procedures	Recommendations
1. The teacher chooses a text with rich sentences that would benefit from reflection.	Students could reflect on quotes after reading instead of during reading.
2. The teacher identifies a purpose for selecting quotes (e.g., look for quotes related to animal adaptation).	Rather than writing quotes in a journal as they read, students could highlight quotes, then select 1–3 to reflect on after reading to write into their journal.
3. The teacher comes up with a purpose for reflection and sentence starters to scaffold students' thinking.	The teacher can use sentence starters to support students' reflections.
4. The teacher asks students to read and then write down quotes that relate to that purpose on the left side of the journal template in Handout 7.3.	
5. After identifying a quote, students reflect on that quote to explain how it illuminates the purpose in the right-hand column of their journal.	

List examples of the images that exemplify single stories.	**Reflect on how those images exemplify "single stories."** *Sentence starters: "I found out . . . ," "I was surprised . . . ," "I would ask the author . . . ," "I realized . . . ," and so on.*
"All my characters were white and blue-eyed."	*I realized that all of the characters looked the same, like the single-story version of British children's stories. This reminds me of my own experiences when I read stories when I was young. I am Black, but I was exposed to many stories with white characters.*
"It had not occurred to me that anybody in his family could actually make something. All I had heard about them was how poor they were."	*She also held a single-story version of poverty from her family's domestic helper. This reminds me of how I used to think about poverty, before I got to know some people who have experienced it and realized that they have had different experiences.*
"My American roommate was shocked by me. She asked me where I had learned to speak English so well, and was confused when I said Nigeria happened to have English as its official language."	*Her college roommate had a single-story version of countries in Africa and didn't realize some countries in Africa use English as an official language. This reminds me of how everyone in* The Tempest *looked down on Caliban because they assumed he was only part human, even though he was capable of beautiful speech.*

FIGURE 7.7. Teresa's double-entry journal from Ms. Bartleby's postcolonialism unit.

answers were either affirmed or changed (see Table 7.7). Using anticipation guides can help novices in any subject pay attention to the small ways that authors communicate big ideas within content-area texts.

Let's explore what that looks like. Ms. Anthony decided to use an anticipation guide before reading *Before Columbus: The Americas of 1491* by Charles C. Mann. She specifically focused on statements that orient students to the content in the text, knowing that Mann's text will explode myths about Indigenous peoples. As you can see from Michael's example (Figure 7.8), his thinking was affirmed in his first answer, but his thinking changed in his second answer, noting from the text that "colonists were able to defeat much bigger Indian societies." In this case, the anticipation guide clearly shows how Michael is both activating his prior knowledge but also building knowledge while reading—which prepares him for more successful comprehension of the next texts in Ms. Anthony's text set.

Anticipation guides also work well in ELA, although it looks different with literature than with expository texts. Let's see what this looks like in Mrs. Bartleby's 12th-grade ELA class midway through her postcolonialism unit, after her students have finished exploring master/slave narratives (*The Tempest*) and after they have read a short explanation and definition of postcolonial theory. Before her students begin reading from Chimamanda Ngozi Adichie's *Americanah* (2013), Mrs. Bartleby creates an anticipation guide with statements that will help them connect the histories of Shakespeare and postcolonialism to the themes in *Americanah,* while also connecting

TABLE 7.7. How to Plan and Implement an Anticipation Guide

Procedures	Recommendations
1. Teacher writes statements that students can agree or disagree with prior to and after reading. It's best when the statements are broad and make students think. 2. Prior to reading the text, students read the statements and mark whether they agree or disagree with the statements. 3. The teacher may encourage discussion prior to reading, particularly with a small group or partner, but should not "reveal" their own answers to the statements. 4. Students read the text, considering the statements as they read. 5. After reading, they revisit the statements and indicate whether they agree or disagree with the statement after reading. 6. The teacher then engages students in a discussion about the statements. 7. After the discussion, students can write short reflections on how their thinking was either affirmed or adjusted or explain why they chose agree or disagree after reading.	Work hard to frame anticipation guide statements in an open-ended way to inspire deeper thinking.

to their lives today. She asks them if they agree or disagree with the following statements:

- The racial experiences of Black people in the United States are mostly similar to the racial experiences of Black people born elsewhere around the world.
- The global era of colonization was so long ago that its impacts are not really noticeable in everyday life today.

These statements help surface her students' knowledge about the different experiences of race around the world and about the current impacts of colonization. Because the novel explores the distinct experiences of the white and Black characters from Nigeria, the United Kingdom, and the United States, this anticipation guide prepares them to notice those themes and integrate new cultural and historical knowledge into their evolving understanding of postcolonial reading. See a blank template for creating your own anticipation guide in Handout 7.4.

Provide Brief Explanations or Prompts to Build and Activate Knowledge

Another way that we can help students use relevant knowledge to make sense of texts is by providing short explanations that students read at specific places in the

Statements	Before Reading	After Reading	Justification
1. Indigenous peoples lived lightly on the land and in harmony with nature, leaving little lasting impact on the environment.	**(Agree)** Disagree	**(Agree)** Disagree	·Europeans [illegible] land as [illegible] ·Environmental [illegible] Americas
2. Before Europeans arrived, Indigenous peoples in the Americas lived in very spread-out societies, with low population density.	**(Agree)** Disagree	Agree **(Disagree)**	·Colonists were able to [illegible] bigger Indian [illegible] ·"Native Americans created societies that were older, bigger, more highly developed"
3. Historians are confident in establishing the approximate date of human arrival in the Western Hemisphere.	Agree **(Disagree)**	Agree Disagree	
4. Archaeological evidence, though interesting, does not have the potential to reshape our understanding of Indigenous life in the Western Hemisphere before 1492.	**(Agree)** Disagree	Agree **(Disagree)**	·"New research" shows what life was like in the Americas before ... 1492"

FIGURE 7.8. Michael's anticipation guide from Ms. Anthony's indigenous stereotypes unit.

text. These can provide brief in-the-moment information to help readers understand a particular part of the text (McNamara, 2010; Spires & Donley, 1998). Many textbooks provide this scaffolding, but as teachers craft text sets, they may need to add these explanations themselves. Adding brief explanations is particularly helpful for language learners, who benefit from multiple exposures to new content and vocabulary. One way to do this is to create a reading guide (a technique we introduced in the previous chapter) and embed these explanations or text elaborations into the guide. Reading guides can also be useful in activating knowledge because you can provide specific prompts to help students to use knowledge you know they have (or you have recently built) while reading. For a "how to" on creating reading guides, see Table 6.6 on p. 85.

To explore what this looks like, let's go back to Ms. Astrid's excerpt from *Packing for Mars for Kids* that we shared at the beginning of this chapter. Initially, she worried that there were many things that her students may not know from this passage, including who Neil Armstrong is or what a mammal is. As she considers her learning goals for this unit (understanding gravity's rotation pull) and this text (to engage students' interest in gravity by considering zero-gravity spaceflight situations), she realizes that students need to understand some, but not all of these words. If students don't know who Neil Armstrong or John Glenn are, it will not take away from Ms. Astrid's intended learning; as such, she does not add supports for this. However, the concept of "mammal" and the concept of sending mammals other than humans to space first *are* something that her students need to understand in order to reach her main unit goal of understanding how space travel will affect humans. As a result, she provides a brief definition of "mammal" in her reading guide and a short explanation clarifying that humans are also mammals (see the example in Figure 7.9).

As she looks at the longer passage, she also realizes that students have a lot of knowledge that she wants them to use while reading, but that they may not be able to use this knowledge without help. As such, she adds several prompts to help students activate knowledge to make it more likely they will use it to make sense of the text. For example, she prompts students to remember what they learned in a previous text (the article, "Overview of the Sun," from the NASA website; NASA, 2023b) about how hot the sun is. Additionally, she wants her students to stop and think about how gravity may impact liquids to get them thinking about what they already know about gravity.

Reading Guide Example: Packing for Mars for Kids

Definitions		*Other supports*
	Let's say you boarded a rocket in your backyard, strapped yourself in, and launched. After you'd gone about sixty miles up, you would arrive in space. If you lived in New York City, a journey into space would be about the same distance as a journey to Hackettstown, New Jersey. Sixty miles.	Write: name a place that is 60 miles from your house:
	You don't even need a change of underwear. Yet the idea of going up into space was extremely worrisome back before anyone had done it. Space was the edge of the known world. The temperature out there will kill you, and there's no air to breathe.	Do you remember how hot it is on Venus? On the sun?
Scary idea	Plus, you would no longer experience the effects of Earth's gravity. You'd be weightless. Lighter than a soap bubble. That was an **alarming proposition** way back in the beginning of the space exploration era.	
	Humans evolved for life with gravity.	Write: define gravity:
	We're built for it. No one knew what would happen to the human body without it. What if your blood didn't flow through your blood vessels the way it's supposed to? What if your nerves stopped firing or your organs stopped working?	Write: does gravity have an impact on how liquid flows?
 Retrieved from, nih.gov hairy animal that feeds milk to its young a	Until there were answers to questions like these, it seemed risky to send a person up there. So, a decade before Yuri Gagarin became the first person in space, long before John Glenn and Neil Armstrong, before ham the astrochimp and Laika the space dog, before all of them, was Albert. Albert was a nine-pound **rhesus monkey**. In 1949, dressed in a gauze diaper, little red-haired Albert, one of five spacefaring monkeys named Albert, rode a V-2 rocket into space. He was the first **mammal** to go there.	Did you know that humans are mammals?

FIGURE 7.9. Ms. Astrid's reading guide: *Packing for Mars for Kids*.

SCAFFOLD KNOWLEDGE THROUGH ACTIVATION, CONSTRUCTION, AND INTEGRATION

So how can teachers scaffold knowledge demands? The best way to do this is to build and activate readers' knowledge throughout reading. This scaffolding begins with viewing students' existing knowledge as an *asset*, selecting strategic texts, and initiating activities that facilitate learning from content-area texts. Using the techniques we describe in this chapter can also prepare students to integrate new knowledge gleaned from text with their prior knowledge. By connecting the new and prior knowledge, students will be able to answer the essential questions of the unit and achieve deeper learning in science, social studies, and literature.

HANDOUT 7.1. Template: KWL chart

K Know	W Want to Know	L Learned

HANDOUT 7.2. Template: KLEWS chart

K **What do we think we know?**	L **What are we learning?**	E **What is our evidence?**	W **What do we still wonder about?**	S **What scientific terms or principles explain this phenomenon?**

HANDOUT 7.3. Template: Double-Entry Journal

Write quotes from the text or describe images that . . .	**Reflect on how those quotes or images . . . Use the following sentences starters if you need help starting your thoughts:** *I found out . . .* *I was surprised . . .* *I would ask the author . . .* *I realized . . .*

HANDOUT 7.4. Template: Anticipation Guide

Statements	Before Reading	After Reading	Justification
	Agree Disagree	Agree Disagree	
	Agree Disagree	Agree Disagree	
	Agree Disagree	Agree Disagree	
	Agree Disagree	Agree Disagree	

CHAPTER 8

How Can Teachers Scaffold Text Structure Challenges?

GUIDING QUESTIONS

1. How can a text's organization influence a reader's comprehension?
2. How do we teach students to use text structure to understand a text?
3. How can we support students' understanding of multimodal text structures?

Dr. Perch has started teaching the text from a NOAA article to help his 10th-grade biology class learn more about how to combat algal blooms. He initially asked students to take notes on the reading and is a bit alarmed to see that most students seem to have just randomly listed bullet points of information in a single column in their digital notebook. After the reading, he asks students what it was about and they answer algal blooms and recite several facts about it. No one seems to have understood that as much as the article discussed the problem, it equally discussed the solutions we can all work toward. He can't help wondering how students missed this.

A quality text is not just a random assortment of facts. Rather, authors take care to organize ideas to show the reader how ideas connect, perhaps as problems and solutions, causes and effects, as items in a series, and so on. The way authors organize ideas in a text are reflected in the structure of a text. If a reader can recognize these structures, they can then more fully comprehend the text. If a reader cannot recognize the text structure, they may be able to understand some of the ideas within it, but not how ideas relate to each other, much like Dr. Perch's students above, and comprehension will suffer. In this chapter, we will explain the research and scaffolds for supporting text structure challenges, including understanding how to help readers knit together ideas across a text. We will also address how to support students to read multimodal text structures.

THE INVISIBLE SKELETON

Text structure refers to the way an author has organized ideas in a text to achieve their purpose. As experienced and proficient readers, we tend to take logical text structures for granted. For example, as you are reading this chapter, you are probably not actively reflecting on how each sentence and paragraph is connected to the one before it. If we've done our jobs as authors, the ideas should connect and move together seamlessly. As a result of your experience as reader and (hopefully) our expertise as writers, the text structure has likely faded into the background to become an "invisible skeleton" holding the chapter together. This invisibility of a good text structure can make it particularly challenging to teach—in the same way that you don't think about your skeleton until you tweak your back, we don't really notice a text's organization until it gets wonky. Let's see an example:

Read the following excerpt from the text that Dr. Perch adapted from an article published by the National Oceanographic and Atmospheric Administration (NOAA, 2021), and then try to summarize it:

> Even better, these treatments do not leave leftover chemicals. Studies have examined what happens when such bubbles are released into lakes and burst. These are tiny bubbles even smaller than a human hair. Results show that nanobubbles release oxygen and ozone, which then helps eliminate the cyanobacteria causing the blooms. Scientists investigating how to combat algal blooms have examined the effectiveness of nanobubbles.

Are you confused? Yep, we are too. Was this passage about chemicals? Nanobubbles? Comparing oxygen and ozone? Why was this passage so difficult to comprehend? Well, we changed the order of the sentences from the author's original work. In doing so, we undid the careful work of the author to organize the ideas in ways that connect and make sense. In other words, we removed the text structure. Try reading the original version of the text now:

> Scientists investigating how to combat algal blooms have examined the effectiveness of nanobubbles. These are tiny bubbles even smaller than a human hair. Studies have examined what happens when such bubbles are released into lakes and burst. Results show that nanobubbles release oxygen and ozone, which then helps eliminate the cyanobacteria causing the blooms. Even better, these treatments do not leave leftover chemicals. (Adapted from NOAA, 2021)

Was it easier to read the original version? We think so. That is because in the original version the structure of the text was familiar to you, and the author's clues about how the ideas are connected were present. In the original version, the author begins by explaining the problem: invasive algal blooms. Then, the author defines what nanobubbles are and continues to explain how they can be a solution to protect the Great Lakes ecosystem from the problem of invasive algal blooms.

This text structure is known as problem-solution. When you read texts that have problem-solution structures, your brain recognizes this organization and enables you to use your knowledge of that structure to help you understand the text. In the first version, in which we rearranged the sentences, the information is the same, but because we rearranged the structure of the text, it is hard for the reader to understand the problem the author is describing (algal blooms) and the solution (releasing nanobubbles into the Great Lakes).

In sum, recognizing how texts are organized and using the author's organizational clues can help a reader connect ideas and, ultimately, understand the information in the text. Of course, genre (fiction, nonfiction, poetry) and modality (texts that can contain more than mode, such as pictures, written text, or videos) both play a role in text structure. For example, the structure of a 14 line sonnet can help a student see how the speaker's perspective changes from the first lines to the last lines. Dan has had particular success asking students to unscramble a sonnet with a very formal rhyme scheme, such as John Milton's (1673) "When I Consider How My Light Is Spent." The exercise helps students see how the line breaks show the speaker's change in attitude from despair at his blindness to acceptance of it.

HOW CAN A TEXT'S ORGANIZATION INFLUENCE A READER'S COMPREHENSION?

Teaching text structure begins with understanding how texts are organized. While there are many ways a text can be structured, some tend to require less scaffolding than others. In general, narrative texts, such as stories, memoirs, movies, and plays, follow a similar pattern: exposition–conflict–rising action–climax–resolution. Students tend to learn this explicitly in school through the "witch's hat" graphic organizer with the high point representing the climax. Perhaps more importantly, we tend to internalize how stories are structured far before school through countless bedtime stories, TV shows and movies, and family legends told over supper that use the same structure. Because we use narrative structures frequently in and out of school, narrative text structure often requires less support.

However, nonfiction texts follow several different typical organizational patterns, including comparison, problem-and-solution (like the Great Lakes text we just read), cause-and-effect, chronological, list, topic-subtopic, and description (Pyle et al., 2017). Nonfiction texts can also be particularly challenging for readers as they often use multiple structures across the whole text, and as such, they can require specific instruction and support to help readers make sense of the text (Pyle et al., 2017).

Research indicates that brief instruction in the various ways that expository texts are organized may be helpful (Reed et al., 2020; Taylor & Beach, 1984). However, some studies have not shown gains for students who receive text structure instruction, likely because text structure instruction devoid of content and meaning is unhelpful

(Tierney & Readance, 2005). Thus, we recommend teaching text structure in the context of learning from the texts, as we show throughout this book with units about ecosystems, Indigenous stereotypes, and postcolonialism.

HOW DO WE TEACH STUDENTS TO USE TEXT STRUCTURE TO UNDERSTAND A TEXT?

Researchers identify key factors for teaching text structure (McGee & Richgels, 1986). First, teachers must carefully choose passages that are consistently organized in the particular type of structure the teacher wants to teach. Many texts follow multiple organizational patterns or may simply be poorly organized; those texts are not ideal for teaching students about a specific text structure. Similarly, as we discussed in Chapter 7, sometimes authors simply assume a reader already has knowledge of how ideas are related and, as a result, may not include as many organizational clues. We call these texts inconsiderate texts because readers are left to figure out how ideas are related. Considerate texts, on the other hand, give clear textual clues about how ideas are related, although readers need to know how to recognize those clues in order to use them to understand the text. These texts are much better choices for teaching text structure. Second, teachers need to analyze the text prior to instruction so that they are familiar with the text structure and can easily direct students to the "clues" that indicate the type of structure. Third, it is usually best to begin by teaching problem-solution, cause-and-effect, and chronological text patterns, as these three are easier to identify than list or description structures.

After ensuring those factors are in place, we suggest a three-step process for teaching text structure adapted from McGee and Richgels (1986). The first step is for the teacher to model, or demonstrate, what the structure of the text is by thinking out loud (remember think-alouds from Chapter 6?). During the think-aloud, it is key for teachers to point out both why a text is structured the way it is, and also, how they noticed specific textual clues to determine its structure. Teachers use the think-aloud to show students clues that the author has provided about the text structure, such as identifying signal words (*however, because,* or *therefore*). For example, as Dr. Perch reads the excerpt from the beginning of this chapter, he might pause and say: "I notice two seemingly simple words: 'which then'—these words specifically connect the solution (the ozone nanobubbles) to the problem (algal blooms)." While his ninth graders already know the meaning of "which then," they may not notice their structural importance in the passage. Therefore, Dr. Perch's brief think-aloud scaffolds their understanding of text structure. To make this even more visible, he might structure the note taking that he asked of students to mirror this structure, perhaps by using a two-column chart labeled "problem" and "solution."

After a think-aloud, the teacher asks students to recognize the text structure of a similar text on their own. Teachers are encouraged to begin with short passages (a few sentences) and then move onto larger passages. It is important in this step that students verbalize how and why the text is structured in a particular way (Readance & Tierney, 2005). For example, after tackling the five-sentence excerpt at the beginning of this chapter, Dr. Perch moves on to the next paragraph in the NOAA article on algal blooms. He asks students to read and explain to each other how that part of the text is organized (remember that informational texts usually follow multiple organizational patterns) and how the knowledge of the text structures helps them understand how scientists manage Great Lakes ecosystems and fight algal blooms.

Lastly, once students can identify a particular text structure, they produce a text of their own that reflects this structure. For example, Dr. Perch's class might write about one cause of the Great Lakes pollution and then describe a proposed solution. This step will help students solidify their text structure knowledge, and, as a result, they will not only be improving as writers but also be better able to understand text structures in the future. And, in the example we shared, students are also able to process the biology content knowledge in the texts, which helps support their text understanding too.

Support Students to Use the Text Structure to Help Them Understand

After we teach these types of organization, then what? Support students in using the structure of the text to help them comprehend and learn from the text. What does that look like? One scaffold you can use is called an organizational walk through, which helps students identify the text structure and use that structure to help them comprehend. In this instructional scaffold, teachers preview the text with students prior to reading, with the purpose of understanding the organization of the text. Aukerman (1972) suggests starting by analyzing the chapter title and engaging in a discussion about how that topic relates to other topics they have recently read. Then, the students can preview the subtitles and visuals, and they can even make predictions about what the text will be about. Next, the students should read the introductory paragraph and concluding paragraph, the latter of which often provides a summary of the chapter. With this information, students should be primed to identify the overall structure of the text. The teacher can help students use this text structure to make sense of the text by emphasizing what they will learn based on this structure. For example, if students have observed that the text is organized as a cause–effect text, then the teacher can remind them that they will read about a specific issue related to the topic, then look for its consequences. This information can help students better understand how the ideas in a passage are related and digest what they are reading.

A more in-depth and structured way to support students to identify and use text structure is through a technique called SQ3R, which stands for Survey, Question, Read, Recite, and Review (McGee & Richgels, 1986). Using this technique, students begin by surveying the text before they read it, which is the same procedure as the organizational walk through described in the previous paragraph. It can be helpful to begin text structure instruction with organizational walk throughs, then "graduate" students to SQ3R once they have mastered this technique (see Table 8.1 for how to plan and implement an SQ3R). After students have learned SQ3R, they can repeat it until they are experts in detecting text structure and no longer need the scaffold.

Next, the reader forms questions about the text based on their survey. This could look like turning the headings into questions, or simply asking questions about the

TABLE 8.1. How to Plan and Implement an SQ3R

Procedures	Recommendations
1. The teacher selects a sufficiently challenging text that is structured in a way that students can use the text structure to understand the author's meaning. 2. The teacher should familiarize themselves with the passage and the steps of SQ3R so that they are prepared to support students who struggle with any of the steps. For example, the teacher should note text features they want students to notice in the survey step, and consider how to articulate the purpose for reading this text to support students in developing strong questions before reading. 3. The students first **survey** the text, meaning they look over the whole text and consider its title, topic, and text features. This step can either be done as a whole class or individually, followed by a whole-class discussion. 4. Next the teacher explains a purpose for reading and asks students to generate **questions** to give purpose and curiosity to their reading. This may occur as a group, or individually but requires some teacher support to help students formulate relevant text-based questions. 5. Students then **read** the passage, looking for answers to their questions. 6. After reading, students **recite**, or summarize the passage in writing. Opportunities to share their summaries with a partner are encouraged. 7. Finally, students **review** their understanding of the passage by answering their questions.	Be sure to review the text ahead of time to determine the text features students must notice during the "survey" phase and consider how to support students in developing text-based questions while reading.

topic that the student hopes to learn about. For example, while reading the textbook chapter entitled Gravity (CK-12, 2020) in Ms. Astrid's sixth-grade science class, one student, Andreas, had previewed the heading "Earth's Gravity" and asked the question "How is Earth's gravity affected by the other planets?"

In Ms. Anthony's eighth-grade history class, a student, Eleanor, was reading a book section with the heading "The Case of the Carved Gourd" (Mann, 2011, p. 11). While surveying the passage, Eleanor noticed that there were pictures carved onto the gourd and that the heading sounded mysterious, which led her to ask, "What do the pictures on the gourd mean?" See Figure 8.1 for Eleanor's example.

In both cases, the teacher asked students to identify the text structure before reading and explain how that structure helps them understand the text. For example, in both of the examples above, the text is organized by description, and Eleanor's SQ3R prepares her to notice that. The teacher can explain to students that the gravity chapter is going to describe gravity, and the section on the carved gourd is going to describe how and why the gourd is carved.

Next, primed by their initial survey and questions, students actually read the whole text and then "recite" a summary of the text. Finally, students review by trying to answer the questions they asked prior to reading. This helps students reflect on what they learned through reading (similar to the KWL chart we described in Chapter 7).

Support Students to Understand Subject-Specific Text Structures

What does teaching text structure look like with science journals or lab reports? These types of texts follow a particular organizational pattern that many secondary students are unfamiliar with. These subject-specific structures will likely require more support. A lab report structure, for example, follows the scientific method and includes the conventions (e.g., third-person writing) and elements (e.g., abstracts, methods) consistent

1. Survey
   Think about what you are going to read.
   Title: "The Case of the Carved Gourd" sounds like a mystery
   Topic: Artifacts from the ancient Andes and their connection to today
   Text features: Pictures of carved gourds
   Questions before you begin: What do the pictures on the gourds mean?
2. Question
   Record three questions that you want to answer by the end of your reading.
   - What do the pictures on the gourds mean?
   - Why is this a mystery?
   - Why are ancient carved gourds important?
3. Read
   Read the passage carefully. You are going to need to write a summary of it afterward, so make sure you are paying attention to the details.
4. Recite
   Write three summary statements and make sure to give details.
   - Carved gourds can be hard to date because of conflicts between carbon dating and layering.
   - They can show connections between ancient Andean religion and today.
   - Hard to know for sure what an ancient artifact means.
5. Review
   Go back to the questions you had before you read and answer them in complete sentences.
   - They are pictures of the Andean Staff God.
   - Historians and archaeologists are sure the gourds were important cultural artifacts but don't know exactly how old they are.
   - They could show connections between the Andean religious traditions over thousands of years.

FIGURE 8.1. Eleanor's SQ3R around "The Case of the Carved Gourd."

with scientific argumentation in science journals. A scaffold called **unscrambling texts** is a great way to get adolescents to notice the structural features of these reports or other subject-specific text structures. How does it work? Similar to what we did at the beginning of this chapter, simply break the science article into sections, then scramble them up (either cutting and pasting the paper or digitally) and ask students to unscramble them into the correct order consistent with the scientific method. Watching different partners compare their unscrambled versions often leads to productive discussions as students explain to each other how they think the text's ideas develop.

Once the students have unscrambled the texts, teachers can ask, "How does this organization support what the author is conveying?" This helps students see the connections between the specific science content and the bigger scientific methods that generate the knowledge. Because the structure of a text and its purpose are so closely tied together in texts in all content areas, helping students see the intricacies of disciplinary text structure helps them see the larger picture.

Teach Students to Summarize Using Text Structure

Another way to support students in identifying and using text structure to make sense of a text is to use a scaffolded summary technique. Two different scaffolded summarizing techniques can be used: one for narrative and one for expository texts.

If the text is narrative in nature, **Somebody Wants But So (and Then) (SWBST)** can help students identify and understand the structure of the story. In this technique students identify a character from the text (*somebody*) and what that character *wants* (indicative of the character's motivation, or what drives the plot). Next, the reader identifies the central tension or conflict that is preventing the character from getting what they want (*but*) and the resolution (*so*). Teachers have the option of adding "and *then*" to explain what happens next, which can help students see how the plot connects to deeper thematic elements. This technique can be used multiple times throughout a longer work with multiple conflicts and resolutions to help students use their knowledge of text structure to keep track of a story.

For example, in *The Tempest*, Mrs. Bartleby uses this scaffold at different points in the play to guide students through multiple storylines and to track different protagonists, such as Prospero or Caliban. As you can see in Table 8.2, Angelica determined that Prospero wanted to "be restored to his dukedom and find happiness for his daughter" but was initially unable to achieve this goal due to his exile at sea, but that this desire motivates him throughout the play. In this way, Angelica can rely on the familiar narrative story structure to help her make sense of this complicated play and trace the evolution of its complex characters.

For expository texts, the **ABC summary technique** helps students summarize a text using this formula: (a) identify the author, (b) select a verb, and (c) finish the thought. Where does text structure come into play? In b, select a verb, students need to think about the structure of the text to select an appropriate verb that describes what the author is doing. For example, in texts using the description text structure, the students may pick verbs like *explain* or *describe*. In compare–contrast structures, students

TABLE 8.2. Angelica's SWBST Organizer using *The Tempest*

Somebody (List a character)	Wanted (What was their desire?)	But (What stood in the way?)	So (What did they do?)	Then (What did it mean?)
Prospero	To be restored to his dukedom and find happiness for his daughter.	He'd been exiled and cast to sea and ended up on the island.	He uses his magic to orchestrate the downfall of his usurpers and the marriage of his daughter.	He can give up his books and magic and his desire for power and revenge.
Caliban	Freedom like he had before Prospero arrived.	Prospero's enslaving books and magic.	Plotted to kill Prospero but was unsuccessful.	Remains in bondage, unclear how he feels about it.
Ariel	Freedom.	Prospero's enslaving books and magic.	Obeyed Prospero's orders and was granted freedom.	Gains his freedom, but this contrasts with Caliban remaining in bondage.

may use *compare* or *contrast*. In problem-solution structures, the student may use verbs like *argues*, *defends*, or *presents*. This technique is beneficial for teaching students how to use the text structure to make sense of the text, in addition to helping students process and summarize the text. Once students identify the text structure and can explain what the author is trying to do in a passage, the summary is much easier. This technique helps readers solidify their understanding of text structure and also use text structure to understand the text (see Table 8.3 for how to use this scaffold).

Let's explore what this looks like in Dr. Perch's 10th-grade biology classroom as students are reading the following text, adapted from the U.S. Geological Survey's article about zebra mussels:

> Zebra mussels are an invasive, fingernail-sized mollusk that is native to fresh waters in Eurasia. Their name comes from the dark, zig-zagged stripes on each shell. Zebra mussels probably arrived in the Great Lakes in the 1980s via ballast water that was discharged by large ships from Europe. They have spread rapidly throughout the Great Lakes region and into the large rivers of the eastern Mississippi drainage. They have also been found in Texas, Colorado, Utah, Nevada, and California.
>
> Zebra mussels negatively impact ecosystems in many ways. They filter out algae that native species need for food and they attach to—and incapacitate—native mussels. Power plants must also spend millions of dollars removing zebra mussels from clogged water intakes. To prevent the spread, the USGS highly discourages catching and transporting zebra mussels for use as bait, food, and aquarium pets. They also encourage good boat hygiene, including washing the boat with warm, soapy water and disposing of leftover bait in the trash. This can prevent bait that is not native to the water, like zebra mussels, from spreading unnecessarily and becoming invasive in a new space. (Adapted from U.S. Geological Survey, n.d.)

TABLE 8.3. How to Plan and Implement ABC Summary Sentences

Procedures	Recommendations
1. Chunk text to determine stop points where students can stop and summarize. Consider stopping at the end of a dense section or complicated piece of the text so that students have a chance to stop and process. 2. At the end of the first chunk, direct students to identify the author (A). 3. Then, students select a verb while considering the structure of the text (B). The teacher may provide verbs and ask students to pick from the list. 4. The student finishes the sentence by adding the big idea (C). Prompt students to reread the author and add a verb to help them finish the thought. 5. Repeat these steps with the remaining chunks.	A fun game to play to help students review the text and solidify their understanding of ABC summary sentences is to ask students to choose one summary statement and read it out loud to the class. The class then has to guess which paragraph or excerpt the summary sentences are describing. The class can also offer feedback on the summary sentence to improve it.

Dr. Perch asks his students to stop and summarize after each paragraph. For example, as you see in Table 8.4, Marshall's ABC summary identified the first paragraph as descriptive, for it explains what a zebra mussel is and how it came to the United States and spread. However, he then realized that the second paragraph was organized to describe the problem and solution, in that zebra mussels are negatively impacting the ecosystem, but with good boat hygiene and other practices, the damage can be mitigated. Calling students' attention to the structure and purpose of each paragraph helps them break down complex texts.

Some people use graphic organizers to teach text structure (using a Venn diagram to teach comparative structure, for example), but this approach can be limiting because complex texts are often structured in multiple ways that a single graphic organizer cannot accommodate. As such, this can detract from focusing on making meaning of

TABLE 8.4. Marshall's Example of ABC Summary Sentences

Paragraph Number	A: Identify author	B: Consider text structure and select a verb (e.g., *defends, presents, contrasts, suggests, argues*)	C: Finish Your Thought (big idea, main concept)
1	The USGS article	defines	what a zebra mussel is and how it arrived and spread around the United States.
2	The USGS article	argues	that the mussel has a negative impact on the ecosystem of the Great Lakes, but this problem can be solved by observing good boat hygiene and limiting the use of zebra mussels as bait.

the text (a key element of teaching text structure). Thus, we prefer more flexible techniques such as ABC summary sentences because students can select different verbs to summarize different parts of the text, reflecting different organizational patterns.

However, graphic organizers can still be helpful for teaching students particular types of text structures. For example, understanding a chronological order structure is a critical aspect of historical thinking—and helping students use timelines as graphic organizers may support them in seeing how texts' chronological information documents the evolution of a historical phenomenon. Specific graphic organizers also might support students in noticing the links to the scientific method in science texts. That's why it's always important to consider the specific content objective when designing text structure scaffolds.

Support Students in Understanding How Ideas Are Connected across Sentences

Another aspect of text structure is how well the reader can connect ideas across a text and understand how the various sentences are related to each other. The author usually provides clues about how the ideas are connected across the text. However, sometimes these clues are challenging for novice readers to identify and use when reading, particularly when texts are really challenging.

For example, sometimes authors use words, such as *although* or *thus* to show how ideas are *connected* in the passage. If students are unfamiliar with these words, they may have trouble understanding how the ideas across those sentences are related to each other. These students benefit from brief instruction in how to notice these scaffolds that the author has provided for readers in the text, as Dr. Perch did in his think-aloud with the text at the beginning of this chapter.

What can that look like? One way teachers can do this is to draw attention to words that the author has used to reflect the relationship between ideas. This can be done through **teaching connectives** (Crosson & Lesaux, 2013). Connectives are words like *if, however, but, similarly,* or *nonetheless* that show relationships between the ideas in a passage. To use this scaffold, teachers remove the connectives from a text and leave a blank where each connector was. See Table 8.5 for guidelines on how to do it. For example, Ms. Astrid takes out the words "after" and "if" in the following sentences:

> *Let's say you boarded a rocket in your backyard, strapped yourself in, and launched. _____ you'd gone about sixty miles up, you would arrive in space. ____ you lived in New York City, a journey into space would be about the same distance as a journey to Hackettstown, New Jersey.*

Then, students can figure out what goes in the blanks, which causes them to determine how the ideas are connected in the passage. The teacher then reveals the author's choice of connective at the end. In this way, students can learn the meaning of various connectives while also helping them understand that the author has placed clues to show how ideas are related in the passage.

Ms. Astrid knows that science texts are rich in connectives that show the relationship between science ideas. She chooses a paragraph from *Packing for Mars for*

TABLE 8.5. How to Teach Connectives

Procedures	Recommendations
1. Select a short piece of text rich in connective words, such as conjunctions or transitions like *however, if, after, then.*	Teachers can offer a word bank to help students who can't think of words.
2. Remove the connectives from the passage and replace them with a blank, creating a student version without connectives.	
3. Provide brief teaching on the connectives that were removed prior to reading. Explain the word briefly and show students a different example sentence using that word.	
4. Then ask students to read the student version and fill in the blanks with a connective they think shows the relationship between the ideas.	
5. When students are finished, have them compare their connectives with a partner, looking for similarities and differences.	
6. Finally, share the original version with students and ask them to compare their version to the original version. What's different?	

Kids to provide practice for her students. She selects a passage rich in connectives and removes them, then has her students fill in the blanks. Students then compare their answers to the original text.

As you can see from Figure 8.2, Mary used the same word as the author in the second and fifth blanks (*if*) but chose different words in the other blanks. For instance, she used the word *when* instead of *after*. Ms. Astrid used this as a teaching point to communicate how the word *after* provided more specific information to more precisely communicate the arrival in space.

Another way that teachers can support students' in connecting ideas across the text is using annotations to help students understand anaphoric references (Knecht et al., 2023). Anaphoric references are words in a sentence that connect them to previous sentences—often pronouns, but sometimes other nouns too. For example, consider this excerpt from *The Evolution of Calpurnia Tate* by Jacqueline Kelly (a book Ms. Bennett is reading with her sixth-grade ELA class):

> I had one of the small green grasshoppers in a jar on my vanity, and I stared at **it** for inspiration. I had been unable to catch one of the big yellow ones, even though they were much slower. "Why are you different?" I asked, but **it** refused to answer. (Kelly, 2009, p. 12)

In this example, the author introduces the antecedent "green grasshoppers" in the first sentence. She uses a pronoun later in the sentence, but also, two sentences

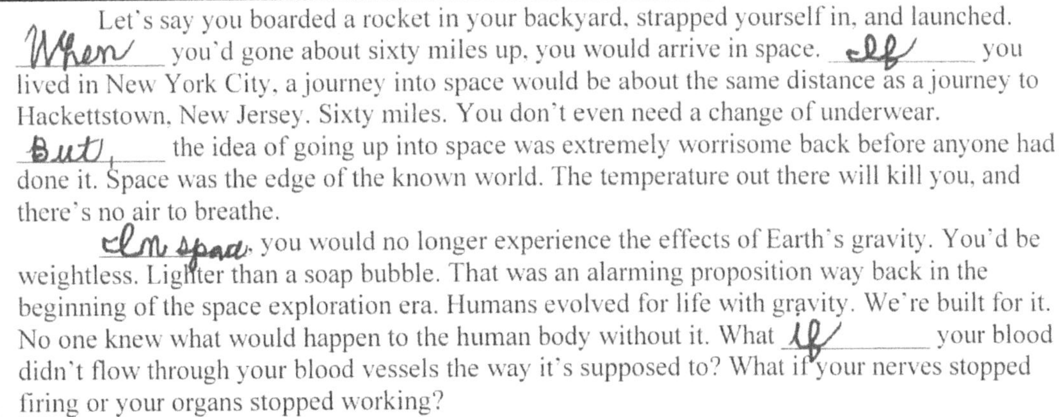

Let's say you boarded a rocket in your backyard, strapped yourself in, and launched. When you'd gone about sixty miles up, you would arrive in space. If you lived in New York City, a journey into space would be about the same distance as a journey to Hackettstown, New Jersey. Sixty miles. You don't even need a change of underwear.

But, the idea of going up into space was extremely worrisome back before anyone had done it. Space was the edge of the known world. The temperature out there will kill you, and there's no air to breathe.

In space, you would no longer experience the effects of Earth's gravity. You'd be weightless. Lighter than a soap bubble. That was an alarming proposition way back in the beginning of the space exploration era. Humans evolved for life with gravity. We're built for it. No one knew what would happen to the human body without it. What if your blood didn't flow through your blood vessels the way it's supposed to? What if your nerves stopped firing or your organs stopped working?

FIGURE 8.2. Mary's example of teaching connectives with *Packing for Mars for Kids.*

later, the reader still needs to remember that the pronoun *it* is referring back to the entrapped grasshopper.

Tracking these anaphoric references is something that expert readers do automatically, but it is often hard for novice readers who are engaging with tough texts for the first time. To make this aspect of the "invisible skeleton" of text structure visible, we can teach students to track anaphoric references using a protocol called **annotating anaphoric references** (see Table 8.6). What does it look like to teach this strategy? Ms. Bennett could offer her students the version of the text above, where she has underlined the pronouns and antecedents. As she reads, she stops at the pronouns (*it*) and asks her students to track what *it* refers to. She asks her students to explain how they figured out what "it" meant to help them solidify this autonomous process. If her students have trouble, she will show them and explain how she found the reference for the pronoun to make the process visible through a think-aloud (see Chapter 6 for directions on how to plan a think-aloud).

TABLE 8.6. How to Annotate Anaphoric References

Procedures
1. Select a short piece of text rich in anaphoric references.
2. Underline the anaphoric references and pronouns that refer back to them before distributing to students.
3. Read the text aloud and stop when you get to the underlined pronouns.
4. Ask students to identify what the pronoun is referring back to.
5. When students are having trouble identifying the reference, model and explain how you figured it out.
6. Next provide similar practice but without underlining the anaphoric references ahead of time.

HOW CAN WE SUPPORT STUDENTS IN UNDERSTANDING MULTIMODAL TEXT STRUCTURES?

Modalities are different ways of conveying information, such as a written text or a picture, or a video. Today, texts are much more than printed books: They contain audio, images, video, and other types of digital modalities. Teaching students how to read texts that incorporate multiple modalities strikes at the core of what contemporary literacy *is*. It's true that today's students are likely experienced in using interactive and digital modalities, but equally true is that students need to be taught effective ways to critically analyze and extract information from those sources, and text structure plays an important role.

But how can we support students in understanding structures of texts that contain nonprint aspects? Two strategies that we have already shared with you can be helpful: the notice and wonder protocol (introduced in Chapter 6; see Table 6.1 for directions) and the organizational walkthrough (see above).

What does the notice and wonder protocol look like? Teachers can use the noticing protocol to help students understand maps and even use digital features of interactive online maps. For example, if reading a digital map that has a zoom feature, such as the U.S. Census Bureau's 2020 Demographic Viewer, Ms. Anthony asks her students, "Where do Indigenous people live in the US today?" She uses a noticing protocol to guide students through examining the state level, where the map shows variation across states, with a higher concentration of Indigenous people living in the western states. Understanding the population distribution of Indigenous people will enrich her students' reading of *Before Columbus*. This kind of scaffolding helps students not only to learn facts about Indigenous peoples today but also develop important skills in digital map reading.

Next, we will explore how to use an organizational walkthrough to help students understand multimodal text structures. The key here is to remember that those texts have structures, too. For example, Ms. Astrid wants her students to use the PhEt gravity simulation so that they can not only explain the general idea of gravity, but also see how gravity works with multiple bodies at once (sun, Earth, and moon), and how gravity is affected by the masses of the bodies. Figure 8.3 shows a five-step process by which Ms. Astrid can guide her students through the digital features of this text so that they can then do systematic inquiry about the ways gravity works. By walking her students through the digital features of this text, she ensures that they will use the structure of this stimulation to help them understand orbital patterns and universal gravitation across the sun, Earth, the moon, and satellites.

CONNECTING TEXT STRUCTURE TO CONTENT LEARNING

In this chapter, we provide a number of techniques for helping students identify how authors connect ideas across texts as well as how to use that knowledge to draw meaning from texts and make conclusions about how ideas within the text are connected to

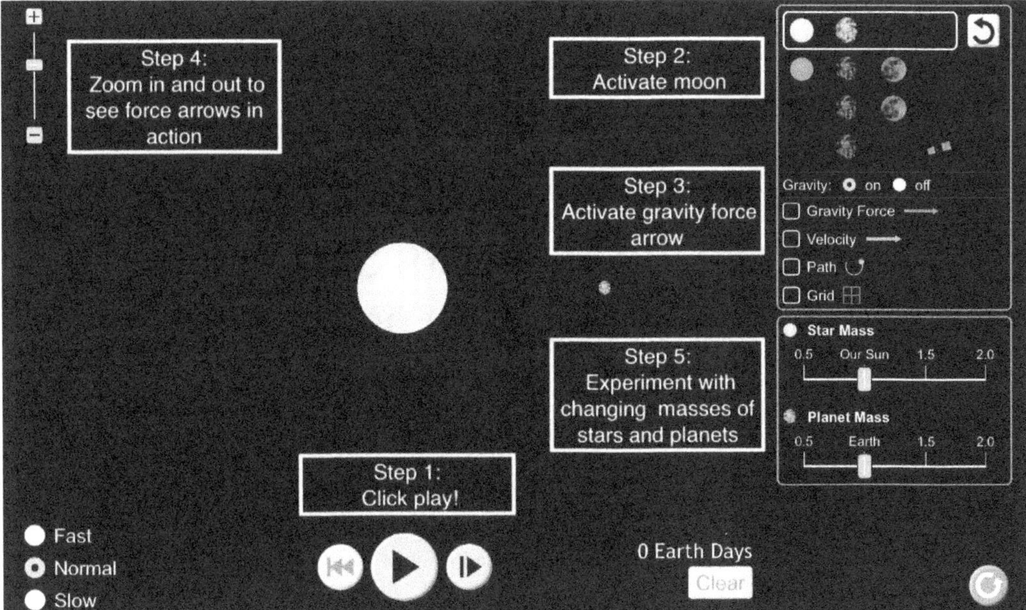

FIGURE 8.3. Example of organizational walkthrough for Ms. Astrid's gravity unit.

each other. After all, the structure of the text is at the very heart of a text's meaning, and it is tied closely to the very nature of the content-area ideas it conveys. Teaching students about text structure is, as Fisher and Frey (2015) put it, doing more than just teaching students what texts *say*, but rather teaching them how texts *work*. When breaking down the structures of texts for students, you are teaching students to use the text structure or organization of the text to learn.

CHAPTER 9

How Can Teachers Scaffold Challenging Vocabulary and Language?

GUIDING QUESTIONS

1. What does the research say about how we learn words?
2. How should teachers select which words to teach?
3. What do we do when students don't understand the words in texts?

"[Postcolonial theorists] also examine ways in which the literature of the colonial powers is used to justify colonialism through the perpetuation *of images of the colonized as inferior." (University of Washington, n.d.)*

Mrs. Bartleby, a 12th-grade ELA teacher, considers this line of this text about postcolonialism and wonders how her students will understand this sentence if they don't know the meaning of the word "perpetuation" or how to unpack this sentence. She looks up the term in the dictionary, which provides the following unhelpful definition: "to make perpetual or cause to last indefinitely" (Merriam-Webster, 2023). She wonders if her students even need to understand the word "perpetuation" to take away the larger understanding of the statement that colonial literature intentionally portrayed colonized peoples as inferior to justify their poor treatment. If she does need to teach this word, how can she go about helping her students understand this abstract concept?

If you, like Mrs. Bartleby, are feeling overwhelmed by how to support students in understanding the unfamiliar words abundant in science, history, and ELA texts, you are not alone. When we speak with teachers, they often mention that students are unfamiliar with a large number of words in the passages they need to assign. In this chapter, we will examine what the research reveals about how people learn new words and what teachers can do to support vocabulary development while reading.

We will also address how teachers can help students use their knowledge of sentence structure to support their understanding of challenging language.

WHAT DOES THE RESEARCH SAY ABOUT HOW WE LEARN WORDS?

We often approach vocabulary instruction with the question "Do students know this word or not?" However, vocabulary instruction is not black and white. The depth, specificity, and accuracy of students' word knowledge all play an important role here (McCarthy & McNamara, 2021). A better question that teachers can ask is how *well* do students know this word? As such, viewing word knowledge along a continuum is a more helpful way to capture students' understanding of words.

At one end of the continuum (see Figure 9.1), a word is completely unfamiliar to a student, meaning they have never heard of or seen that word before. Slightly farther along the continuum, a student might mark that they have heard the word but cannot use it in a sentence or define it. Here, readers may rely on connotations. For example, they hear the word "adverse" and remember that it means something negative, but they can't remember what it means. Or they may rely on roots and affixes knowledge. For example, they see the word "colonialism" and know it is related to a colony, but they aren't sure how to define it.

Toward the middle of the continuum, a student may know a word's meaning when they encounter that word in a rich context. In that context, they might be able to define that word or explain its meaning. For example, they see the sentence "The colonists experienced a lot of 'adversity' in their early years of settlement in the colony of Jamestown." Here, using their knowledge of early colonists' experiences of hardship in Jamestown, they would understand that adversity is akin to hardship, and so they would ascertain that meaning. And at the far end of the continuum, a student easily uses a word in speech or writing as a regular part of their vocabulary. With this level of rich word knowledge, students can even use the word figuratively or apply it to entirely new contexts.

As a teacher, we know it is tempting to want to quickly "teach" students unfamiliar words prior to reading. However, the research on word learning reveals that adolescents (and adults, too, for that matter) can't learn words all that quickly, and we require many examples and different exposures to words to really learn them.

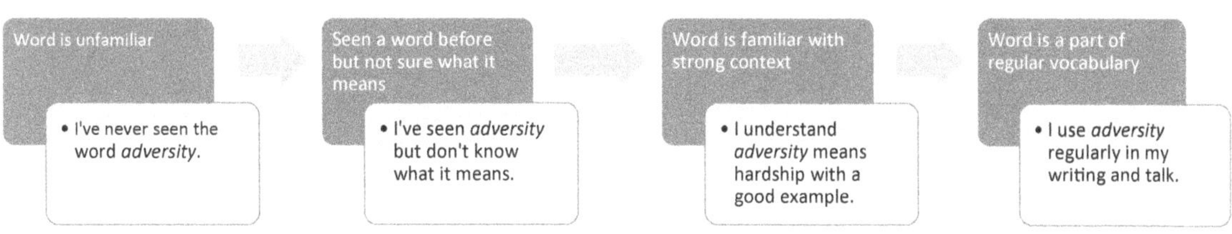

FIGURE 9.1. Continuum of word knowledge. Based on Beck et al. (2013).

Rather, word learning happens incrementally, over time, with repeated exposure to words in varying contexts with strong examples that add shades of meaning (Irvin, 1997).

Additionally, it is important for teachers to understand how people store word meanings in their brains. Often in vocabulary instruction, we focus on providing definitions for students to help them understand words. However, research reveals that we don't store word meanings as definitions in our brains. Rather, we store words as *connections* (Willingham, 2017). These connections grow as we are exposed to words in different sentences and contexts and use them with different groups of people.

Let's look at the passage entitled *The First Americans: The Olmec* (OpenStax, n.d.) on page 133 of this chapter. Let's consider the word "culture." When I (Sarah) think about this word, I can imagine so many connections. I think about things that are specific to my own culture, like Fourth of July celebrations, Halloween, and the idea of equality. I think about other places that I have visited that have very different cultural perspectives from my own, such as in Istanbul, where tea drinking and hospitality are ubiquitous, people take off their shoes and wear slippers in each other's houses, and the religious celebrations center around Islam. I think about other places I visited, like Nepal and India, and the unique cultural celebrations they participate in, such as cremation ceremonies along the Ganges River in Varanasi. I also think about workplace culture, the culture of a family, and so on. I think about making yogurt (a favorite activity of mine!) and the culture that I use to make yogurt as well as cultures that scientists grow in their labs. When you have deep knowledge of a word, you can make a lot of connections (see Figure 9.2).

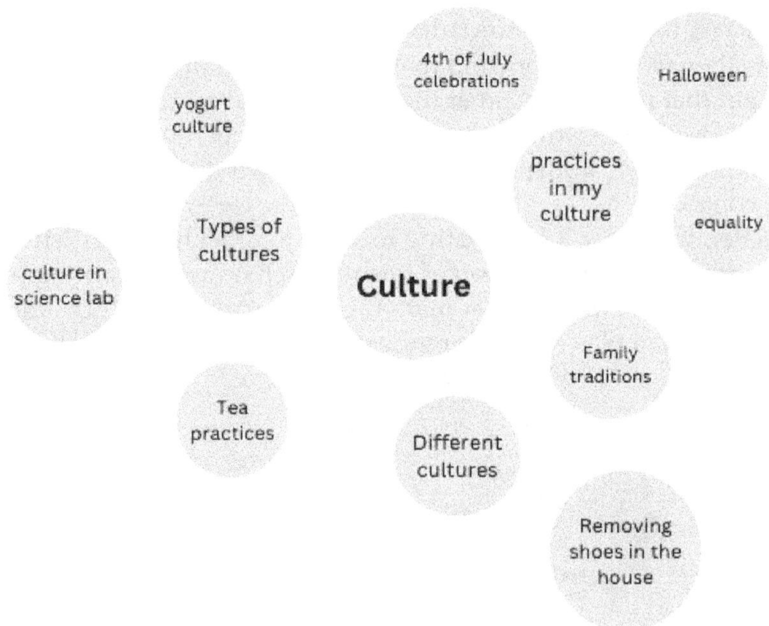

FIGURE 9.2. Word map: Culture.

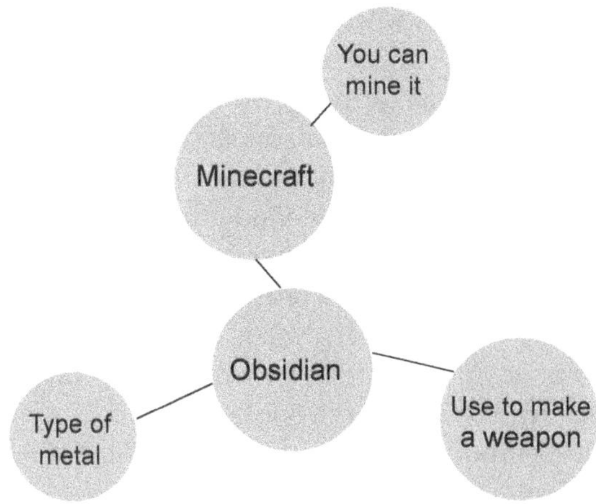

FIGURE 9.3. Word map: Obsidian.

In contrast, let's explore another word that I (Sarah) know less about, the word *obsidian*. Honestly, I know very little about this word, and most of what I know comes from my own children's discussions about the game Minecraft. I *think* obsidian is a type of metal? I am pretty sure, based on the contexts of my children's mentions of it, that it can be used to make weapons. I suspect obsidian can be mined, but I really don't know much more about it. Because I know less about this word, I can make far fewer connections than I might be able to with a word I know deeply, like *culture*, as you can see in Figures 9.2 and 9.3.

What about students' understanding of word parts, such as Latin and Greek roots or affixes? According to the research, the benefits of morphology instruction, in particular, explicit teaching of affixes and roots, are vast, having a positive influence not only on students' word learning, but also on their word recognition and fluency (Bowers & Bowers, 2017; Kirby & Bowers, 2017). As such, this chapter focuses on how to support students in reading the specific words in a text, and the next chapter (which addresses word reading) emphasizes the benefits and instructional techniques of morphology instruction.

Now that we understand how people learn and store word meanings, let's explore what that means for how to support students as they encounter unfamiliar words in tough texts.

HOW SHOULD TEACHERS SELECT WHICH WORDS TO TEACH?

When selecting words to teach from a text, less is really, in fact, more. Research suggests that teachers should select between six and eight words per text to teach in depth per lesson (Baumann et al., 2007; Nagy & Herman, 1987). These are your "focus words," which are words that are key to learning the content in your subject (Kearns et al., 2021). As you select which focus words to teach, consider your two goals: supporting vocabulary development and supporting learning and comprehension of the text. Consider selecting focus words that support both of these goals.

In addition to focus words, you may also teach "fast" words, or words that you quickly define but don't teach in depth (Kearns et al., 2021). Remember not every word in a text needs to be deeply understood for students to comprehend the text. As you come across other unfamiliar vocabulary that are not your focus words, you may quickly define or share examples of other words to help students in the moment understand the word. How do we decide which words are "fast" words? If you are reading a text and students ask about the meaning of a word that is not a focus word, this can become a "fast" word. Additionally, you may notice a word that is not one of your focus words but is key for understanding a sentence that describes a key concept—this may become a "fast" word as well.

Additionally, as teachers consider the goal of helping students to learn more vocabulary, the kinds of words they pick for both fast and focus words matter. Teachers often select subject-specific words, such as *photosynthesis* or *postcolonialism*. Beck and colleagues (2013) call these Tier 3 words, which are content- or domain-specific vocabulary. These are indeed important words to teach. However, we also need to teach high-frequency academic vocabulary such as *conclude* and *infer*, which are what Beck and colleagues (2013) call Tier 2 words. General academic vocabulary words are not specific to any particular subject but are essential for students to navigate the school curriculum. Additionally, Tier 2 words are often difficult to learn because they are abstract; for example, you cannot show a picture of the word *infer*. As such, it is important for teachers to include these words in their instruction alongside content-specific words. To help teachers discern which focus words to teach in a text, we present the following questions:

- How often does the word occur in a text or unit?
- How often will this word occur in future instruction?
- Do students need to know the word to learn the content?
- Is the word part of a larger morphological family?
- Is this a word that students will see across disciplines?

What does this look like? Let's visit Ms. Anthony, an eighth-grade history teacher, as she plans how to teach the textbook chapter about the first Americans that she's assigning her students tomorrow in her unit on Indigenous stereotypes (see the excerpt below). She's overwhelmed by the challenging vocabulary in the passage and isn't sure where to begin. She sees words such as *topographic, polytheistic, domesticated, edifices*, and *diffuse*, and she's unsure how to support her students in understanding so many unfamiliar words in one passage.

Ms. Anthony reviews the selection and settles on six focus words to teach in depth (bolded and underlined below). She chooses *topographic* and *commerce* because both words will appear in other units. She chooses *polytheistic* because this word is needed to understand cultural practices of the Mesoamerican people and *inscriptions* since students need to understand this word to learn about how the Mesoamerican people recorded their stories. She decides to teach *domesticated* both because it is critical to learning, but it also has a root word that is valuable across contexts, and because she thinks students know other similar words that she can connect it to. Lastly, she chooses the word *diffuse*, a Tier 2 academic word, because it is critical to understanding the history content (how culture spread in the early complex civilizations).

> **The First Americans: The Olmec**
>
> Mesoamerica is the geographic area stretching from north of Panama up to the desert of central Mexico. Although marked by great **topographic**, **linguistic**, and cultural diversity, this region cradled a number of civilizations with similar characteristics. Mesoamericans were **polytheistic**; their gods possessed both male and female traits and demanded blood sacrifices of enemies taken in battle or ritual **bloodletting**. Corn, or maize, **domesticated** by 5000 BCE, formed the basis of their diet. They developed a mathematical system, built huge **edifices**, and devised a calendar that accurately predicted eclipses and solstices and that priest-astronomers used to direct the planting and harvesting of crops. Most important for our knowledge of these peoples, they created the only known written language in the Western Hemisphere; researchers have made much progress in interpreting the **inscriptions** on their temples and pyramids. Though the area had no overarching political structure, trade over long distances helped **diffuse** culture. Weapons made of **obsidian**, jewelry crafted from jade, feathers woven into clothing and ornaments, and cacao beans that were whipped into a chocolate drink formed the basis of **commerce**. The mother of Mesoamerican cultures was the Olmec civilization. (OpenStax, n.d.)

Additionally, Ms. Anthony notes several other "fast" words that her students may be unfamiliar with that she could quickly define or explain as she reads this passage: *linguistic, bloodletting, edifices*, and *obsidian* (bolded but not underlined). None of these words are crucial to learning the content, nor will the words appear in future history learning, so she decides not to teach them in depth.

WHAT DO WE DO WHEN STUDENTS DON'T UNDERSTAND WORDS IN TEXTS?

Although unfamiliar vocabulary in content-area texts can seem overwhelming, do not fear. There are a number of techniques, all supported by research that can support students' word learning while reading science, history, and ELA texts.

VOCABULARY: WHAT NOT TO DO

Research has also identified several strategies that are not helpful for supporting vocabulary development. Avoid these techniques:

- Copying definitions from the dictionary
- Matching activities
- Providing definitions but no context or examples or explicit teaching of the word
- Providing definitions that aren't student-friendly
- Word searches
- Using context clues to find the meaning of words in place of regular and explicit vocabulary instruction

Help Students Make Connections between Words

Keeping in mind that our brains store words as connections rather than as definitions, vocabulary supports should focus on helping students see how words they know are related to new words (Willingham, 2017). One way we can do that is to use a technique called **list–group–label** (see Table 9.1). This technique was designed to help students learn technical vocabulary in science and social studies classes by helping them categorize and organize words into logical groups (Taba, 1967). In this technique, the teacher tells students a topic and asks students to identify words that are related to that topic. Then, after reading, students group those words into logical categories and label them. The process of listing words related to the topic, grouping them, and labeling them builds semantic connections for the words.

What does this look like? Let's visit Ms. Anthony and her eighth-grade history class again. Her students are reading a chapter on the American West, which she has chosen so that students can contrast that chapter's incomplete picture of Indigenous life this text portrays with the more complete story told in *Before Columbus*.

Ms. Anthony decides to use a list–group–label scaffold because it will capture the ideas that perpetuate stereotypes of Indigenous people that she wants her students to critique. As such, she wants her students to read the chapter and identify

TABLE 9.1. How to Plan and Implement a List–Group–Label

Procedures	Recommendations
1. The teacher reviews the text and identifies a topic that can be conveyed to students in which there are a number of related words or phrases in the text. 2. Students read the text and *list* words related to that topic. The teacher may also do this whole group by eliciting words from students during a whole-group read-aloud of the text or after reading. If students list words, it can be helpful for them to list them on sticky notes or index cards so that they can manipulate them in the next step. 3. After reading, either alone, or even better, with a partner, small group, or as a whole class, students group their words into logical categories. 4. Then, students come up with a label for each group of related words. The label may be a word from their list, or they may come up with a new word as a label. 5. If students complete this in groups or pairs, they can then view how others have grouped words and look for similarities or differences between words, groupings, and labels.	This strategy requires modeling the first few times that students use it. Allowing students to group and label words in partners or groups is a great way to scaffold the high-level thinking needed to complete this strategy.

(list) words or phrases that are related to Indigenous peoples' experiences in the American West, to draw her students' attention to these concepts. They will read with a partner and write each word they identify on a small sticky note to create their "list."

As you can see in Figure 9.4, Mai and Fatima worked together and listed words such as *transcontinental railroad, bullets,* and *ancestral land.* Before moving on to the next step, Ms. Anthony provides her own short list of words that she asks her students to add to their list if they didn't have them already, including *frontier, Crazy Horse, immunity, migration, westward,* and *Sandy Creek, Colorado.* This step is optional, but Ms. Anthony chooses to do it to ensure that her students will grapple with some of the key concepts she needs them to understand to ensure learning objectives.

Next, she asks her students to group the words into logical "groups." She had them create their lists on sticky notes (index cards work well too) because they can easily manipulate them to form "groups" of words. In this step, students look for words in their list that are related to each other and "group" those words together. As students work, Ms. Anthony monitors them so that she can provide support if they are struggling to see logical groups for any of their words. For example, she visits Mai and Fatima when she notices that they are having trouble figuring out what to do with the word *frontier.* They know it's not a person and doesn't seem to go with the words that relate to technology like *rifles* or *railroads.* Finally, with some in-the-moment prompting from Ms. Anthony, the girls realize that frontier is a place, so they group it with other locations, like Sandy Creek, Colorado, and Montana, even though it's not a proper noun. (Note: more on how to scaffold in action like this in Chapter 11.)

Locations	**People**	**Technology**	**Means of Destruction**	**Reasons for War**
Sandy Creek, Colorado	Native Americans	Conestoga wagon	European plagues	transcontinental railroad
Wounded Knee, South Dakota	Geronimo	repeating rifles	bullets	ancestral land
Idaho	Sitting Bull	railroad systems	rifles	migration westward
Montana	Crazy Horse		immunity	
frontier	settlers		buffalo extermination	
	Apache warriors			

FIGURE 9.4. Mai and Fatima's example of a list–group–label.

The beautiful part of this strategy is the discussion that Mai and Fatima engaged in to decide where to group the word *frontier*, in which they drew upon their knowledge of the word frontier to realize it was a place and belonged with the proper nouns describing specific locations.

Lastly, Ms. Anthony asks students to create a "label" for each group of words. In this step, students may find that one of the words in their list is a label, or they may use a sticky note to add a new word as a label. For example, Mai and Fatima used the word "locations" as a label for their group that included frontier, Sandy Creek, and Colorado. As students work, Ms. Anthony provides additional in-the-moment scaffolding to help students achieve this metacognitively difficult task.

After the class has finished, Ms. Anthony asks her students to walk around and view how others have listed, grouped, and labeled words. She finishes with a discussion on the similarities and differences they noticed across list–group–labels, and when possible, connecting the labels to her larger goals about unpacking stereotypes about Indigenous peoples. Although list–group–label is a challenging task, it is an incredible way for students to truly integrate and learn content as well as become more familiar with challenging vocabulary.

Another way to help students see connections between words is to use **graphic organizers**, such as a **Venn diagram**, a **labeled picture**, or a **timeline** or **continuum** to help students see how ideas are connected (see Table 9.2). The National Reading Panel (2000) found that graphic organizers are highly effective for teaching vocabulary, especially in science, social studies, and math, as they help students see how words are related.

Let's explore what this looks like by visiting Ms. Anthony's eighth-grade history class again. Ms. Anthony considers the three Ohio-related texts she is asking students to read that all retell the state's Indigenous history: one from a newspaper (the *Columbus Dispatch*), one from Wikipedia, and one from a blog that publishes creative digital stories (Midstory) written by Jessie Walton, an Indigenous author. Each story includes some details about the "Indian Removals" in Ohio but leaves out others.

Ms. Anthony decides that using a Venn diagram would allow her students to compare perspectives on Indigenous populations across the articles. She provides students with a list of key vocabulary, such as *Kickapoo, Shawnee, Wyandot, removal, forced out, migration*, and *Treaty of Fort Harmar.* She then asks students to consider which articles mentioned these words, and which left them out. In this way, Ms. Anthony prepares students not only to learn agreed-upon facts, but also to recognize the deeper questions about historical perspective and naming. She places particular emphasis on the names of the Indigenous peoples as a way to avoid essentializing them into one group, and she invites students to discuss ways in which they represent their identities so as to avoid being essentialized. See how Marissa, one of Ms. Anthony's students, completed the Venn diagram in Figure 9.5.

Another way to help students see connections between words is through **semantic mapping.** Several types of maps are helpful for showing students how words are related. This strategy is helpful because the structure of the map shows the relationship between the words or concepts, and this provides a visual for students. A

TABLE 9.2. How to Plan and Implement Graphic Organizers to Show How Words Are Related

Procedures	Recommendations
1. The teacher reviews the text and related unit words and decides on the type of organizer to use (Venn diagram, timeline or continuum, labeled picture) that will help students connect the new vocabulary.	This activity can be completed in partners or in small groups or even as a whole class.
2. The teacher then selects the words that will be included in the organizer and any structure to the organizer that is needed (i.e., finding a picture to label).	
3. During or after reading a related text, students complete the organizer.	
4. The teacher reviews with the class.	

common type of map is called a spider map. In this type of map, students write down key words or concepts, and then draw connections between words.

Another less well-known type of map is called a **hierarchical map**, which shows students the hierarchy of ideas. According to Thelen (1982), understanding the hierarchy of ideas is an important step in helping students learn new concepts. This map can be particularly helpful in supporting students in understanding the challenging vocabulary in science and social studies texts that often uses a hierarchical structure to organize ideas.

Let's explore what this type of map looks like in Dr. Perch's 10th-grade biology class as he nears the end of his unit on Great Lakes ecosystem management while reading from the *Death and the Life of the Great Lakes*. Dr. Perch wants his students to connect their knowledge of lake species to the concept of *energy pyramids*, which is perfect for a hierarchical diagram. He invites students to compile lists of the organisms they encounter in his unit, matching them to the corresponding level of the trophic pyramid (see a student's example in Figure 9.6). This way, he connects their existing vocabulary knowledge to new conceptual categories, enriching both. This also helps build students' conceptual infrastructure for understanding invasive species: What happens, for example, when a zebra mussel (a primary consumer) reshapes the energy pyramid because it has no natural predator? This question will build specific vocabulary that will help students answer the larger unit question determining how scientists should design systems to protect the stability and balance of the Great Lakes.

Use Examples and Nonexamples to Teach Word Meanings

Another way to support vocabulary development is to use examples and nonexamples to teach word meanings. One way you can do that is with the tried-and-true **Frayer model** (Frayer et al., 1969). Frayer models are useful for defining vocabulary words by

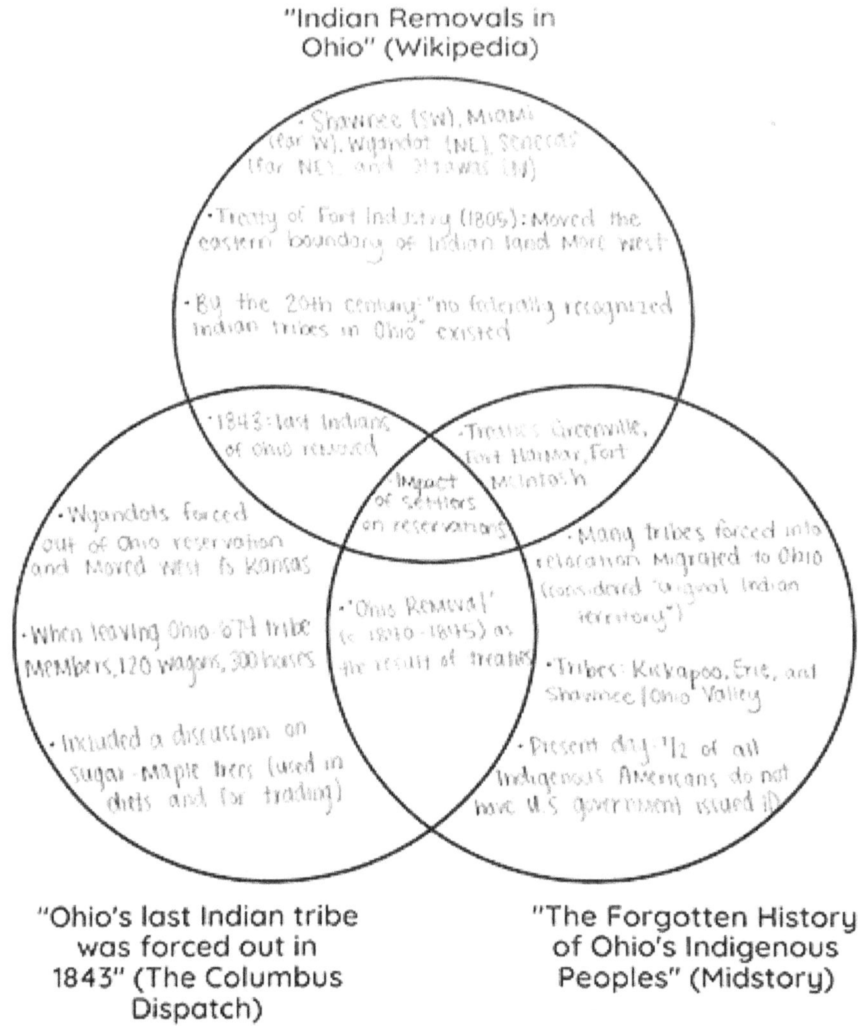

FIGURE 9.5. Student example of Venn diagram.

asking students to come up with examples, nonexamples, definitions, and a sentence using the key word or concept.

What does this look like? Let's explore how Ms. Astrid, when teaching a unit on gravity for her sixth-grade science class, used a Frayer model for the word *sun* using the text "NASA's Overview of the Sun's Role in the Solar System." Ms. Astrid knows that even a simple word like *sun* is a good choice because it is central to the concept; moreover, students may not be aware that the sun is classified as a particular type of star and that it is distinct from other celestial bodies (e.g., moons, planets). Thus, asking her students to come up with other examples of *sun* helps them understand the richness of the astronomy concepts she is teaching. She also sees the Frayer model as a good opportunity to build cross-linguistic connections between English/Spanish

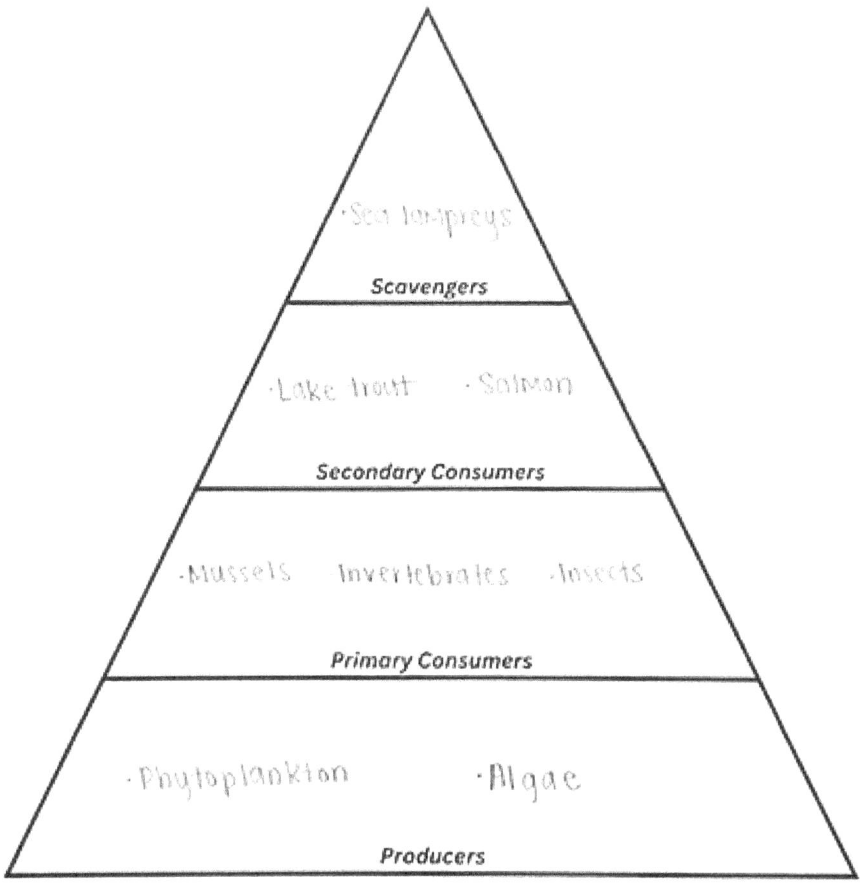

FIGURE 9.6. Marissa's energy pyramid diagram around the *Death and Life of the Great Lakes.*

cognates like *planet* and *planeta* and noncognates like *dwarf* and *enana,* so she offers opportunities for her students to write in Spanish (see Figure 9.7 for Lupita's example). The non-examples also clarify important concepts by defining the boundaries of the original word and helping her students differentiate moon or plants from the sun (or other stars). A blank template you can use is provided in Handout 9.1 at the end of this chapter.

Concept of definition maps (Schwartz & Raphael, 1985) are another way to use examples and nonexamples to teach word meaning and are useful for explaining more sophisticated concepts. For example, Ms. Bennett, a sixth-grade English teacher, is teaching her students about the concept of marginalization so that they can better understand the character's experiences in a story they are reading. This is a challenging concept for her students, and so she decides to have them read a short text about it, followed by creating a whole-class **concept of definition map** to teach the word (Schwartz & Raphael, 1985).

As shown in Figure 9.8, in a concept of definition map, students would list the

Vocab Word: Sun (*el Sol*)			
Definition and Picture	Sentence	Example/Synonym	Non-Example/Antonym
A 4.5 billion-year-old star at the center of our universe	The day/night cycle happens because the Earth orbits around the *sun*	Sun—el *Sol* Yellow Dwarf—*una enana amarilla* Star—*una estrella*	Moon—*la luna* Planet—*una planeta*

FIGURE 9.7. Lupita's example of Frayer model of the sun.

key concept at the center (*marginalization*), define the category this concept falls under (*oppression*), providing non-examples that are nonetheless part of the overarching category (*discrimination*), list characteristics of the concept, and finally, list examples of the concept (e.g., *voter suppression*). See Handout 9.2 for a blank template. It may take a little more class time to do a concept of definition map for a single word, but doing such a map can be an anchor for a network of conceptual vocabulary words that a teacher scaffolds throughout a unit.

Provide Direct Vocabulary Instruction

Direct and explicit instruction of vocabulary is key for learning. This is done best by providing opportunities for students to engage with words through activities

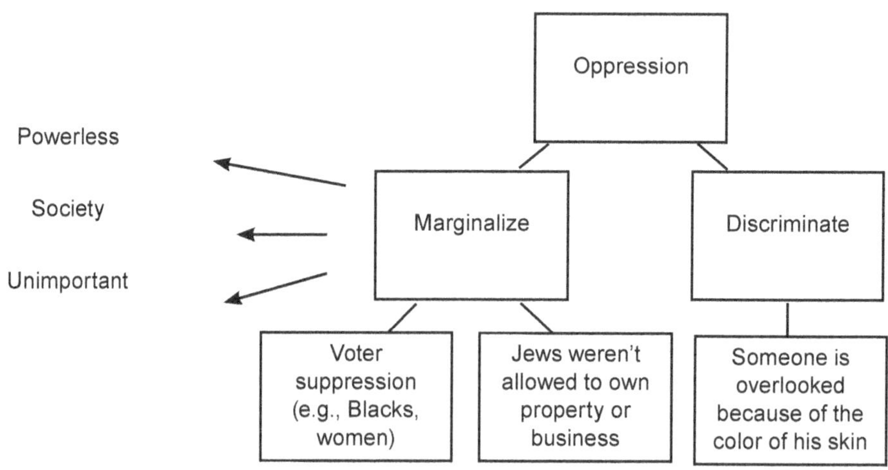

FIGURE 9.8. Concept of definition map example: Marginalization.

and discussion that provide context and relevant examples for students (Beck et al., 2013). Providing student-friendly definitions for the words is important, but definitions alone are not enough to support students in moving from never having seen a word before to integrating it into their vocabulary. Activities should focus on helping students compare words and engage in discussion about words with each other. Activities can occur before reading a text, but often, it is best to explicitly teach words *after* reading as the text can provide an introduction of the word in a relevant context (Beck et al., 2013). This is particularly relevant when reading fiction texts and studying groups of unrelated words (Flanigan & Greenwood, 2007).

One way to provide direct and explicit instruction is through a technique called **probable passage** (Wood, 1984; see Table 9.3). In probable passage, students are given a list of eight to twelve words prior to reading. and they sort those words into categories. This technique varies from list–group–label as you (the teacher) provide the words for students and the labels and students only group the words. After reading, students recategorize words based on what they have learned from the passage. Probable passage works well for explicitly teaching students new vocabulary because it provides students with three opportunities for encountering the words (before, during, and after reading) and helps them see how words are related to each other, while using the context of the text to teach the words. A blank template is available in Handout 9.3.

Let's explore what probable passage looks like in Ms. Bennet's sixth-grade English class. She is reading *The Evolution of Calpurnia Tate* with her students in which the main character, Calpurnia, known as "Callie Vee" wants to learn about the process of speciation, or how different species evolve over time from a common ancestor. However, it's 1899, and women didn't generally become scientists during this period of time. Further, Darwin's book *On the Origin of Species* was a controversial book that most

TABLE 9.3. How to Plan and Implement Probable Passage

Procedures	Recommendations
1. List 8–12 key words related to a passage. 2. Determine three to four categories. In social studies and ELA, categories usually include characters, setting, problem, and resolution. In science, categories may include substances, processes, location, circumstances, problem, or solution. 3. Prior to reading or learning about a topic, students place each of the 8–12 words into one of the categories. 4. They then write a gist statement, predicting what the passage will be about. 5. After reading, students revisit the words and move words to different categories based on what they learned in the text. 6. They also revisit their gist statement, adjusting it to reflect what the passage was about.	Optional features include adding a category for unknown words or a section for questions that arise. Probable passage works well in groups or pairs and creates excellent opportunities for discussion.

Christians rejected—and Callie is drawn to its scientific explanations but also aware of how her community views its ideas.

Ms. Bennett decides to use probable passage with the typical narrative text categories (Characters, Settings, Problems, and Solutions) to help her students understand the first chapter. She selects words that she knows will help her students understand the story, such as *pecan farm* (where Callie Vee lived) and *yellow grasshoppers* (the unique species she discovers, which are different from the typical green ones). She also chooses words that will help her students understand the problem in the first chapter, such as *mortified* (how Callie Vee felt at the library when she was scolded as she tried to check out Darwin's book), *conundrum* (describes the confusion Callie Vee feels about finding yellow grasshoppers), and *ceremoniously* (the manner in which her grandfather presents her with a copy of *On the Origin of Species*).

Ms. Bennett's students place these words into the categories before reading. Then, after reading, they recategorize them, based on what they have understood from the text. Figure 9.9 shows an example of this strategy in action. In Annabelle's work, the words that are moved are crossed out, then underlined in their new place. You can see that Annabelle moved *conundrum* from Solutions to Problems. When Ms. Bennett asked her why, Annabelle explained that she did not understand what the word meant before reading, but after seeing it in context (Callie reflects: "I stumbled through my grasshopper conundrum"), Annabelle understood that this word described Callie's problem. Although Annabelle was still not able to easily and precisely define *conundrum*, it's clear that her understanding of it grew through this activity and the reading.

Additionally, it is not important that all students have words in the same place; what matters more is that students have a good reason for why they put a word in a certain place. For example, Annabelle moved the word *librarian* from Characters to Problems, since in the story the librarian caused problems for Callie Vee. Although others may not have seen it this way, this move helped Annabelle understand the story.

In science texts, probable passage categories can vary to capture science concepts, such as substances, location, data, or circumstances. Let's explore a science example of probable passage from Dr. Perch's class. Before reading the NOAA (2019) article on algal blooms, he asked the students to sort the words in Figure 9.10 and predict which of the four categories (Causes, Problems, Types, and Data) the words belonged in. Dr. Perch knows his students have some knowledge of the Lake Erie ecosystem, but he also wants them to think about the complex interactions in the ecosystem (as his biology content standards require). That means he not only wants them to learn the vocabulary in this scaffold, but also connect them to the causes and effects of algal blooms.

After reading the NOAA text, Dr. Perch's students moved words around to demonstrate their understanding of how the specific vocabulary in the passage relates to larger scientific concepts. See Figure 9.10 for his student Jacob's work with this scaffold. For example, Jacob had placed *cyanobacteria* under Problems but realized it was actually part of the makeup for algal blooms, so he moved it under the category Types. He also had *swimming* under Causes but realized that swimming didn't cause the algal blooms to happen, but instead, the algal blooms made swimming dangerous, and so he moved *swimming* to Problems. For a blank template, see Handout 9.4.

Key words: Callie Vee, grandfather, librarian, *Origin of Species*, yellow grasshoppers, pecan farm, public library, theory, ceremoniously, conundrum, mortified

Characters	Settings
Callie Vee Grandfather ~~librarian~~	pecan farm public library

Problems	Solutions
mortified ~~specimen~~ yellow grasshoppers conundrum librarian	theory *Origin of Species* ceremoniously ~~yellow grasshoppers~~ ~~conundrum~~

Gist Statement (What do you think the passage will be about?)

Before Reading
Callie Vee and her grandfather live on a pecan farm and go to the public library. They check out a book *On the Origin of Species* so they can learn about yellow grasshoppers and other theories and specimens.

Revised After Reading
Callie Vee and her grandfather live on a pecan farm and wanted to learn about a conundrum: why there was a sudden surge in yellow grasshoppers during a drought. The librarian at the public library wouldn't lend her the book *On the Origin of Species*, which mortified Callie Vee. Her grandfather encouraged her to observe, which she did, and formed her own theory, before he ceremoniously gave her the book to see if she's right.

FIGURE 9.9. Annabelle's example of probable passage with Chapter 1 of *The Evolution of Calpurnia Tate*.

Semantic feature analysis is another technique that can be used to explicitly teach words and build connections between them (Bos & Anders, 1990; Johnson & Pearson, 1984). This strategy, like list–group–label and probable passage, also helps students improve their categorization skills, as well as understand the similarities and differences between related words. Table 9.4 contains instructions for planning and implementing a semantic feature analysis.

Let's explore what this looks like in Mr. Douglass's AP U.S. History class. While he's teaching some of the same content as Ms. Anthony's eighth-grade U.S. History class, his advanced students are reading the more challenging adult version of the book, entitled *1491: New Revelations of the Americas Before Columbus*. (Ms. Anthony is using the version of the same text written specifically for adolescents, titled *Before*

Words: winds, cyanobacteria, microcystin, winds, severity index, drinking water, swimming, fishing, lake temperature, tourism, fishing, rainfall

Causes	**Problems**
~~Swimming~~ ~~Severity index~~ ~~Rainfall~~ Winds Runoff Nutrients	~~Cyanobacteria~~ Drinking water Tourism Fishing Swimming
Types	**Data**
~~Nutrients~~ Microcystin Blue-green algae Cyanobacteria	~~Runoff~~ Lake temperature Severity index Rainfall

Gist Statement (What do you think the passage will be about?)

I think this passage will describe the causes and effects of algal blooms, like being caused by runoff and affecting drinking water, swimming, and fishing. The scientists will also describe what algal blooms are made of, like cyanobacterial, and how they measure the bloom with data like the severity index, rainfall, or temperature.

FIGURE 9.10. Jacob's example of probable passage in science.

Columbus.) Mr. Douglass had his students read a selection from the book's appendix entitled, "Laying the Land," in which the author, Charles Mann, lays out the complex decisions that historians and authors must make when deciding how to name Indigenous peoples they are writing about.

Mr. Douglass realizes that some of the words in the passage do not initially appear to be difficult vocabulary words. He also realizes that they reveal much about *how* history is written—and how those histories affect popular conceptions of Indigenous people today. For example, Mr. Douglass asks his students about how Mann depicts the differences between historians' approaches to naming, such as the common method of referring to Indigenous peoples as *tribes* versus European peoples as *kingdoms*, and Indigenous leaders as *chiefs* versus European leaders as *kings*. These words, though

TABLE 9.4. How to Plan and Implement a Semantic Feature Analysis

Procedures	Recommendations
1. The teacher selects a category related to their teaching topic and lists the words in that category along the left-hand column (see Handout 9.6 at the end of this chapter for an example of a blank organizer). 2. Then the teacher lists the features of those words along the top of the organizer. Teachers check to make sure that each category has at least one feature present and that each feature is related to at least one category. 3. Students read the text and then complete the organizer, placing a check in each box that contains a relevant feature. 4. The teacher then reviews the feature analysis with students.	It works well individually or in pairs. Categories can be descriptions of scenarios rather than individual words. When categorization is more complex, such as when features may sometimes be present, but not always, it can be helpful to include a yes, sometimes, or no system for analyzing features, rather than simply placing a check or not.

they don't appear complex and are not likely to be new to the students, nevertheless reveal much about historians' biases toward Indigenous peoples. Unpacking the connotations of these vocabulary words is a great exercise for his AP U.S. History class, which will be examining historical documents and critiquing the perspectives of secondary source authors all year long. So, in designing the semantic feature analysis you see in Figure 9.11, Mr. Douglass first selects the terms and names in the left row and designs the column headers to consider how those names are used. He also includes the reflection question at the bottom to make sure students pull together the big idea from the word-specific semantic feature analysis. Handout 9.5 provides a blank template and Handout 9.6 shows an additional example of a semantic feature analysis from a U.S. government class.

Teach Students to Use Grammatical Knowledge to Understand Unfamiliar Language

We have often heard teachers refer to context clue instruction, which means teaching students to use the context to figure out a vocabulary word. Research has shown that context is an important way that readers learn new words (Nagy et al., 1985). However, context clues are not a perfect solution: context can also be misleading and frustrate readers. So, how can readers know if the context is going to help them understand unfamiliar language?

Simple: their knowledge of grammar and syntax will help them. (More on this in Chapter 10.) Syntax refers to the way words are arranged in a sentence. Knowledge of syntax can be used to deepen readers' understanding of a text (Greenwood & Flanigan, 2007). How? Well, understanding the structure of sentences is the ability to understand how words work together to communicate meaning in sentences,

Directions: When reading the Appendix to *1491*, the author asks an interesting question: By what names should today's historians, writing in English, refer to Indigenous peoples? As you read, consider the names in the far left column, but also put check marks in the boxes about how those names are used (or not used) by different people involved in the writing of Indigenous history.				
Names/terms	Historically used to refer to European groups	Historically used to refer to Indigenous groups	Used by Charles Mann in *1491* to describe Indigenous groups	Used by some Indigenous peoples themselves
Indian		x	x	x
Native American			x	
Names of specific groups (e.g., Wampanoag)			x	x
Civilization	x	x		
Chief/tribe		x		
King/nation	x		x	x

FIGURE 9.11. Example from Mr. Douglass's Indigenous history and stereotypes unit.

including how they function as parts of speech and how phrases and clauses work to form complete thoughts and indicate more or less important ideas (Mackay et al., 2021). For example, some sentences might hint at a word's meaning by contrast: "*Even though* most of his friends hated the new school lunch menu options, the boy actually found them *scrumptious*." The way the words *even though* sets up the contrast in the first part of the sentence prepares a reader to know that *scrumptious* must mean that he did not hate, but rather enjoyed, the new menu. The fact that the first part of the sentence ("Even though . . . options") is the subordinate clause indicates that the friends' opinions about the lunch menu was not the author's main point; rather, the boy's opinion is the main point.

Thus, students can use their knowledge of grammar to help them use context to understand unfamiliar words. What does this look like? The **make it fit** scaffold is a fun way to have students use their knowledge of grammar to deepen their vocabulary. In this technique, the teacher selects a text excerpt and then removes some key words. Next the teacher asks students to place a word that goes into the blank (see Table 9.5). In this way, students have to consider the grammatical aspects of the sentence to determine the part of speech and the meaning of the missing words, as well as keep the meaning of the larger sentence and whole passage in mind. Make it fit, then, is a way to teach specific words essential to a unit that supports students in using their knowledge of grammar to help them figure out unfamiliar words.

Let's explore what this looks like in Mrs. Bartleby's class as they read about

TABLE 9.5. How to Create a Make It Fit Exercise

Procedures	Recommendations
1. The teacher selects a short passage that has a high density of critical conceptual vocabulary words.	You can make this easier or harder by including more or fewer words, or adding words that don't match the passage, or adding a word bank.
2. The teacher removes several key vocabulary words from the passage and leaves blanks where the words were.	
3. As students read, they invent their own words and phrases that fit in those blanks.	
4. Students read the text, seeing the words that should go in the blanks.	
5. After reading, the teacher reviews the synonyms that students had created, discussing how close the words are to the meaning in the text.	

postcolonial theory. The word *postcolonial* is central to the success of Mrs. Bartleby's unit, so she designs this scaffold to get to the very heart of this concept. She selects a passage and eliminates a few key words that are related to the word *colonial,* including *postcolonial, colonized,* and *colonizing,* but also *inferiority* and *oppression* (see Figure 9.12). She then asks her students to read through the passage once and fill in the blanks with words or phrases that make the sentence make sense. Next she encourages students to read the passage again out loud and make sure the words they chose make sense in context.

Afterward, Mrs. Bartleby asks her students to compare their answers with a partner. She suggests that if they came up with different words than their partner, they should explain why. Finally, Mrs. Bartleby reveals the original passage and asks students to compare their word choice with the author's. By asking students to make a word "fit," the teacher helps students connect new words to their existing vocabulary networks.

ENGAGE STUDENTS WITH WORDS AND MAKE CONNECTIONS TO SUPPORT LEARNING

How can teachers scaffold challenging vocabulary and language? The research we highlight in this chapter demonstrates that we can scaffold readers' understanding of difficult vocabulary and language by providing opportunities for students to thoughtfully engage with vocabulary. Our scaffolds focus on helping students make connections with words, rather than memorize definitions, to align with what we know about brain research on how people learn and store word meanings. Through meaningful encounters, opportunities to use words, and making connections between familiar and unfamiliar words, we can scaffold students to tackle challenging language and deepen their vocabulary knowledge to support their content learning.

Probable Passage

_________ theory deals with the reading and writing of literature written in previously or currently _________ countries, or literature written in _______ countries which deals with colonization or colonized peoples. It focuses particularly on the way in which literature by the colonizing culture _______ the experience and realities, and inscribes the _______, of the colonized people on literature by colonized peoples which attempts to articulate their identity and ________ their past in the face of that past's inevitable otherness. It can also deal with the way in which literature in colonizing countries _________ the language, images, scenes, traditions and so forth of colonized countries.

Original passage:

Postcolonial theory deals with the reading and writing of literature written in previously or currently **colonized** countries, or literature written in **colonizing** countries which deals with colonization or colonized peoples. It focuses particularly on the way in which literature by the colonizing culture **distorts** the experience and realities, and inscribes the **inferiority,** of the colonized people on literature by colonized peoples which attempts to articulate their identity and **reclaim** their past in the face of that past's inevitable otherness. It can also deal with the way in which literature in colonizing countries **appropriates** the language, images, scenes, traditions and so forth of colonized countries.

FIGURE 9.12. Example of make it fit in Ms. Bartleby's postcolonialism unit.

HANDOUT 9.1. Frayer Model Template

Vocabulary Word:			
Definition and Picture	Sentence	Example/Synonym	Non-Example/Antonym

HANDOUT 9.2. Concept of Definition Map Template

Concept of Definition

Name: ______________________________

Date: __________________

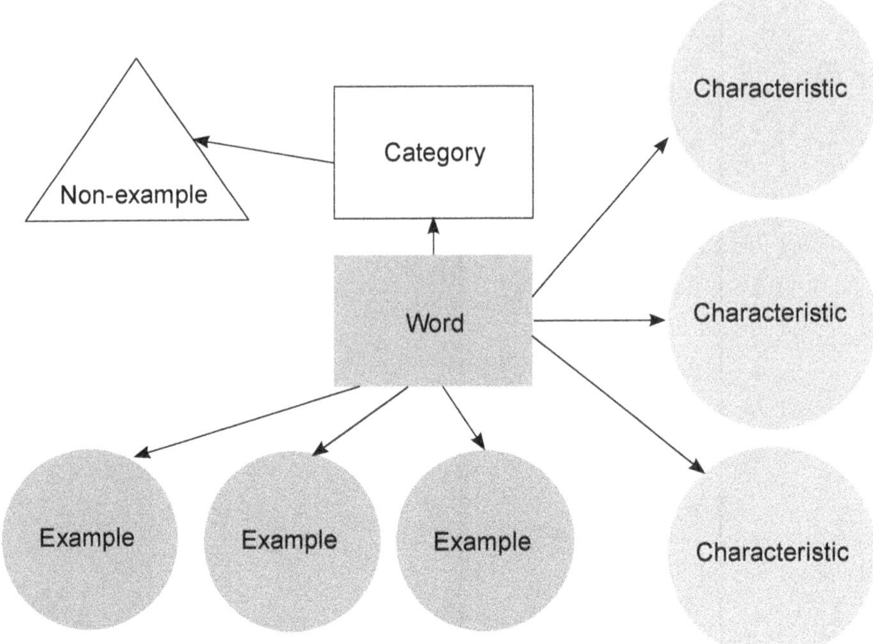

HANDOUT 9.3. Probable Passage Template

Key words:

Characters	**Settings**
Problems	**Solutions**

Gist Statement (What do you think the passage will be about?)

HANDOUT 9.4. Template for Probable Passage in Science

Words:	
Causes	**Problems**
Types	**Data**
Gist Statement (What do you think the passage will be about?)	

HANDOUT 9.5. Semantic Feature Analysis Template

Features → **Vocabulary** **Terms ↓**				

HANDOUT 9.6. Additional Example of Semantic Feature Analysis for U.S. History or Government

This semantic feature analysis (SFA) doesn't just ask students to memorize what these documents were or when they were created. It asks them to think about how the documents functioned in the early days of the United States. In this way, the SFA enriches vocabulary instruction in history and government.

Features → Documents ↓	**Inspired by the Magna Carta**	**Proposed a form of government**	**Addressed individual rights**	**Reflected fear over a strong central government**	**Eventually replaced**
Declaration of Independence					
Articles of Confederation					
Constitution					
Bill of Rights					

CHAPTER 10

How Can Teachers Scaffold Word Reading?

GUIDING QUESTIONS

1. What are word-reading skills for adolescents?
2. How can teachers determine who needs word-reading support?
3. How do we support word-reading needs for adolescents?

"But my students can't read; how can I incorporate challenging texts into my classroom?"

We have often heard secondary teachers complain that their students "can't read." What we think teachers mean is that some students have trouble sounding out the words in the text. Many teachers know the terrible feeling—for students, peers, and teachers alike—of listening to a secondary student read aloud who struggles to accurately pronounce the words.

Is it always necessary to have correct pronunciation? Not necessarily. Take this sentence from *1491:* "The name of the Mayan ruler . . . has been rendered as, among other things Toh-Chak-Ich'ak, Chak Toh Ich'ak, and Chak Tok Ich'aak" (Mann, 2011, p. 396). These proper nouns pose an extraordinary challenge even for strong readers; additionally, correct pronunciation is not necessary for the history-learning goals in this lesson: Learning different kinds of Mayan spellings in English is not the purpose of Mr. Douglass's unit. However, in Dr. Perch's class, words like *cyanobacteria* and *microcystins* are also difficult to pronounce, but they are crucial to his essential questions and unit goals.

Further, some adolescents, even in middle and high school, still have underdeveloped skills around word reading, particularly in the area of *decoding* (the ability to sound out the words on the page) and *fluency* (the ability to read quickly and accurately with good expression) (e.g., Cutting & Scarborough, 2006). While elementary teachers have a background in teaching children how to read the words, secondary teachers largely do not.

Are we saying it is the job of the ELA, science, or social studies secondary teachers to teach their students with underdeveloped word-reading skills how to read? Absolutely not! However, content-area teachers need to know how to support readers who have trouble sounding out the words. This chapter will define word-reading skills and how to figure out who needs support with sounding out words. Then, we will share researched-based and age-appropriate scaffolds to help adolescents sound out difficult words while reading challenging content-area texts.

WHAT ARE WORD-READING SKILLS FOR ADOLESCENTS?

As noted above, word-reading skills are made up primarily of decoding and fluency abilities. Let's explore decoding first. For a reader to sound out the words on the page, they must first possess knowledge of letters and their associated sounds. For example, readers must know that the letter *c* can make the /s/ sound as in *city* or the /k/ sound as in *cake*. Additionally, to sound out words, readers must know more complex letter patterns and those sounds, such as that the letters *dge* make the /j/ sound in the word *hedge*, or the letters *ea* make the long *e* sound in the word *mean*. Decoding skill also consists of the ability to break up a word into syllables (meaningful chunks) so that it can be read more easily.

In addition, for adolescents, decoding skills go beyond simply knowing letters and patterns. Research reveals that adolescents also need to understand roots and affixes. We call this *morphology*, which is defined as the study of the meaning of word parts. For example, the word *reteach* consists of the prefix *re*, which means again, and the base word *teach*. Understanding the meaning of words and chunks of words is effective in supporting adolescents' word recognition skills (Bowers & Bowers, 2017; Toste et al., 2017, 2019). Later in this chapter we share a number of ways that teachers across content areas can support adolescents with weak decoding skills by drawing attention to the roots and affixes that make up words.

Word reading also includes fluency, which is a reader's ability to read orally with accuracy, speed, and meaningful expression. Let's explore *accuracy* first, which is a reader's ability to sound out the words correctly. Accuracy includes a strong foundation in decoding. That is, to read accurately, readers need to sound out letters and patterns of letters (including roots and affixes) correctly. As readers learn these patterns, they become embedded into their brains, and become automatic, meaning that readers do not have to sound things out letter by letter. The ability to read words without sounding them out is called *automaticity*. You are likely not sounding out any words as you are reading this chapter because your reading is effortless, autonomous, and unconscious. This is because you are an automatic word reader. You have not memorized all the words in the English language; rather, you have learned the letter patterns, roots, and affixes we use, and they are familiar enough that you can read them accurately without your needing to stop and sound them out.

Thus, considering how accurately someone reads is one way to determine if they need the word-reading scaffolds described in this chapter. If adolescents can read most of the words, meaning roughly 90% of the words in a text, fluency support is likely not needed. However, if a reader is reading fewer than 90% of the words, that reader may benefit from the fluency scaffolds we describe in this chapter. Do you remember the difficult passage you read in Chapter 2? You were able to read 87% of those words correctly, and that passage was difficult as a result.

These numbers are based on the most recent research on fluency instruction. In the past, many people thought that readers needed to be able to read approximately 95% or more of the words to be able to make sense of the passage, but more recent research has shown that with fluency support, students can make sense of much more challenging passages, particularly older readers (Kuhn & Stahl, 2003). And, if they read these more challenging passages with support—over time—their fluency improves. It actually improves at greater rates than if we keep readers with word-reading difficulties in easier passages (Vaughn et al., 2022).

The next element of fluency is *speed*. Automaticity is a key aspect of speed, and as such, in early elementary grades, there is a strong correlation between reading speed and comprehension. At this age, students who read faster show that they also better understand the text, likely because they have developed more automaticity than their less speedy peers. However, this correlation between speed and comprehension is much smaller in later elementary grades and even smaller yet for middle and high school students (Wang et al., 2019; Washburn, 2022). This means that adolescents (and adults) can read more difficult things slowly and still understand them.

Why is this? When texts get harder, as they do across the subjects in middle and high school, readers often slow down their reading, and many have to slow down in order to sound out more difficult words. Therefore, this doesn't mean that every student who reads slowly and is having trouble sounding words out has weak word-reading skills. Imagine if I handed you a medical journal article meant for practicing surgeons. It would contain mostly words unfamiliar to you and likely even many roots and affixes new to you. It may also have long, complicated sentences structured in ways that you are not familiar with (this is called *syntax*—more on this in a bit).

If you were asked to read that text aloud, you would read slowly, perhaps awkwardly, and certainly you would lack good expression. This does not mean that you didn't learn how to read. Rather, the *vocabulary* of the text is unfamiliar to you, which slows down your reading. This happens to many adolescents across the disciplines because content-area texts contain a lot of new and difficult words or even complex jargon. Thus, supporting vocabulary (as we discussed in Chapter 9) is crucial for text understanding.

However, despite the lower correlation between speed and comprehension for adolescents, there still *is* a small association. That means that we do need to pay attention to adolescent readers' speed, albeit less attention than for younger readers. We can measure speed by looking at how many words a person can correctly read in one minute. Table 10.1 displays typical reading rates (words read correctly in one minute) for readers in grades 3–12. These rates are based on Hasbrouck and Tindal's (2017) research of K–sixth graders. Little research has explored typical rates for students beyond sixth grade, so an informed estimation is made here based on research. A score below the benchmark indicates a possible need for the fluency supports described in this chapter.

The last piece of the fluency puzzle is *expression*, which we also call *prosody*. Prosody is the ability to read smoothly with the right emotion, expression, and intonation; in other words, readers know to pause at periods or commas, their voice goes up when they ask a question, and so on. As such, to read prosodically, a reader needs to understand what they read. Prosody is one of the most powerful aspects of fluency and a great focus of instruction for readers with word recognition difficulties (Paige et al., 2014).

What does prosodic reading look like? Figure 10.1 includes a prosody rubric that describes what less prosodic reading and more prosodic reading look like. As you can see, less prosodic reading includes reading word-by-word or even sound-by-sound in a monotone voice. As readers improve, they start to read some phrases, but their reading is still choppy. They eventually read with more expression or emotion and they regularly attend to punctuation, sounding natural and smooth. Many of the instructional techniques we will share in this chapter support readers' prosody.

What about sentence fluency? One factor that influences readers' prosody, particularly for older readers, is syntax, which we introduced in Chapter 6 and discussed again in Chapter 9. As we previously mentioned, syntax refers to the way words are arranged in a sentence (Paris & Hamilton, 2009). Longer sentences, which contain more complex grammatical features, are more challenging to read prosodically, such as:

> So, a decade before Yuri Gagarin became the first person in space, long before John Glenn and Neil Armstrong, before Ham the astrochimp and Laika the space dog, before all of them, was Albert (Roach, 2022, p. 11).

In contrast, sentences with simpler grammar are easier to read with good expression and intonation: "Albert was a nine-pound rhesus monkey" (Roach, 2022, p. 11).

Thus, supporting readers' prosody includes supporting readers' ability to digest more complex sentences. The supports include sentence-level scaffolds such as the vocabulary cloze (or a fill-in-the-blank style) exercise **make it fit** or **the who did what?** scaffold, both of which help students focus on the meaning and grammatical aspects

TABLE 10.1. Typical Reading Rates by Grade Level

	Fall	Winter	Spring
3rd grade	**59–104**	**79–137**	**91–139**
4th grade	**75–125**	**95–143**	**105–160**
5th grade	**87–153**	**109–160**	**119–169**
6th grade	**112–159**	**116–166**	**122–173**
7th–8th grades*	***135+***	***n/a***	***n/a***
9th–12th grades*	***150+***	***n/a***	***n/a***

Note. Adapted from Hasbrouck and Tindal (2017). *Fall, winter, spring norms not established; rather, a score below this benchmark indicates a fluency need.

1	2	3	4
Most of the passage is read slowly, choppily, in a monotone voice, sounding words out word-by-word.	Most of the passage is read choppily in a monotone voice, read in phrases of two-to-three words.	Reads with a mixture of smoothness and choppiness, sometimes uses expressions and sometimes attends to punctuation.	Reading sounds natural and smooth, has expression, and attends consistently to punctuation.

FIGURE 10.1. Prosody rubric. Derived from *https://nces.ed.gov/nationsreportcard/studies/orf/scoring.aspx.*

of the sentence. However, many of the fluency strategies we share later in this chapter also help students digest longer sentences with more complex syntax by including multiple reads of a sentence.

HOW CAN TEACHERS DETERMINE WHO NEEDS WORD-READING SUPPORT?

Middle and high school teachers have a unique situation that differs from elementary teachers. Rather than teaching one class of 15–30 students, secondary teachers usually have five- or more large classes with roster numbers typically totaling over 100 students. And rather than having most of the day with the same students, secondary teachers may have just 45 minutes a day with their classes, which makes figuring out students' reading needs quite difficult.

We have a simple and pragmatic solution. We suggest that teachers listen to their students read a grade-level passage, one typical for your content-area, for at least one minute. This can be done informally as part of your class instruction.

To make this approach simple, teachers ask students to read a passage out loud with a small group, taking turns at each paragraph. As students read, the teacher circulates, listening to students informally. The teacher has a sheet of paper with all of the students' names on it (see Figure 10.2 for an example and Form 10.1 for a blank template). As students read, the teacher can take notes to indicate whether students are reading accurately and quickly, with good prosody. We suggest a simple system to indicate "yes" or "no" whether or not they have a need, and jotting down some notes if needed for prosody. For example, as Ms. Anthony circulated in her room, she heard Rebecca reading out loud and making a great many mistakes. She wrote a "no" in the accuracy column, indicating that this student did not read accurately (see Figure 10.2). She heard another student, Caleb, reading with great expression and wrote "yes" in the prosody column, indicating that he did not need prosody support. If you don't catch everyone's reading the first time you do this, repeat with another reading on a different day.

How can you get everyone comfortable reading aloud in a small group? We have found that culture building is key for regularly incorporating this practice into your

Students	Notes on Accuracy *Does the student read most of the words accurately?*	Notes on Speed *Does the student read quickly?*	Notes on Prosody *Does the student read sound-by-sound, word-by-word, or phrase-by-phrase?* *Are students pausing appropriately at punctuation?* *Does the student use good expression and intonation?* *Are students making a lot of self-corrections?*
Rebecca	No	No	No, many self-corrections, read phrase-by-phrase
Caleb	Yes	Yes	Yes, great expression and emotion
Nasli	No	Yes	No, read through periods/commas, little emotion
Ena	No	No	No, little to no expression, no emotion
Jacob	Yes	No	Yes, read smoothly
Arthur	Yes	Yes	Yes, great expression and emotion
Annabelle	No	No	No, many self-corrections, poor intonation
Patience	Yes	Yes	Yes, read smoothly, good intonation

FIGURE 10.2. Whole-class fluency reading in Ms. Anthony's class.

classroom and building a caring environment in which students are allowed to take risks and make mistakes. Still, if some students are resistant to reading out loud, you could ask those readers to come into the hall with you and read to you for a minute so that you could listen to their reading privately, or ask them to stay after class or join you at lunch.

I (Sarah) have used this method for years and have found that this informal way of listening to students read is simple and effective. All teachers, including science, social studies (and even math teachers!), should listen to their students read, as it provides a great deal of insight into whether or not students are struggling to sound out the words—and whether or not they need to use the scaffolds in this chapter.

HOW DO WE SUPPORT WORD-READING NEEDS FOR ADOLESCENTS?

We have often heard teachers say that not much research has been done on how to support word-reading skills for older readers with reading difficulties, or that the research is not clear on what works. We have excellent news for you: Neither of those statements is true. A great deal of research has been done on how to support adolescents' word reading *and* the findings are robust; in other words, there is clear guidance on what to do, supported by many, many studies.

Additionally, it is important to note that the guidelines from the research on supporting older readers' word reading are quite different from how to support elementary students with seemingly similar issues with regard to sounding out words. For example, one of the most important differences is that all word-reading support for

FORM 10.1. Fluency Chart for Whole-Class Reading

Students	**Notes on Accuracy** *Does the student read most of the words correctly?*	**Notes on Speed** *Does the student read quickly?*	**Notes on Prosody** *Does the student read sound-by-sound, word-by-word, or phrase-by-phrase?* *Are students pausing appropriately at punctuation?* *Does the student use good expression and intonation?* *Are students making a lot of self-corrections?*

adolescents should be meaning-based. This means that while we support readers in accurately, quickly, and prosodically sounding out words, we must keep our attention on helping students *understand* the passage (Vaughn et al., 2022; Wexler et al., 2008). Thus, all of the scaffolds we discuss in this section will support students' word reading while also supporting their text understanding.

Provide Morphology Instruction

One way teachers can support adolescents' word reading is by providing morphology instruction. This means teaching students about relevant roots or affixes that are typical for your content area (Bowers & Bowers, 2017; Kim et al., 2017; Toste et al., 2017, 2019). Teachers can do this by having students create **morphology posters** (see Table 10.2). In these posters, students define a root, prefix, or suffix, provide example words with that root or affix, a sentence using one of the words, and illustrate their poster.

What does this look like? Let's explore morphology posters in Dr. Perch's 10th-grade biology class in his unit around the Great Lakes ecosystems. Dr. Perch chooses the word *cyanobacteria,* which has two roots: *bacteria* (a single-celled organism) and *cyano* (meaning blue-green). Cyanobacteria is commonly called *blue-green algae* (hence the *cyano*). In the example poster in Figure 10.3, Wyatt split the word into two morphemes by color code (using blue for *cyano*), defined each morpheme, and drew pictures to help remember what *cyanobacteria* really are: not plants but blue-green, single-celled organisms. Understanding what cyanobacteria really are will help Dr. Perch's students understand their role in the Lake Erie ecosystem and how scientists can recommend solutions to potentially harmful algal blooms.

Another way to support students in learning vocabulary is a **morphology Frayer model**, which is similar to the traditional Frayer model we shared in the previous chapter. In this technique, instead of writing a key word at the center, students write a root, such as *vade*. Then, students define the root (to go for a walk) and provide examples of words with that root (*invasive, evade*). Next, students find, or the teacher provides, an example sentence from the text, and finally students write their own sentence using a word with this root (see Figure 10.4).

Similar to the morphology Frayer model, another way to teach students about how

TABLE 10.2. How to Create Morphology Posters

Procedures	Recommendations
1. Teacher selects a root or affix for study and defines that root/affix.	Select roots or affixes that are core to the unit or that students will encounter in future units.
2. Students write the root/affix and definition on their poster.	Have students briefly present the posters after making them.
3. Students list words that contain that root or affix.	
4. Students write a sentence with that root or affix.	
5. Students illustrate the poster.	

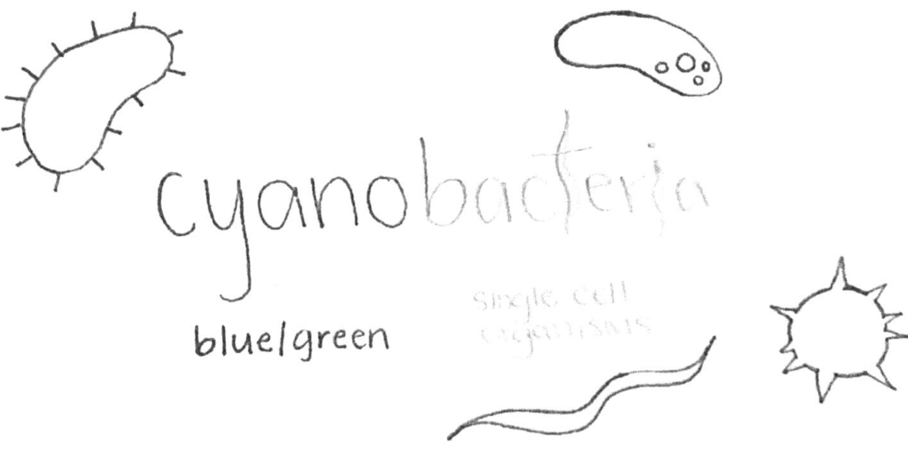

FIGURE 10.3. Wyatt's example of morphology poster of the word "cyanobacteria."

words work is to create a **root-word wall.** In this technique, teachers write a relevant root word in the center of the wall, with its derivations in different parts of speech in a web around it. For example, Mrs. Bartleby creates a root-word wall around "colony" because this root has many possible connections to the core concept of the unit: postcolonialism. She decides to organize it by parts of speech to illustrate how suffixes can change how words are used. For example, students who have already seen the word *colonize* are likely to be less intimidated by the rarer verb form *decolonize* (see Figure 10.5, for example). Starting this word wall early in the unit can give students space to add in words as they go and eventually add relevant examples of each word related to various texts in the unit. For example, in *The Tempest*, students can add an example of what Caliban's precolonial life was like before Prospero's arrival.

Another way to teach morphology is to focus on spelling. Yes, you read that right, spelling! Research shows that spelling instruction has a positive effect on adolescents' word-reading skill (Graham, 2020; Levesque et al., 2021).

One way to weave spelling instruction into rich content-area texts is to use the

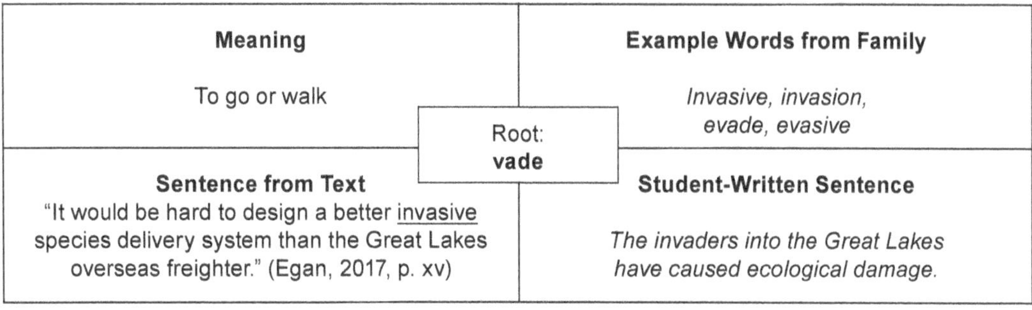

FIGURE 10.4. Will's example of a morphology Frayer model.

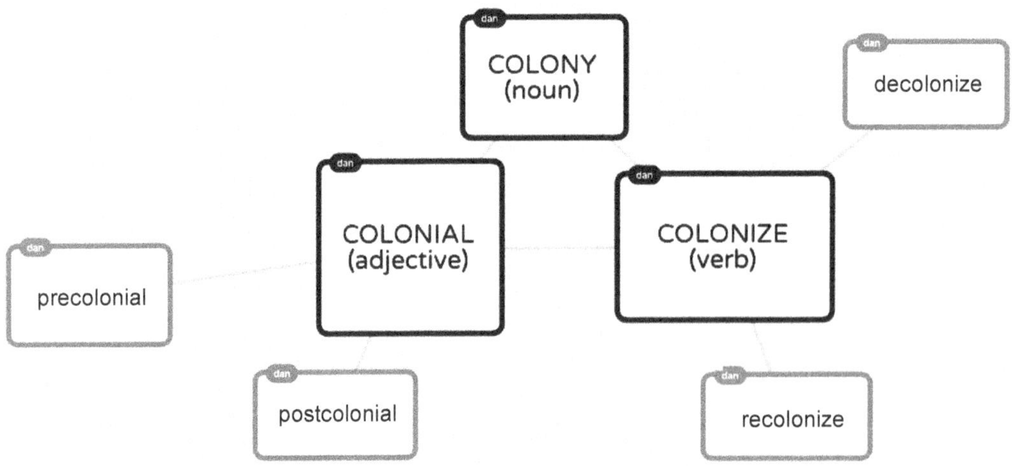

FIGURE 10.5. Example from Mrs. Bartleby's postcolonialism unit.

badd spelling protocol (see Table 10.3). To use this technique, the teacher selects a passage with key words that have important spelling, morphology, or phonics patterns (for example, *-tion, enviro-,* or *ances-*). Then, the teacher replaces those words with phonologically plausible misspelled versions (the "badd"ly spelled words) and asks the students to work in pairs to replace those words with their correct spellings. This approach helps students see the connections between a word's sound, its morphemes, and its meaning in the passage.

Let's explore what this looks like in Ms. Anthony's eighth-grade history class. She is reading *Before Columbus* with her students, which contains many multisyllabic words with roots and affixes. Ms. Anthony selects a short passage that contains four words with the roots *enviro-, ances-, wild-,* and *touch-*. She modifies the passage to misspell those roots. Before reading, Ms. Anthony briefly introduces the roots and their definitions to her students. Next, she asks her students to read the modified text and correct the "badd" spellings:

> Today, the invayronmentl laws in the United States are designed to bring the country's rivers, fields, and forests back to the way they were when only Indians lived in the Americas. Before my ansester Billington arrived, my history books told me, this whole half of the world was basically a willdurnes: an empty landscape, nature in the raw. Again I wondered, could that possibly be true? Did Indians live here for so long and leave the land almost uhntucht? Part Three of this book looks at that question. (Mann, 2009, p. vii)

She then asks students to identify the misspelled words and asks them to reflect on how the correct spellings reveal the root word's connection to the word's meaning. For example, one student, Jade, pointed out that the suffix *-ness* was spelled incorrectly in the word *willdurnes*. Another student, Xavier, noticed that the root *wild* was

TABLE 10.3. How to Use the Badd Spelling Protocol

Procedures	Recommendations
1. Pick a short excerpt (1–3 paragraphs) of text that has vocabulary words with key roots or affixes. 2. Put in misspelled versions of those words, focusing on misspelling the roots and affixes. 3. Teach the idea that the spelling can tell us which root or affix is in a word, which can help us determine meaning. 4. Preteach the roots or affixes in your excerpt, focusing on both spelling and meaning. 5. Have students read your excerpt, find the misspelled words, and explain what the roots mean.	Be sure to clarify why spelling is important: it helps us see morphemes and meanings. Explain that this will help students be both better spellers and readers. Have fun with the "badd" spelling game—for enrichment, have students make up their own "badd" versions. You can even have students read excerpts and write the "badd" versions.

also spelled wrong in this word, lamenting that the idea of "wild" was important in describing the meaning of *wilderness*. Together they pieced together how to spell wilderness, but they also explained how the roots and affixes worked together to form a meaning.

Teach Readers How to Break Down Multisyllabic Words

Another way to support adolescent word readers is to teach readers how to break down multisyllabic words into more manageable chunks (Toste et al., 2017, 2019; Vaughn et al., 2022). Here the research suggests teaching students one strategy for how to do this and sticking with that one strategy to reinforce it. We describe a strategy for **chunking words** (see Table 10.4) that helps students to break down multisyllabic words. This strategy builds on effective morphology instruction by helping students first recognize roots and affixes as they break the word apart.

Let's explore what this looks like in practice by visiting Mrs. Bartleby's eighth-grade history class, where students are reading the textbook chapter "The American West"—in particular, this sentence: "The *Transcontinental* Railroad became the catalyst for the last war and the last assimilation of the Native American people" (CK-12, 2019). Ms. Anthony stops at the word *transcontinental* to practice chunking words with her students. She first has her students circle the roots or affixes they recognize (*trans*), then underline any remaining vowels (*o, i, e,* and *a*). Next, she has students draw a loop under each word part as they say that part of the word out loud (see Figure 10.6). Finally, she has them say the whole word. After practicing this word, one of her students, Alejandra, points out: "This text is wrong; it suggests that Native Americans are completely assimilated, but they still exist today. We heard that on that podcast we listened to, remember?" Ms. Anthony smiles, as her purpose for this unit is being

TABLE 10.4. How to Chunk Words to Support Word Reading

Procedures	Recommendations
1. Circle the roots or affixes that you recognize in the word.	This strategy pairs well with scaffolded partner reading.
2. Underline the remaining single vowels or vowel combinations.	This strategy can be modeled by the teacher with more complicated words during a read-aloud.
3. Draw a loop under each word part as you say it out loud.	This strategy can reinforce morphology instruction by specifically targeting words with roots or affixes that were studied.
4. Say the whole word by blending the parts together.	

Note. Adapted from Vaughn et al. (2022).

fulfilled: Alejandra is using the information they gained in the other texts to read this one with a more critical lens.

Engage in Multiple Readings of a Text

Another way to support adolescents' word reading is to have students read a passage multiple times to support their fluency (Vaughn et al., 2022; Wexler, 2008). When students have the chance to read the passage through once just to determine pronunciation, once to clarify vocabulary meanings, and another time to perform it with emotion and intonation, students develop better word recognition skills. We suggest pairing multiple reads with syntax and text structure scaffolds from Chapters 8 and 9.

Our favorite technique for engaging in multiple text reads to improve word-reading skills is to use a protocol called **scaffolded partner reading.** In this approach, a teacher begins by chunking the passage (remember this scaffold from Chapter 6?) and

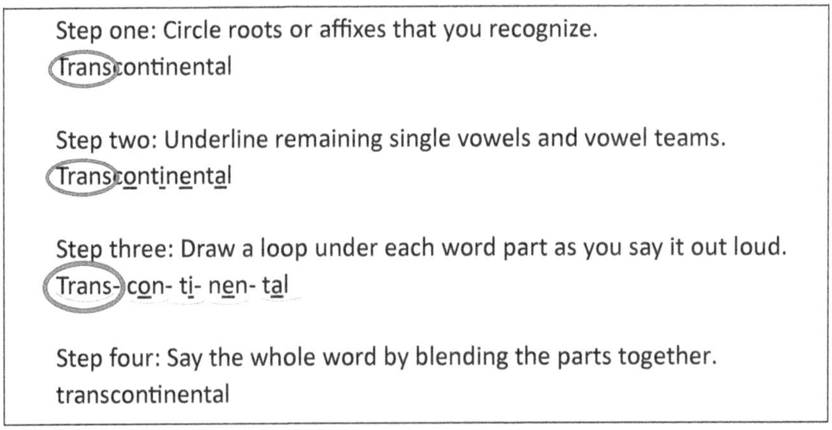

Step one: Circle roots or affixes that you recognize.
Transcontinental

Step two: Underline remaining single vowels and vowel teams.
Transcontinental

Step three: Draw a loop under each word part as you say it out loud.
Trans- con- ti- nen- tal

Step four: Say the whole word by blending the parts together.
transcontinental

FIGURE 10.6. Example chunking words.

TABLE 10.5. How to Do Scaffolded Partner Reading

Procedures	Recommendations
1. Divide text into chunks (1–3 paragraphs). 2. Assign partners (more fluent with less fluent if a lot of fluency support is needed). 3. Students read the first chunk silently and independently with the purpose of underlining any words they don't know or can't read. 4. The teacher watches and selects three to five words that many students underline. 5. Then, the teacher decides how to practice the three to five words with students. This may include: dividing the word into chunks, repeating the word and pointing at it in the text, providing a quick definition or example of the word, or defining affixes or roots. 6. Next, students read the chunk a second time, this time out loud with a partner. They take turns, or if the chunk is short, they can both read it once all the way through. Before reading, the teacher provides a specific purpose for reading. For example, the teacher might say, "as you read, think about what is the first life cycle stage for a spider?" Students focus on this purpose as they read the second time. 7. After students have finished reading the chunk a second time out loud, they discuss the chunk first with a partner, then as a whole class, focusing on the content-specific purpose the teacher provided (i.e., describe the first life cycle stage of the spider) to ensure understanding. 8. Repeat the entire procedure with remaining chunks.	It is important to keep the prereading word review brief. As students learn this protocol, it takes a long time to administer, but once students know it this protocol can be implemented quickly.

having students complete two reads of the passage with two different foci to help support fluency (see Table 10.5).

Let's explore what this looks like in Dr. Perch's 10th-grade biology class. Students are reading about sea lamprey control in a text from the Great Lakes Fishery Commission (n.d.) website. Dr. Perch has strategically paired more fluent readers with less fluent readers. He then asks students to read the first chunk alone and underline unfamiliar words. Below is an example of what one student underlined.

> The sea lamprey is an incredibly destructive <u>invasive</u> species. Since entering Lake Ontario in the mid-1800s, and the upper Great Lakes beginning in 1921, sea lampreys have <u>inflicted</u> significant <u>economic</u> damage, harmed the fishery and ecosystem, and changed the way of life in the region.

> Of the more than 180 non-native species in the Great Lakes basin, sea lampreys are the only invader that is controlled basin-wide and is the only example in the world of a successful aquatic vertebrate pest control program at an ecosystem scale. Sea lampreys must be controlled to maintain and improve the fishery as we know it and to protect the integrity of the ecosystem. The good news is they can be controlled! The Great Lakes Fishery Commission, pursuant to the Convention on Great Lakes Fisheries, delivers sea lamprey control in partnership with the US Fish and Wildlife Service, Fisheries and Oceans Canada, and the US Army Corps of Engineers. The US Geological Survey conducts critical sea lamprey research to aid in control. This control program has reduced sea lamprey populations by 90% in most areas of the Great Lakes, a remarkable success! (Great Lakes Fishery Commission, n.d.)

As students are reading and underlining, Dr. Perch is circulating the room to identify three to five words (maximum) that multiple students are underlining.

Dr. Perch notices that many students underline *invasive, inflicted, aquatic,* and *vertebrae.* He now decides in the moment what students need to help them be able to read those words. To review the four words, he does the following:

1. *Invasive.* Dr. Perch first supports students in breaking this word into syllables using the technique they learned in their ELA class. They start by circling roots (*in*) and underlining vowels (*a, i/e*). Then they loop under each syllable to practice reading the syllables (*in-va-sive*). Lastly, they point to the word in the text and say it. Dr. Perch quickly defines the word (spreading in a way that is harmful).
2. *Inflicted.* Dr. Perch provides a quick definition (to cause something unpleasant) and example of this word (getting someone else sick: inflicting a disease upon them) to help students understand the meaning. Then he asks students to point and say the word twice to help students say the word correctly.
3. *Aquatic.* Dr. Perch asks students to find the root of the word (*aqua*) and helps them define it (water). Then they point to the word in the text and say it. Dr. Perch provides a quick definition (something that lives in the water).
4. *Vertebrae.* Dr. Perch again supports students in breaking the word into chunks and then quickly defines the word for students (back bones), and he mentions that sea lampreys are considered aquatic vertebrates because they have backbones and live in the water.

Dr. Perch has been using scaffolded partner reading for a while, so his students are used to it, and as such, his review of those four words takes him only a few quick minutes. Then, he asks students to read this chunk aloud with their partner, taking turns reading every other sentence with the content-specific purpose: to explain why sea lampreys are harmful and what we can do to reduce their existence.

After reading, Dr. Perch engages students in a quick discussion about why sea lampreys are harmful and elicits ideas from students about how they can be controlled. Then Dr. Perch repeats the procedure with the remaining chunks of the text, providing a content-specific purpose for each chunk:

Heading of Text Chunk	Purpose for Reading
"How are sea lampreys controlled?"	Ask students to answer the question "How are sea lampreys controlled?"
"Lampricides"	Ask students "What are lampricides, and how do they help control sea lamprey?"
"Barriers, traps, and pheromones"	Ask students "How can we use barriers and traps to reduce the sea lamprey population?"

When supporting fluency, emphasizing prosody—which is the smoothness, intonation, and expression of reading—has been shown to have a large influence on students' text understanding (Paige, 2014; Shanahan, 2022). One way to do this is to engage students in **podcaster reading**. In this technique, the student can self-select a passage from a text they have already read together. Then, they record themselves reading that passage as if they were a podcaster. Next, students listen back and see how they can improve upon their reading to sound more like a podcaster announcer. They then re-record themselves and listen again (see Table 10.6 for step-by-step directions).

Let's explore what this looks like in Ms. Astrid's sixth-grade science class. The teacher has recently read the following excerpt from *Packing for Mars for Kids* and asks them to read it again and think about how a podcaster would read it.

> To a rocket scientist, the human being is a problem. We are the most irritating piece of machinery a rocket scientist could ever have to deal with. We need food and water and eight hours of sleep to function. Our memory is puny. We're moody and unpredictable. A circuit board or a propulsion nozzle, on the other hand, is stable and undemanding. It does not eat or forget to shut the airlock, and it never complains. (Roach, 2022, p. 3)

TABLE 10.6. How to Engage in Podcaster Reading

Procedures	Recommendations
1. Students select a passage from the text they have been reading.	This technique also works well when students read their own writing.
2. They record themselves reading that section, reading it how a podcaster would read it.	A prosody rubric (see Figure 10.1) can be used to help students understand what prosodic reading looks like.
3. Next, students listen back and see how they can improve their reading to make it more similar to a podcaster.	
4. They read it again, recording it a second time.	
5. Optional: Students listen to each other's recordings and provide feedback.	

Then, Ms. Astrid asks her students to record themselves using their school-issued laptop devices reading the text aloud as a podcaster would. After recording, students listen to the recording and consider how they could improve their reading to sound more like a podcaster. They record a second time. Ms. Astrid listens for excellent examples and then she plays a few of those examples to the class. Ms. Astrid likes this technique because she has observed that her students are better able to comprehend after reading a passage this way. She suspects it is because in order to read with the intonation and expression of a podcaster, students have to understand what they are reading.

A similar way to support prosody is using a technique called **say it like a character** (see Table 10.7). In this approach, Mrs. Bartleby wants to help her students to become more fluent readers while they tackle their unit goals to understand the subtleties of how Caliban reacts to his enslavement. So she selects a passage from *The Tempest* when Caliban reflects on the dreams that enchant him—but the audience knows that those dreams are also signs of his imprisonment. Mrs. Bartleby asks the students to practice reading this speech a few times and consider how Caliban would say it at that point in the play:

> Be not afeard. The isle is full of noises,
> Sounds and sweet airs that give delight and hurt not.
> Sometimes a thousand twangling instruments
> Will hum about mine ears, and sometimes voices
> That, if I then had waked after long sleep,
> Will make me sleep again; and then, in dreaming,
> The clouds methought would open, and show riches
> Ready to drop upon me, that when I waked
> I cried to dream again. (*The Tempest*, III.ii, 148–156)

The partners read their interpretations out loud to each other and discuss, explaining their interpretations to each other. As they discuss, they consider aspects of the plot and how that influenced how the character would say that passage. For example, students considered, is Caliban aware that his dreams are also part of his imprisonment? How should an actor perform these lines to evoke a sense of sympathy for the enslaved Caliban?

While students are reading, Mrs. Bartleby circulates and listens to two students who have particularly excellent readings share their readings with the class. After they share their interpretations, the class discusses the emotions conveyed and why they read it that way, and how Caliban's shifting voice from prose to blank verse adds to the complexity of his character and to the play's themes around master–slave narratives.

Another way to support prosody with multiple readings is to engage in the **emotions reading game.** In this approach, teachers or students select a passage from a text for students to reread out loud in a small group or with a partner, and their classmates have to guess what emotion they were trying to convey (see Table 10.8).

Let's explore what this looks like in Mrs. Bartleby's 12th grade ELA class. She selects a passage of dialogue from *Americanah* by Chimamanda Ngozi Adichie in

TABLE 10.7. How to Plan for and Implement Say It Like a Character

Procedures	Recommendations
1. The teacher selects a short passage that conveys deep emotion(s). 2. Students read the text silently, thinking about the emotions the characters are trying to convey in the passage. 3. Students silently reread the passage, this time just the way they think the character would say it. 4. Students read their interpretation aloud to a partner or the class. 5. Ask students a few questions. a. What emotion were you trying to convey? b. What made you think that you should have read it that way? 6. Students share interpretations and discuss.	Works best with fiction and narrative nonfiction. An alternative: ask students to select a passage that conveys deep emotion and then have them perform it.

TABLE 10.8. How to Play the Emotions Reading Game

Procedures	Recommendations
1. The teacher or students select a passage from a text to reread. The passage can be one that students enjoyed, or one that teachers want students to read again to gain deeper meaning from it. 2. The teacher puts students in small groups, and each group has a jar with slips of paper with different emotion words written on them (sad, morose, happy, ecstatic, joyful, rage-filled, nervous, etc.). 3. Students take turns: whoever goes first draws a piece of paper with an emotion word written on it out of a jar (sad, ecstatic). 4. Students then read the selected passage with that emotion. 5. The other students in the group guess what emotion the student drew. 6. Students discuss their interpretations and then analyze the text for meaning.	This technique works best with fiction or narrative nonfiction.

which the narrator and protagonist, Ifemelu, has immigrated to the United States from Nigeria, and she has come to her first day at a university to register for classes. She encounters a university employee (Cristina Tomas) who judges her for her Nigerian accent. Mrs. Bartleby's students have to consider how to perform Ms. Tomas's clipped voice, Ifemelu's dialogue, and Ifemelu's interior narration.

> It was a warm day. Ifemelu had walked past students sprawled on green lawns; cheery balloons were clustered below a WELCOME FRESHMEN sign.
>
> "Good afternoon. Is this the right place for registration?" Ifemelu asked Cristina Tomas, whose name she did not then know.
>
> "Yes. Now. Are. You. An. International. Student?"
>
> "Yes."
>
> "You. Will. First. Need. To. Get. A. Letter. From. The. International. Students. Office."
>
> Ifemelu half smiled in empathy, because Cristina Tomas had to have some sort of illness that made her speak so slowly, lips scrunching and puckering, as she gave directions to the international students office. But when Ifemelu returned with the letter, Cristina Tomas said, "I. Need. You. To. Fill. Out. A. Couple. Of. Forms. Do. You. Understand. How. To. Fill. These. Out?" and she realized that Cristina Tomas was speaking like that because of her, her foreign accent, and she felt for a moment like a small child, lazy-limbed and drooling.
>
> "I speak English," she said.
>
> "I bet you do," Cristina Tomas said. "I just don't know how well."
>
> Ifemelu shrank. In that strained, still second when her eyes met Cristina Tomas's before she took the forms, she shrank. She shrank like a dried leaf. She had spoken English all her life, led the debating society in secondary school, and always thought the American twang inchoate; she should not have cowered and shrunk, but she did. And in the following weeks, as autumn's coolness descended, she began to practice an American accent. (Adichie, 2013, p. 163)

Mrs. Bartleby shares a jar with each small group. Inside the jar are several slips of paper with different emotions: polite, reflective, resigned, or frustrated. She considers whether to include some emotions that are not in the passage (e.g., energetic) but decides not to. Students take turns drawing an emotion out of the jar and reading the passage with that emotion. After each group has read the passage aloud with their selected emotion, the group first tries to guess what emotion the person was trying to convey. Then, the group discusses whether or not the emotion they read (polite, frustrated, and so on) best captured the emotions of the characters in the passage. For example, they might recognize how Cristina Tomas's clipped tone might suggest her frustration. They discuss how Ifemelu's emotions change during the passage from her initial politeness to her final resignation. Finally, students discuss how the tone and emotions in this passage reflect the larger themes in the novel about how language and identity shape the experiences of immigrants to the United States—especially given the colonial histories of language.

It should also be noted that teachers should take care when asking students to read aloud character voices whose dialects are different from their own. Reading aloud various dialects can be helpful for making sense of the different print conventions, rhythms, and intonations, but it can also be fertile ground for stereotyping, particularly if a student has never heard the dialect authentically. If students feel uncomfortable speaking the words of the character, it may be helpful to use an audio book to hear the text from a professional narrator.

TEACHERS CAN SUPPORT WORD READING BY INCLUDING MORPHOLOGY AND FLUENCY SCAFFOLDS

In this chapter we tackle the question "How can teachers support adolescents with word reading?" While secondary ELA, science, and history teachers are not expected to teach word reading, the scaffolds presented in this chapter offer opportunities for teachers to provide support in this area to make texts accessible. By scaffolding word knowledge through thoughtful morphology instruction, teachers are helping students improve their ability to sound out words *and* understand the meaning of those words. Focusing on reading with expression and intonation truly helps adolescents improve both their fluency *and* their understanding of tough texts.

CHAPTER 11

From Planning to Implementation

What Does Scaffolding in Action Look Like?

GUIDING QUESTIONS

1. How do we support students' reading comprehension *in the moment*?
2. What do we do when students struggle with planned scaffolds?
3. Can we scaffold too much?

Ms. Anthony is proud of the immense effort she put into creating the perfect lesson for her eighth-grade history unit on Indigenous stereotypes. She has chosen her text carefully while considering her students' knowledge and identities. She has created authentic and meaningful tasks. And she has provided scaffolds at every step of the way. However, some students are still struggling to understand the text (despite her carefully planned scaffolds), and they are not connecting with the topic the way she had hoped (in spite of her thoughtfully chosen texts). Suddenly, the task she wants them to achieve seems impossible. On the day of what should be the vibrant debate demystifying Indigenous stereotypes, discussion has fallen flat. Ms. Anthony panics: all that planning for nothing?

We have all been there. We get to the lesson and . . . it doesn't quite go the way we planned. But we don't panic: We support readers *in the moment* to learn from and make sense of the text in front of them. In this chapter, we show you how to support students' when it all goes live.

HOW DO WE SUPPORT STUDENTS' READING COMPREHENSION *IN THE MOMENT*?

In the previous chapters, we discussed many varieties of planned scaffolding. As you have read, developing planned scaffolds is a critical part of lesson planning.

Informed by assessments, theory, knowledge, and expertise, teachers make decisions about how to scaffold *before* the lesson begins. However, as teachers know, each class—and furthermore, each reader—is unique, and that means that students can take up the texts and learning activities that we have so carefully prepared in different ways. This way of acknowledging the human, messy, and unpredictable nature of teaching—as teaching *with* students, rather than *at* students—is informed by the theory of *dialogic teaching.* Dialogic teaching is goals-aligned instruction that invites teachers and students to address learning tasks together by listening to each other, sharing and building ideas, and considering alternative viewpoints. This style of teaching relies on supporting students to articulate their ideas freely, without fear of embarrassment over "wrong" answers. In this theory, the teacher is not a fountain of information that fills up the students' empty heads; instead, classes collectively work together to build knowledge. One of the ways that teachers work in a dialogic classroom is by building a *repertoire,* or a toolkit, of in-the-moment scaffolds to address the unexpected.

In this chapter, we consider these in-the-moment techniques that we call *scaffolding in action*. These are the instructional moves that the teacher makes in the moment to support individual readers. The metaphor of scaffolding means being responsive—consider that physical scaffolding isn't permanent but adjusted to the changing structure of a building. The goal of scaffolding in action is to deepen students' thinking about the text to improve their text understanding and/or learning from the text. This concept draws on the theories of contingent responses (van de Pol et al., 2010) and interactional scaffolding (Hammond & Gibbons, 2005). In this chapter we show exactly what this can look like in your classrooms.

Contingent Scaffolding

To successfully scaffold students' comprehension in the moment, teacher's responses must be *contingent* on the student's initial response, which means it has to address the student's real-time response (Reynolds & Daniel, 2018; van de Pol et al., 2010). This is the part of the lesson that cannot be totally preplanned because it depends on what students do in reaction to the learning activity.

Let's explore what that looks like in Ms. Anthony's class as they engage in a whole-class discussion about Indigenous stereotypes. Prior to the discussion, students read the text *Before Columbus: The Americas of 1491* and completed a pre–post journal outlining the students' assumptions about Indigenous life before European settlers arrived (see Chapter 7 for that scaffold). Let's see how Ms. Anthony provides contingent scaffolding during the discussion:

Ms. Anthony: Tell us about how Indigenous people grew food. What practices did they engage in?

Hannah: Native Americans didn't grow things; they hunted and gathered.

Ms. Anthony: What evidence do you have that they hunted and gathered?

As we can see from this example, a *contingent* response isn't just any response given in the moment or "teaching on the fly." A contingent response supports students to think more deeply about their responses and their reasoning.

But not all responses given in the moment are contingent. Let's review this example as if the teacher had responded with a yes-or-no question in the following hypothetical but familiar situation:

TEACHER: What did you get for question 1, Bobby?

BOBBY: Abraham Lincoln

TEACHER: Incorrect. It was George Washington.

In this interaction, the teacher's response is in the moment, that is, not necessarily planned, and may respond to the student's knowledge but doesn't ask about Bobby's reasoning or help him understand why he was wrong or what he may have missed in a text. Teacher responses like this can seriously limit students' opportunities to learn from complex texts (Daniel et al., 2016). Here, the teacher merely evaluates the response as right or wrong in what is often referred to as an initiate–respond–evaluate (IRE) sequence (Cazden, 2001) rather than addressing *why* Bobby answered Abraham Lincoln instead of George Washington.

Scaffolding in Action Moves

So, what should teachers do in the moment, precisely, to scaffold in action? Teachers need to take quick action to respond contingently to students' emerging comprehension. These quick actions are *instructional moves* that support students' comprehension that respond specifically to challenges they are facing. Instructional moves include verbal responses, like asking a question, or physical responses, like drawing a picture or using a gesture. The key here is that they're quick responses in the moment reacting to students' needs that arise during instruction with challenging texts.

Learning how to provide contingent responses to students' needs is a difficult part of teaching in general, although more so for novice teachers. To that end, Dan has developed a menu of 29 instructional moves to help teachers better support students' text reading in the moment (see Table 11.1). This menu is a scaffold for you, the teachers. Using this menu can help your in-the-moment scaffolding complement your planned scaffolding.

How can you use this menu? We suggest different approaches depending on your skill and comfort with scaffolding in action. If you are a novice teacher, we suggest reviewing this list before teaching and perhaps even printing it out and keeping it nearby as students are reading. As students struggle and you feel unsure, look over this list to see if there is a move you can employ.

For more experienced teachers who want to hone their scaffolding skills, we suggest that you review this list and reflect on these moves. Which ones are you using regularly? Which ones have you never tried? When might you try these moves?

For novice and experienced teachers alike, we suggest engaging in reflection *after* you have taught students to engage with complex texts. You can think about your

TABLE 11.1. Menu of Contingent Instructional Moves

Category	#	Scaffolding Move
Extending talk (Ch. 6)	1	Ask students to say more or elaborate on their ideas.
	2	Ask students to comment on a classmate's thinking.
	3	Re-voice a student's comment and ask them to verify its accuracy.
Pressing for evidence (Ch. 6)	4	Ask students to provide evidence for a claim (theirs or a peer's).
	5	Provide evidence and ask students to incorporate it into a claim.
	6	Ask students to think of other evidence that might strengthen or weaken a claim.
Supporting knowledge (Ch. 7)	7	Activate students' prior knowledge by asking what they already know about a topic.
	8	Stabilize knowledge by correcting a student misconception or inaccuracy, or providing a missing piece of prior knowledge or definition of vocabulary word.
	9	Act the text out or use a hand gesture to demonstrate a concept.
	10	Explain an idea or concept by drawing a picture on the board or showing a picture/photo to visualize the idea.
	11	Create a concept map to show relationships of ideas.
	12	Use an analogy to explain an idea (__________ is like __________).
Analyzing structure (Ch. 8)	13	Ask students to determine the structure of a text.
	14	Highlight text structure cue words or phrases (e.g., *first*, *on the other hand*, or *therefore*).
	15	Ask students to consider why an author included a detail or what its function is.
Connecting ideas (Ch. 8)	16	Ask students how a sentence fits in with earlier sentences/paragraphs.
	17	Ask students how a character or idea has changed compared to earlier points in the text.
Tracking participants (Ch. 8)	18	Point to a verb and ask students, "Who or what did this action?"
	19	Point to a pronoun or a nominalization and ask, "What does this refer to?"
Unpacking morphology (Ch. 9)	20	Ask students to highlight the morphemes in a word to help them see their meanings.
	21	Highlight a morpheme, and then ask students to consider what it means in context.
Highlighting vocabulary and language (Ch. 9)	22	Point out punctuation that communicates tone and register (e.g., quotation marks indicating sarcasm, italics to communicate emphasis on a concept).
	23	Ask students to consider metaphorical language ("Is X literally happening here?" or connotation of word choice ["what does this word convey?"]).
	24	Point out patterns in language that reveal register (e.g., multiple informal words).
Breaking down syntax (Ch. 9)	25	Break a complex sentence into parts and ask students to paraphrase each part. Then ask how the parts of the sentence work together.
	26	Note words within sentences that indicate relationships (e.g., *however*).
Developing word reading and fluency (Ch. 10)	27	Ask students to read a passage multiple times to improve fluency.
	28	Provide a correct pronunciation or correct a mispronunciation of a conceptually important word.
	29	Discuss the prosody, emotion, or intonation that a text should be read with.

Adapted from Reynolds (2021) and Reynolds and Fisher (2022).

recent instruction and review this list of moves. How did those go? Are there moves that may have worked better than others that you might try next time?

WHAT DO WE DO WHEN STUDENTS STRUGGLE WITH PLANNED SCAFFOLDS?

Now let's see real-life examples of what these moves look like with actual students. Dan did a study in which he looked at tutors working with small groups of 11th graders reading tough disciplinary texts (Reynolds, 2021). He developed this menu of scaffolding moves that teachers might make, but insisted that the tutors' responses remain *contingent* on the content of the students' responses, using the scaffolding moves from Table 11.1.

Let's look at an example of scaffolding a student response related to the following sentence from Bharati Mukherjee's essay "A Four-Hundred-Year-Old Woman." In this sentence, Mukherjee describes her complex history as an immigrant from South Asia who has adopted a completely American identity:

> "My 'country'—called in Bengali*desh*—I have never seen. It is the ancestral home of my father, and is now in Bangladesh." (p. 33)

This single sentence contains all sorts of complexities we've described in this book. It has dense ideas: Mukherjee is describing a "country" as a social, cultural, and geographical entity, much more complex than simply a shape on a map, and her use of paradox hints at that complexity (how can she have never seen her own country?). Truly understanding this sentence also requires relevant background knowledge: Bengali is a language, and Bangladesh is a country in Southeast Asia, and its history is intimately tied up with India's, as it was an Indian province until it became independent in 1971. It also requires understanding of grammar (including punctuation): the single quotations indicating a nonliteral meaning, the italicization of *desh* to indicate that it's not a word in English, and the paired em dashes are three distinct tonal devices (in one sentence) that altogether communicate the complexity of Mukherjee's identity.

To help the students comprehend the density of this sentence, the tutors planned a sentence paraphrasing scaffold (remember this from Chapter 6?). When the scaffolding went live, one 11th grader paraphrased Mukherjee's sentence by saying: "So her dad grew up here, and he can consider it home, but it's changed, and now it's Bangladesh."

This student shows some understanding of the text (Bangladesh is a country; *ancestral* means related), but also seems to lack depth in interpreting this dense sentence (the depth of the meaning of *country* or *here* in the narrator's location and her father's history). So, if you were the teacher, how would you respond in the moment? And how can you make your response *contingent* upon this student's response?

Let's look at one example of an experienced English teacher's scaffolding choices from one of Dan's studies (Reynolds & Fisher, 2022). The tutor, Laura, used scaffold #22 from our menu, which points out punctuation that communicates an idea. In this case, the use of quotes around the word country communicates the density of that idea—all the possible meanings of *country* packed into one word. How did Laura actually respond contingently with scaffold #22? She said to the student "Her country is in Bangladesh. Her 'country' . . . " and made an air quotes hand motion (also borrowing from scaffold #9). Notice how she decided to focus on the idea of *country*, which is key to both understanding the larger geopolitical complexity of the sentence and also attending to the linguistic complexity of the quotation marks. It was an educated guess in the moment. Did it work? Decide for yourself. Here's how the student responded:

> So she's using the . . . okay, I get it. So she's using the word country as a more . . . less like politically defined borders and more like where her culture comes from. More like where her family and ancestors come from?

The student's second response is a much more sophisticated paraphrase than his initial paraphrase attempt ("So her dad grew up . . . "). While the student is still a little unsure (note the ellipses and question mark), his grasp of the complexity of the sentence is much stronger thanks to Laura's scaffolding move. That shows how contingent scaffolding can help students comprehend and learn with complex text, even when students bring varying levels of skills, prior knowledge, and vocabulary.

Though we've written each scaffold in the Table 11.1 menu distinctly to address specific text challenges, you can see in the Mukherjee example above that the challenging aspects of a text can happen simultaneously. Teachers might plan, for example, to address the dense ideas in a text, but an unexpected vocabulary or word-reading challenge may arise during the teaching of the lesson. The menu of scaffolding options can help teachers be prepared to meet these challenges in the moment.

CAN WE SCAFFOLD TOO MUCH?

How much scaffolding is *too much*? Should teachers jump in and help every time a student struggles? No! What is challenging about scaffolding in action is that you, the teacher, have to make decisions in the moment when you see students struggling about whether or not to provide *additional* scaffolding.

Not every mistake that students make needs an in-the-moment learning scaffold. For example, students may not know the meaning of a word, but if the word isn't critical to the overall learning goals of the passage, skip it. However, if the word students misunderstand or mispronounce is key, or is a word that highlights a key phonological or morphological rule, it is worth spending time on it. For example, a tutor Dan observed in a different study was leading students through a discussion of an excerpt from Sally Ride's book *To Space and Back*, which describes what it is like to be weightless in orbit aboard the space shuttle (Reynolds & Goodwin, 2016). The tutor was helping the students identify root words and prefixes. A student pronounced the word *midair* as *meatier*. In this case, the tutor immediately stepped in to correct the pronunciation. Not only was the word critical to the concept of the space-themed text, but the mispronunciation of the morpheme *mid* jeopardized the student's ability to understand the morphological lesson.

Do we need to correct every mispronunciation? If the word is critical to the passage's understanding, yes. However, if a particular word is not critical to the passage's understanding, it's not worth interrupting students to correct their mispronunciation. This is especially true of proper names that are only briefly referenced in a passage, such as those in *1491*, which names a variety of anthropology scholars who have debated about the origins of Indigenous arrivals in America. Repeatedly correcting possible mispronunciations might actually lead students to think that the purpose of the lesson is to accurately read proper names aloud—but that's not related to the essential question of the Indigenous history text set. Further, if we define every word and correct every mispronunciation, we may be overscaffolding. Providing *too many* scaffolds has been shown to limit students' opportunities to engage in open-ended discussions and explore ideas deeply (Daniel et al., 2016).

However, if the correction can serve a larger purpose for understanding cultural and linguistic differences, it may be worth the time to correct it. For example, helping students correctly pronounce the names of Mayan rulers can show students that it is important to cross cultural boundaries and respect cultural differences. Even stopping to ask, "Why is it hard for us to pronounce Toh-Chak-Ich'ak?" (remember that example from Chapter 10?) can also be an opportunity to help students not only to see just the cultural differences but also to develop linguistic knowledge about how languages employ different types of vowel and consonant patterns.

Another mistake to avoid when making decisions about how and when to support readers who are struggling with texts is to lower expectations. Research has revealed that reduced expectations result in teachers not asking students to elaborate on their ideas or to supply evidence for their arguments. The result has been weaker engagement and comprehension outcomes (McElhone, 2012). So, when teachers lower their ambitions, accepting students' initial answers without inspiring richer discussions, they may be limiting the potential for student learning. High challenge should be paired with high support.

How then, can we decide whether or not to scaffold in the moment? How can we make sure we are providing the right amount of challenge? Our advice is that as you observe students struggling with the text, you should ask, "Will students be able to accomplish the goal we have set for this reading?" If they can still accomplish the task, they may not need additional scaffolds in the moment. It is okay if they cannot read every word perfectly or understand the meaning of every single vocabulary word in a text. The goal is that they take away the overall meaning of the text so that they can accomplish the task. Trust your larger purpose.

SCAFFOLDING TOUGH TEXTS: AN ALTERNATIVE TO "JUST DO THE READINGS"

As we've shared throughout this book, scaffolding is a complex process. We wish it were as simple as telling students to "just do the readings," or handing students a generic graphic organizer that will magically help them make sense of a text full of dense ideas, unfamiliar words, or high knowledge demands.

Also, those instructional blunders are rooted in misunderstanding the process of comprehension. Once teachers understand how readers make sense of texts, they can begin to recognize how to support students in learning from content-area texts. Scaffolding begins by identifying what makes a text tough to read so that you can help students tackle them.

Effective scaffolding must also build upon the assumption that every student brings relevant knowledge to the reading experience, and that this knowledge can be used to support learning from the text. More importantly—maybe even most importantly—it means believing your students are capable of learning from tough texts. This means knowing that students will struggle to make sense of the tough texts you are providing for them and understanding that they can do difficult things *with your support.*

Lastly, to scaffold well, teachers must have a toolkit of techniques that will help students understand the tough texts that permeate secondary spaces. These techniques can be planned ahead of time to align with the texts' challenges based on students' needs, which we addressed in Chapters 6–10. But we also need techniques that we can use in the moment, because we know that the best laid plans for teaching can never fully account for how each individual human in our class will take up the lesson. In that case, we need to build our repertoire of scaffolding-in-action techniques that can create dialogic classrooms that lead to comprehension success. When making these moment-to-moment decisions, it's critical to remember the larger design of your text sets, the linguistic assets of your students, and your essential questions and tasks that give purpose to their reading. Aligning your moment-to-moment scaffolding with those larger ideas will reinforce them. As you get to the end of this chapter and this book, you might be thinking, "Wow, scaffolding sure is a lot of work—is it worth it?"

Our response is yes, it is a lot of work. However, it *is* worth it. Why? Let's visit Christine as a teenager to show you why we think the effort of scaffolding is worth it. She shares the following story:

When I was a secondary student, I was a terrific reader, voracious even—a "lunchtimes-in-the-library" kind of reader. Even still, I hated reading for my science and history classes. I usually just skipped the assigned readings, and when I did attempt the long textbook chapters, I quickly got bored and ended up just staring at the book on my lap while the TV blathered on in the background until enough time passed that I could say I was done "studying." As you might guess, this was not an effective way to learn.

Looking back, I can see that I just didn't know what to do with these challenging texts. When I got stuck, I thought, well, I guess this isn't for me, and because I did passably well just paying attention in class, I didn't have to change my "reading" habits . . . until I hit the wall (i.e., started failing reading quizzes) my junior year. Before that, I didn't know there were tools and strategies—scaffolds—that could help me crack these texts and glean information from them. I'm betting a lot of our students feel the same way. And that's why we wrote this book.

When we tell students to "just do the readings," we think many students end up doing what Christine did, which is to say, not much. If we struggled with a math problem, we would not expect a teacher to simply say, "Do the math problem." We think–and suspect you would all agree—that is not stellar math pedagogy. Instead, we would expect a teacher to walk us through the problem step-by-step to explain how to do it. In the same way, telling students to "just do the readings" is not stellar literacy pedagogy.

To learn from challenging texts, students need to know what to do and how to do it. They need to know that reading different types of texts in different content-areas requires overlapping, but often distinct, skills. They need to know what to do when the vocabulary stops making sense to them. They need to know how to build bridges between what they already know and what they need to learn. They need to know how to use all the scaffolds that the author has provided for them in the text, such as cohesive devices, and text features, to make sense of texts. They need to know when and how to use their knowledge to help them learn from texts. They need to know that when they struggle—and that they should struggle—their teacher, *you,* will have scaffolds to support them. And with this book, you will.

Teaching adolescents how to tackle tough texts is ultimately teaching students to empower themselves: You are helping them unlock any challenging text they encounter, not only in your class, but anywhere. Just imagine what they will be able to do next.

Literature Cited

Actively Learn. (n.d.). McGraw Hill. Retrieved from *www.activelylearn.com/about-us*.

Adichie, C. N. (2009). The danger of a single story [Video]. TED. Retrieved from *www.ted.com/talks/chimamanda_ngozi_adichie_the_danger_of_a_single_story/c*.

Adichie, C. N. (2013). *Americanah*. Alfred A. Knopf.

Big History Project: 13.8 billion years of history. (n.d.). OER Project. Retrieved from *www.oerproject.com/Big-History*.

CK-12. (n.d.). CK-12 Foundation. Retrieved from *www.ck12info.org/mission*.

CK-12. (2019). *The American West*. CK-12 Foundation. Retrieved from *https://flexbooks.ck12.org/user:zxbpc2rzcziwmthaz21hawwuy29t/cbook/episd-2019-2020-us-history/section/2.2/primary/lesson/pa-1%3A-the-american-west*.

CK-12. (2020). *2.10 Gravity*. CK-12 Foundation. Retrieved from *www.ck12.org/book/ck-12-fifth-grade-science/section/2.10*.

Classroom Materials. (n.d.). Library of Congress. Retrieved from *www.loc.gov/programs/teachers/classroom-materials*.

CommonLit. (n.d.). CommonLit. Retrieved from *www.commonlit.org*.

Durr, V. F. (1956). *Letter from Virginia Foster Durr to Myles and Zilphia Horton*. Montgomery, AL. Retrieved from *https://historicalthinkingmatters.org/rosaparks/0/inquiry/main/resources/20/index.html*.

Education. (n.d.). National Oceanic and Atmospheric Administration. Retrieved from *www.noaa.gov/education*.

Egan, D. (2017). *The death and life of the Great Lakes*. W. W. Norton.

Eshet, D. (2020). *Teaching American Indian history with primary sources*. Salem State University.

Explore Census Data. (n.d.). United States Census Bureau. Retrieved from *https://data.census.gov*.

Frontiers for Young Minds. (n.d.). Frontiers Media S.A. Retrieved from *https://kids.frontiersin.org*.

Gravity and Orbits. (2023). PhET Interactive Simulations. Retrieved from *https://phet.colorado.edu*.

Great Lakes Fishery Commission. (n.d.). Sea lamprey control in the Great Lakes: A remarkable success! Retrieved from *www.glfc.org/control.php*.

Indian removals in Ohio. (n.d.). In Wikipedia. Retrieved from *https://en.wikipedia.org/wiki/Indian_removals_in_Ohio*.

Kelly, J. (2009). *The evolution of Calpurnia Tate*. Henry Holt.

Mann, C. C. (2009). *Before Columbus: The Americas of 1491*. Scholastic.

Mann, C. C. (2011). *1491: New revelations of the Americas before Columbus*. Second Vintage Books Edition.

Merriam-Webster. (2023). Perpetuate. In *Merriam-Webster Dictionary*. Retrieved from *www.merriam-webster.com/dictionary/perpetuation.*

Milton, J. (1673). *When I consider how my light is spent*. In *The Norton anthology of English literature* (pp. 123–125). W. W. Norton.

Mukherjee, B. (1991). "A four-hundred-year-old-woman." In J. Sternberg (Ed.), *The writer on her work: Volume II. New Essays in New Territory*. W. W. Norton.

Nagle, R. (Host). (2019). *This land* [Audio Podcast]. Crooked Media.

NASA. (2018). Learning Resources Human Research Program. NASA. Retrieved from *www.nasa.gov/learning-resources.*

NASA. (2023a). *Our solar system*. NASA's Jet Propulsion Laboratory. Retrieved from *https://solarsystem.nasa.gov/solar-system/our-solar-system/overview.*

NASA. (2023b). *Overview of the sun*. NASA's Jet Propulsion Laboratory. Retrieved from *https://solarsystem.nasa.gov/solar-system/sun/overview.*

National Museum of the American Indian. (n.d.). Teaching and learning about Native Americans. Retrieved from *https://americanindian.si.edu/nk360/faq/did-you-know.*

National Oceanic and Atmospheric Administration. (2019). NOAA partners predict large summer harmful algal bloom for western Lake Erie. Retrieved from *www.noaa.gov/media-release/noaa-partners-predict-large-summer-harmful-algal-bloom-for-western-lake-erie.*

National Oceanic and Atmospheric Administration. (2021). New program created to test harmful algal bloom control technology in Ohio. Retrieved from *https://coastalscience.noaa.gov/news/nccos-harmful-algal-bloom-control-technology-will-be-tested-in-ohio.*

OpenStax. (n.d.). U.S. History: 1.1 The Americas. Retrieved from *https://openstax.org/books/us-history/pages/1-1-the-americas.*

The Poetry Foundation. (n.d.). Poetry Foundation. Retrieved from *www.poetryfoundation.org.*

Reading Like a Historian. (n.d.). Stanford History Education Group. Retrieved from *https://sheg.stanford.edu/history-lessons.*

ReadWorks. (n.d.). ReadWorks. Retrieved from *www.readworks.org.*

Ride, S., & Okie, S. (1986). *To space and back*. HarperCollins.

Roach, M. (2022). *Packing for Mars for Kids*. National Geographic Books.

Robinson, J. A. (1954). Letter from Jo Ann Robinson. Retrieved from *https://historicalthinkingmatters.org/rosaparks/0/inquiry.*

Schifini, A. (1999). *Reading instruction for older struggling readers*. PREL. Retrieved from *www.prel.org.*

Science Journal for Kids. (n.d.). *Science Journal for Kids*. Retrieved from *www.sciencejournalforkids.org.*

Shakespeare's Birthplace Trust. (n.d.). *The Tempest*: Synopsis and plot overview of Shakespeare's *The Tempest*. Retrieved from *www.shakespeare.org.uk/explore-shakespeare/shakespedia/shakespeares-plays/tempest.*

Shakespeare, W. (c. 1611). *The Tempest*. Folger Shakespeare Library. Retrieved from *www.folger.edu/explore/shakespeares-works/the-tempest/read.*

Staff Writer. (2013). Ohio's last Indian tribe was forced out in 1843. *The Columbus Dispatch*. Retrieved from *www.dispatch.com/story/opinion/cartoons/2013/08/18/ohio-s-last-indian-tribe/23655446007.*

The Tempest: Act V, Scene i and Epilogue. (n.d.). *SparkNotes*. Retrieved from *www.sparknotes.com/shakespeare/tempest/section10.*

University of Minnesota, (n.d.). The Watershed Game: Classroom version. Retrieved from *https://seagrant.umn.edu/classroom-versions.*

University of Washington. (n.d.). An Introduction to Post-Colonialism, Post-colonial Theory and Post-colonial Literature. Retrieved from *https://art.washington.edu/sites/art/files/documents/about/an_introduction_to_post-colonialism_post-colonial_theory_and_post-colonial_literature.pdf.*

U.S. Geological Survey. (n.d.). What are zebra mussels and why should we care about them? Retrieved from *www.usgs.gov/faqs/what-are-zebra-mussels-and-why-should-we-care-about-them.*

Walton, J. (2020). The Forgotten History of Ohio's Indigenous Peoples. Midstory. Retrieved from *www.midstory.org/the-forgotten-history-of-ohios-indigenous-peoples.*

WordGen Weekly. (n.d.). Strategic Education Research Partnership. Retrieved from *www.serpinstitute.org/wordgen-weekly.*

References

Alvermann, D. E., & Hynd, C. (1989). Effects of prior knowledge activation modes and text structure on nonscience majors' comprehension of physics. *Journal of Educational Research, 83*(2), 97–102.

Annie E. Casey Foundation. (2022). Children who speak a language other than English at home, by state. Retrieved from *https://datacenter.aecf.org/data/tables/81-children-who-speak-a-language-other-than-english-at-home*

Athanases, S. Z., & de Oliveira, L. C. (2014). Scaffolding versus routine support for Latina/o youth in an urban school: Tensions in building toward disciplinary literacy. *Journal of Literacy Research, 46*(2), 263–299.

Aukerman, R. C. (1972). *Reading in the secondary school classroom.* McGraw-Hill.

Baker-Bell, A. (2020). *Linguistic justice: Black language, literacy, identity, and pedagogy.* Routledge.

Baumann, J. F., Ware, D., & Edwards, E. C. (2007). "Bumping into spicy, tasty words that catch your tongue": A formative experiment on vocabulary instruction. *The Reading Teacher, 61*(2), 108–122.

Beck, I. L., McKeown, M. G., & Kucan, L. (2013). *Bringing words to life: Robust vocabulary instruction* (2nd ed.). Guilford Press.

Beers, K., & Probst, R. E. (2013). *Notice and note.* Heinemann.

Benner, A. D., & Graham, S. (2011). Latino adolescents' experiences of discrimination across the first 2 years of high school: Correlates and influences on educational outcomes. *Child Development, 82*(2), 508–519.

Biancarosa, G., & Snow, C. E. (2006). *Reading Next: A vision for action and research in middle and high school literacy.* A report to Carnegie Corporation of New York (2nd ed.). Alliance for Excellent Education.

Bos, C. S., & Anders, P. L. (1990). Effects of interactive vocabulary instruction on the vocabulary learning and reading comprehension of junior-high learning disabled students. *Learning Disability Quarterly, 13,* 13–42.

Bowers, J. S., & Bowers, P. N. (2017). Beyond phonics: The case for teaching children the logic of the English spelling system. *Educational Psychologist, 52*(2), 124–141.

Brown, B. A. (2021). *Science in the city: Culturally relevant STEM education.* Harvard Education Press.

Cazden, C. B. (2001). *Classroom discourse: The language of teaching and learning.* Heinemann.

Cenoz, J., Santos, A., & Gorter, D. (2022). Pedagogical translanguaging and teachers' perceptions of anxiety. *International Journal of Bilingual Education and Bilingualism,* 1–12.

Crosson, A., & Lesaux, N. (2013). Connectives: Fitting another piece of the vocabulary instruction puzzle. *The Reading Teacher, 67*(3), 193–200.

Cutting, L. E., & Scarborough, H. S. (2006). Prediction of reading comprehension: Relative contributions of word recognition, language proficiency, and other cognitive skills can depend on how comprehension is measured. *Scientific Studies of Reading, 10*(3), 277–299.

Daniel, S. M., Martin-Beltrán, M., Peercy, M. M., & Silverman, R. (2016). Moving beyond yes or no: Shifting from over-scaffolding to contingent scaffolding in literacy instruction with emergent bilingual students. *TESOL Journal, 7*(2), 393–420.

Daniels, H., Zemelman, S., & Steineke, N. (2007). *Content area writing: Every teacher's guide.* Heinemann.

De Koning, B. B., & van der Schoot, M. (2013). Becoming part of the story! Refueling the interest in visualization strategies for reading comprehension. *Educational Psychology Review, 25*, 261–287.

de Leur, T., Van Boxtel, C., & Wilschut, A. (2020). "When I'm drawing, I see pictures in my head": Secondary school students constructing an image of the past by means of a drawing task and a writing task. *European Journal of Psychology of Education, 35*(1), 155–175.

de los Ríos, C. V., & Molina, A. (2020). Literacies of refuge: "Pidiendo posada" as ritual of justice. *Journal of Literacy Research, 52*(1), 32–54.

Dyches, J. (2018). Critical canon pedagogy: Applying disciplinary inquiry to cultivate canonical critical consciousness. *Harvard Educational Review, 88*(4), 538–564.

Fisher, D., & Frey, N. (2015). Selecting texts and tasks for content area reading and learning. *The Reading Teacher, 68*, 524–529.

Flanigan, K., & Greenwood, S. C. (2007). Effective content vocabulary instruction in the middle: Matching students, purposes, words, and strategies. *Journal of Adolescent and Adult Literacy, 51*(3), 226–238.

Frayer, D., Frederick, W. C., & Klausmeier, H. J. (1969). *A schema for testing the level of cognitive mastery.* Wisconsin Center for Education Research.

Fulmer, S. M., D'Mello, S. K., Strain, A., & Graesser, A. C. (2015). Interest-based text preference moderates the effect of text difficulty on engagement and learning. *Contemporary Educational Psychology, 41*, 98–110.

Gatlin-Nash, B., & Wanzek, J. (2015). Relations among children's use of dialect and literacy skills: A meta-analysis. *Journal of Speech, Language, and Hearing Research, 58*(4), 1306–1318.

Goldenberg, C. (2020). Reading wars, reading science, and English learners. *Reading Research Quarterly, 55*, S131–S144.

Goldman, S. R., Britt, M. A., Brown, W., Cribb, G., George, M., Greenleaf, C., et al. (2016). Disciplinary literacies and learning to read for understanding: A conceptual framework for disciplinary literacy. *Educational Psychologist, 51*(2), 219–246.

Goodwin, A. P., Petscher, Y., & Reynolds, D. (2022). Unraveling adolescent language and reading comprehension: The monster's data. *Scientific Studies of Reading, 26*(4), 305–326.

Graham, S. (2020). The sciences of reading and writing must become more fully integrated. *Reading Research Quarterly, 55*, S35–S44.

Greenwood, S. C., & Flanigan, K. (2007). Overlapping vocabulary and comprehension: Context clues complement semantic gradients. *The Reading Teacher, 61*(3), 249–254.

Hammond, J., & Gibbons, P. (2005). Putting scaffolding to work: The contribution of scaffolding in articulating ESL education. *Prospect, 20*(1), 6–30.

Hasbrouck, J., & Tindal, G. (2017). *An update to compiled ORF norms* (No. 1702). Technical Report. University of Oregon.

Hattan, C., & Lupo, S. M. (2020). Rethinking the role of knowledge in the literacy classroom. *Reading Research Quarterly, 55*, S283–S298.

Hershberger, K., & Zembal-Saul, C. (2015). KLEWS to explanation-building in science. *Science and Children*, 52(6), 66.

Hiebert, E. H. (2017). The text of literacy instruction: Obstacles to or opportunities for educational equity? *Literacy Research: Theory, Method, and Practice, 66*, 117–134.

Hiebert, E. H., & Tortorelli, L. S. (2022). The role of word-, sentence-, and text-level variables in predicting guided reading levels of kindergarten and first-grade texts. *The Elementary School Journal, 122*(4), 557–590.

Irvin, J. L. (1997). *Reading and the middle school student* (2nd ed.). Allyn & Bacon.

Johnson, D. D., & Pearson, P. D. (1984). *Teaching reading vocabulary* (2nd ed.). Holt, Rinehart, & Winston.

Kearns, D., Lyon, C. P., & Pollack, M. S. (2021). Teaching world and word knowledge to access content-area texts in co-taught classrooms. *Intervention in School and Clinic*, 56(4), 208–216.

Keehn, S., Harmon, J., & Shoho, A. (2008). A study of readers theater in eighth grade: Issues of fluency, comprehension, and vocabulary. *Reading & Writing Quarterly, 24*(4), 335–362.

Kim, J. S., Hemphill, L., Troyer, M., Thomson, J. M., Jones, S. M., LaRusso, M. D., & Donovan, S. (2017). Engaging struggling adolescent readers to improve reading skills. *Reading Research Quarterly, 52*(3), 357–382.

Kintsch, W. (1986). Learning from text. *Cognition and Instruction, 3*, 87–108.

Kintsch, W. (2013). Revisiting the construction-integration model of text comprehension and its implication for instruction. In D. E. Alvermann, N. J. Unrau, & R. B. Ruddel (Eds.), *Theoretical models of reading* (6th ed., pp. 807–839). International Reading Association.

Kintsch, W., & Van Dijk, T. A. (1978). Toward a model of text comprehension and production. *Psychological Review, 85*(5), 363.

Kirby, J. R., & Bowers, P. N. (2017). Morphological instruction and literacy. *Theories of Reading Development, 15*, 437.

Klein, A. (1999). What will California's new reading/language arts framework mean for California educators? *Reading Today, 16*(4). International Reading Association.

Knecht, R., Larson, L., & Townsend, D. (2023). Exploring teacher and student knowledge of sentence-level language features. *Journal of Adolescent and Adult Literacy, 66*(6) 344–354.

Kucan, L., Rainey, E., & Cho, B. Y. (2018). Engaging middle school students in disciplinary literacy through culturally relevant historical inquiry. *Journal of Adolescent and Adult Literacy, 63*(1), 15–27.

Kuhn, M. R., & Stahl, S. A. (2003). Fluency: A review of developmental and remedial practices. *Journal of Educational Psychology, 95*(1), 3–21.

Lapp, D., Fisher, D., & Grant, M. (2008). "You can read this text—I'll show you show": Interactive comprehension instruction. *Journal of Adolescent and Adult Literacy, 51*(5), 372–383.

Lechtenberg, K. (2018). Curating against the canon: Collaborative curation for critical literacy. In *Teaching the canon in 21st century classrooms* (pp. 3–17). E. J. Brill.

Lee, C. D. (1995). *Signifying as a scaffold for literary interpretation: The pedagogical implications of an African American discourse genre.* National Council of Teachers of English.

Levesque, K. C., Breadmore, H. L., & Deacon, S. H. (2021). How morphology impacts reading and spelling: Advancing the role of morphology in models of literacy development. *Journal of Research in Reading, 44*(1), 10–26.

Levine, S., Hall, A. H., Goldman, S. R., & Lee, C. D. (2018). A design architecture for engaging middle and high school students in epistemic practices of literary interpretation. In *High literacy in secondary English language arts: Bridging the gap to college and career* (pp. 105–132). Lexington Books.

Lewis, W. E., & Strong, J. Z. (2020). *Literacy instruction with disciplinary texts: Strategies for grades 6–12*. Guilford Press.

Lewis, W., Walpole, S., & McKenna, M. C. (2014). *Cracking the Common Core: Choosing and using texts in grades 6–12*. Guilford Press.

Lupo, S. M., Hardigree, C., Thacker, E., Sawyer, A., & Merritt, J. (2021). *Teaching disciplinary literacy in grades K–6: Infusing content with reading, writing, and language.* Routledge.

Lupo, S. M., Strong, J. Z., Lewis, W., Walpole, S., & McKenna, M. C. (2018). Building background knowledge through reading: Rethinking text sets. *Journal of Adolescent and Adult Literacy, 61*(1), 433–444.

Lupo, S. M., Strong, J. Z., & Smith Conradi, K. (2019). Struggle is not a bad word: Misconceptions about adolescent readers and how to support them. *Journal of Adolescent and Adult Literacy, 62,* 551–560.

Lupo, S. M., Tortorelli, L., Invernizzi, M., Ryoo, J. H., & Strong, J. Z. (2019). An exploration of text difficulty and knowledge support on adolescents' comprehension. *Reading Research Quarterly, 54,* 441–584.

Lupo, S. M., Townsend, D., & Knecht, R. (2022). Enhancing secondary teachers' opportunities to learn about comprehension in culturally sustaining ways. In D. Robertson, C. Brock, & L. Hall, *Innovation, equity, and sustainability in literacy professional learning.* Guilford Press.

Lupo, S. M., Wheatley, B., Koubek, K., Rickabaugh, L, Early, D., Manning, K., et al. (2023). Framework for integrating content and literacy. *Reading in Virginia, 44,* 49–60.

Mackay, E., Lynch, E., Sorenson Duncan, T., & Deacon, S. H. (2021). Informing the science of reading: Students' awareness of sentence-level information is important for reading comprehension. *Reading Research Quarterly, 56,* S221–S230.

Martinez, D. C., Morales, P. Z., & Aldana, U. S. (2017). Leveraging students' communicative repertoires as a tool for equitable learning. *Review of Research in Education, 41*(1), 477–499.

McCarthy, K. S., & McNamara, D. S. (2021). The multidimensional knowledge in text comprehension framework. *Educational Psychologist, 56*(3), 196–214.

McElhone, D. (2012). Tell us more: Reading comprehension, engagement, and conceptual press discourse. *Reading Psychology, 33*(6), 525–561.

McGee, L. M., & Richgels, D. J. (1986). Attending to text structure: A comprehension strategy. In E. K. Dishner, T. W. Bean, & J. E. Readence (Eds.), *Reading in the content areas: Improving classroom instruction* (2nd ed., pp. 234–245). Kendall Hunt.

McNamara, D. S. (2010). Strategies to read and learn: Overcoming learning by consumption. *Medical Education, 44*(4), 340–346.

Moje, E. B. (2008). Foregrounding the disciplines in secondary literacy teaching and learning: A call for change. *Journal for Adolescent and Adult Literacy, 52,* 96–107.

Moje, E. B., Ciechanowski, K. M., Kramer, K., Ellis, L., Carrillo, R., & Collazo, T. (2004). Working toward third space in content area literacy: An examination of everyday funds of knowledge and discourse. *Reading Research Quarterly, 39*(1), 38–70.

Moll, L. C., Amanti, C., Neff, D., & Gonzalez, N. (1992). Funds of knowledge for teaching: Using a qualitative approach to connect homes and classrooms. *Theory Into Practice, 31*(2), 132–141.

Muhammad, G. (2020). *Cultivating genius: An equity framework for culturally and historically responsive literacy.* Scholastic.

Nagy, W. E., & Herman, P. A. (1987). Breadth and depth of vocabulary knowledge: Implications for acquisition and instruction. In M. G. McKeown & M. E. Curtis (Eds.), *The nature of vocabulary acquisition* (pp. 19–35). Erlbaum.

Nagy, W. E., Herman, P. A., & Anderson, R. C. (1985). Learning words from context. *Reading Research Quarterly,* 233–253.

National Assessment of Educational Progress. (n.d.). *Oral Reading Fluency.* National Center for Education Statistics. Retrieved from *https://nces.ed.gov/nationsreportcard/studies/orf/scoring.aspx.*

National Center for Education Statistics. (2015). The Condition of Education 2015. Retrieved from *https://nces.ed.gov/pubs2015/2015144.pdf.*

National Governors Association Center for Best Practices & Council of Chief State School Officers. (2010). *Common Core State Standards for English language arts and literacy in history/social studies, science, and technical subjects.* Authors.

National Reading Panel. (2000). *Teaching children to read: An evidence-based assessment of the scientific research literature on reading and its implications for reading instruction. Reports of the subgroups.* National Institute of Child Health and Human Development.

Ness, M. (2017). *Think big with think alouds, grades K–5: A three-step planning process that develops strategic readers.* Corwin Press.

Next Generation Science Standards. (2013, June). *High School Life Science.* Retrieved from *www.nextgenscience.org.*

Nokes, J. D., Dole, J. A., & Hacker, D. J. (2007). Teaching high school students to use heuristics while reading historical texts. *Journal of Educational Psychology, 99*(3), 492.

Ogle, D. M. (1986). KWL: A teaching model that develops active reading of expository text. *The Reading Teacher, 39,* 564–570.

O'Reilly, T., Wang, Z., & Sabatini, J. (2019). How much knowledge is too little? When a lack of knowledge becomes a barrier to comprehension. *Psychological Science, 30*(9), 1344–1351.

Orellana, M. F. (2003). Responsibilities of children in Latino immigrant homes. *New Directions for Youth Development, 2003*(100), 25–39.

Paige, D. D., Rasinski, T., Magpuri-Lavell, T., & Smith, G. S. (2014). Interpreting the relationships among prosody, automaticity, accuracy, and silent reading comprehension in secondary students. *Journal of Literacy Research, 46*(2), 123–156.

Paris, D. (2012). Culturally sustaining pedagogy: A needed change in stance, terminology, and practice. *Educational Researcher, 41*(3), 93–97.

Paris, S. G., & Hamilton, E. E. (2009). The development of children's reading comprehension. In S. Israel & G. Duffy, (Eds.), *Handbook of research of reading* (pp. 58–105). Routledge.

Pea, R. D. (2004) The social and technological dimensions of scaffolding and related theoretical concepts for learning, education, and human activity. *Journal of the Learning Sciences, 13*(3), 423–451.

Pearson, P. D., & Fielding, L. (1991). Comprehension instruction. In R. Barr, M. L. Kamil, P. B. Mosenthal, & P. D. Pearson (Eds.), *Handbook of reading research* (2nd ed., pp. 815–860). Longman.

Pew Research Center. (2020, September 10). Religious beliefs among American adolescents. Retrieved from *www.pewresearch.org/religion/2020/09/10/religious-beliefs-among-american-adolescents.*

Powers, R. (2008, September 30). Reading shouldn't be a numbers game. *Los Angeles Times.* Retrieved from *www.latimes.com/archives/la-xpm-2008-sep-30-oe-powers30-story.html.*

Pyle, N., Vasquez, A. C., Lignugaris/Kraft, B., Gillam, S. L., Reutzel, D. R., Olszewski, A., et al. (2017). Effects of expository text structure interventions on comprehension: A meta-analysis. *Reading Research Quarterly, 52*(4), 469–501.

Rackley, E. D. (2014). Scripture-based discourses of Latter-day Saint and Methodist youths. *Reading Research Quarterly, 49*(4), 417–435.

RAND Reading Study Group (RRSG). (2002). *Reading for understanding: Toward an R&D program in reading comprehension.* RAND. Retrieved from *www.rand.org/pubs/monograph_reports/MR1465.*

Reed, D. K., Zimmermann, L. M., & Gibbs, A. (2020). Teaching key reading skills. In R. Boon, M. Burke, & L. Bowman-Perrott (Eds.), *Literacy instruction for students with emotional and behavioral disorders (EBD): Research-based interventions for the classroom* (pp. 17–54). Information Age Publishing.

Reisman, A. (2012). Reading like a historian: A document-based history curriculum intervention in urban high schools. *Cognition and Instruction, 30*(1), 86–112.

Reynolds, D. (2021). Scaffolding the academic language of complex text: An intervention for late secondary students. *Journal of Research in Reading, 44*(3), 508–528.

Reynolds, D. (2022). What is an ELA text set? Surveying and integrating cognitive, critical and disciplinary lenses. *English Teaching: Practice and Critique, 21*(2), 98–110.

Reynolds, D., & Daniel, S. (2018). Toward contingency in scaffolding reading comprehension: Next steps for research. *Reading Research Quarterly, 53*(3), 367–373.

Reynolds, D., & Fisher, W. (2022). What happens when adolescents meet complex texts? Describing moments of scaffolding textual encounters. *Literacy, 56*(4), 277–287.

Reynolds, D., & Goodwin, A. P. (2016). Making complex texts a reality for all students: Dynamic scaffolding that bridges the gaps between student and text. *Voices from the Middle, 23*(4), 25.

Scarborough, H. S. (2001). Connecting early language and literacy to later reading (dis)abilities: Evidence, theory, and practice. In S. Neuman & D. Dickinson (Eds.), *Handbook for research in early literacy* (pp. 97–110). Guilford Press.

Schwartz, R. M., & Raphael, T. E. (1985). Concept of definition: A key to improving students' vocabulary. *The Reading Teacher, 39,* 198–205.

Shanahan, T. (2022). Trying again—What teachers need to know about sentence comprehension. Retrieved from: *www.shanahanonliteracy.com/blog/trying-again-what-teachers-need-to-know-about-sentence-comprehension.*

Shanahan, T., Fisher, D., & Frey, N. (2016). The challenge of challenging text. In *On developing readers: Readings from educational leadership (EL Essentials)* (pp. 100–109). ASCD.

Siebert, D. K., Draper, R. J., Barney, D., Broomhead, P., Grierson, S., et al. (2016). Characteristics of literacy instruction that supports reform in content area classrooms. *Journal of Adolescent and Adult Literacy, 60*(1), 25–33.

Skerrett, A. (2014). Religious literacies in a secular literacy classroom. *Reading Research Quarterly, 49*(2), 233–250.

Spires, H. A., & Donley, J. (1998). Prior knowledge activation: Inducing engagement with informational texts. *Journal of Educational Psychology, 90*(2), 249–260.

Stanovich, K. E. (1986). Matthew effects in reading: Some consequences of individual differences in the acquisition of literacy. *Reading Research Quarterly, 21,* 360–407.

Stewart, M. A., Hansen-Thomas, H., Flint, P., & Núñez, M. (2022). Translingual disciplinary literacies: Equitable language environments to support literacy engagement. *Reading Research Quarterly, 57*(1), 181–203.

Sutton, K., Grafmeyer, A. D., & Reynolds, D. (2023). The beam in our own eyes: Antiracism and YA literature through a Catholic lens. *Journal of Catholic Education, 26*(1), 102–118.

Swanson, E., Wanzek, J, McCulley, L., Stillman-Spisak, S., Vaughn, S., Simmons, D., Fogarty, M., & Hairrel, A. (2016). Literacy and text reading in middle and high school social studies and English language arts classrooms. Reading & Writing Quarterly, 32, 199–222.

Taba, H. (1967). *Teacher's handbook for elementary social studies.* Addison-Wesley.

Taylor, B. M., & Beach, R. W. (1984). The effects of text structure instruction on middle-grade students' comprehension and production of expository text. *Reading Research Quarterly, 19*(2), 134–146.

Thelen, J. (1982). Preparing students for content assignments. *Journal of Reading, 25,* 544–549.

Tierney, R. J., & Readence, J. E. (2005). *Reading strategies and practices: A compendium* (6th ed.). Allyn & Bacon.

Toste, J. R., Capin, P., Vaughn, S., Roberts, G. J., & Kearns, D. M. (2017). Multisyllabic word reading instruction with and without motivational beliefs training for struggling readers in the upper elementary grades: A pilot investigation. *The Elementary School Journal, 117*(4), 593–615.

Toste, J. R., Capin, P., Williams, K. J., Cho, E., & Vaughn, S. (2019). Replication of an experimental study investigating the efficacy of a multisyllabic word reading intervention with and without motivational beliefs training for struggling readers. *Journal of Learning Disabilities, 52*(1), 45–58.

Uccelli, P., & Phillips Galloway, E. (2017). Academic language across content areas: Lessons from an innovative assessment and from students' reflections about language. *Journal of Adolescent and Adult Literacy, 60*(4), 395–404.

Uccelli, P., Phillips Galloway, E., Aguilar, G., & Allen, M. (2020). Amplifying and affirming students' voices through CALS-informed instruction. *Theory Into Practice, 59*(1), 75–88.

U.S. Department of Education. (2023). Guidance on constitutionally protected prayer and religious expression in public elementary and secondary schools. Retrieved from *www2.ed.gov/policy/gen/guid/religionandschools/prayer_guidance.html*

van de Pol, J., Volman, M., & Beishuizen, J. (2010). Scaffolding in teacher–student interaction: A decade of research. *Educational Psychology Review, 22*, 271–296.

Vaughn, S., Kieffer, M. J., McKeown, M., Reed, D. K., Sanchez, M., St Martin, K., et al. (2022). Providing reading interventions for students in grades 4–9. *Educator's Practice Guide*. WWC 2022007. What Works Clearinghouse.

Wang, Z., Sabatini, J., O'Reilly, T., & Weeks, J. (2019). Decoding and reading comprehension: A test of the decoding threshold hypothesis. *Journal of Educational Psychology, 111*(3), 387–401.

Washburn, J. (2022). Reviewing evidence on the relations between oral reading fluency and reading comprehension for adolescents. *Journal of Learning Disabilities, 55*(1), 22–42.

Wexler, J., Vaughn, S., Edmonds, M., & Reutebuch, C. K. (2008). A synthesis of fluency interventions for secondary struggling readers. *Reading and Writing, 21*, 317–347.

Wiggins, G. P., & McTighe, J. (2005). *Understanding by design*. Association for Supervision and Curriculum Development.

Willingham, D. T. (2017). *The reading mind: A cognitive approach to understanding how the mind reads*. Wiley.

Wineburg, S. S., Martin, D., & Monte-Sano, C. (2012). *Reading like a historian: Teaching literacy in middle and high school history classrooms*. Teachers College Press.

Wix, H. E. (1927). Education is a life. *Parents Review (48)* 461-468.

Wood, D., Bruner, J. S., & Ross, G. (1976). The role of tutoring in problem solving. *Journal of Child Psychology and Psychiatry, 17*(2), 89–100.

Wood, K. D. (1984). Probable passages: A writing strategy. *The Reading Teacher, 37*(6), 496–499.

Young, C., Durham, P., Miller, M., Rasinski, T. V., & Lane, F. (2019). Improving reading comprehension with readers theater. *The Journal of Educational Research, 112*(5), 615–626.

Young, C., Stokes, F., & Rasinski, T. (2017). Readers theatre plus comprehension and word study. *The Reading Teacher, 71*(3), 351–355.

Index

Note. *f* or *t* following a page number indicates a figure or a table.

S

T